Industrial districts and inter-firm co-operation in Italy

Edited by F. Pyke, G. Becattini and W. Sengenberger

International Institute for Labour Studies, Geneva

ISBN 92-9014-467-X

First published 1990

Copies can be ordered from: ILO publications, International Labour Office, CH - 1211 Geneva 22 (Switzerland).

Preface

This book is a product of research we have been carrying out on the subject of "industrial districts and inter-firm co-operation" since 1987 under the auspices of the "New Industrial Organisation" programme of the International Institute for Labour Studies (IILS). Over the last three years a large number of scholars from around the world have assisted the IILS with our studies, participating in our seminars and conferences and writing papers for us. The work of some of these scholars is presented in this book. That of others is not included in this particular publication but we would like to thank all of them for their help.

We would also like to acknowledge the help given by Alan Mayhew, Martin Harvey, and others in Directorate XXIII of the European Commission in Brussels. Directorate XXIII has provided valuable financial support for the holding of meetings and the commissioning of papers, including several of the contributions in this publication.

Other people whose help we wish to acknowledge include Ximena Subercaseaux for the design of the cover, Christopher Woodall for initial translation work on Chapter 8, Hilary Mueller for typing and Hazel Cecconi for light editing, formatting and proof-reading.

Frank Pyke,
Giacomo Becattini,
Werner Sengenberger

Geneva, July 1990

Contributors

Ash Amin: Lecturer, Centre for Urban and Regional Development Studies of the University of Newcastle-upon-Tyne, U. K.

Giacomo Becattini: Professor of Economics, University of Florence, Italy.

Sebastiano Brusco: Professor of Industrial Economics, University of Modena, Italy.

Paulo Brutti: General Manager, Confederazione Generale Italiana del Lavoro, Rome, Italy.

Franco Calistri: Researcher, Economics Department, Confederazione Generale Italiana del Lavoro, Rome, Italy.

Vittorio Capecchi: Professor of Sociology, University of Bologna, Italy.

Mark Lazerson: Assistant Professor, Department of Sociology, State University of New York, Stony Brook, U.S.A.

Michael Piore: Professor of Economics, Massachusetts Institute of Technology, Boston, U.S.A.

Mario Pezzini: Senior Researcher, Nomisma Research Centre, Bologna, Italy.

Frank Pyke: Research Officer, International Institute for Labour Studies, Geneva, Switzerland.

Kevin Robins: Senior Research Associate, Centre for Urban and Regional Development Studies, University of Newcastle-upon-Tyne, U.K.

Charles Sabel: Professor of Political Science, Massachusetts Institute of Technology, Boston, U.S.A.

Werner Sengenberger: Head, New Industrial Organisation Programme, International Institute for Labour Studies, Geneva, Switzerland.

Fabio Sforzi: Research Fellow, IRPET and Lecturer, Department of Economics, University of Florence, Italy.

Michael Storper: Associate Professor, Graduate School of Architecture and Urban Planning, University of California, Los Angeles, U.S.A.

Carlo Trigilia: Associate Professor of Sociology, University of Palermo, Italy.

Table of contents

Debate

1 Introduction

Frank Pyke and Werner Sengenberger

Whilst economies all over the world in the late 1970s and 1980s set into recession and stagnation, frequently accompanied by serious deteriorations in labour and social conditions, rising unemployment, and insecurity, a few localities stood out as exhibiting a remarkable resilience and even growth. They were engaged in a variety of industries, and included not only advanced sectors but also more traditional, labour-intensive ones, and thereby posed a challenge to those who have argued that such economic activities can no longer succeed in high wage industrialised countries. Thus, places like Oyonnax in France, Jutland in Denmark, Baden-Württemberg in the Federal Republic of Germany, Småland in Sweden, the Barcelona area in Spain, Silicon Valley and around Los Angeles in the United States of America, Cambridge in England, parts of Japan, and areas of Central and North-East Italy, were highlighted as being localised economic constellations that "were beating the recession".

Many of these were said to have a sufficient similarity in their mode of economic operation to permit them to be categorised under one generic heading: "Industrial Districts". Of particular interest to us at the International Institute for Labour Studies was the claim that such districts could combine both economic efficiency and superior standards of employment, and act as a model for promotion elsewhere. This persuaded us to look further into the subject and to evaluate its potential. Thus was set in motion a programme of enquiry that has involved collaboration with researchers in many industrialised countries. This book, put together by ourselves and one of our collaborators, Professor Becattini, is a product of this ongoing research; it reflects, to some extent, the point we have reached with our enquiry.

The focus is on the industrial districts of North Central and North-Eastern Italy; this is partly a reflection of the way our research programme has been organised - a country by country approach, beginning with Italy - and also partly reflecting the fact that the districts in this country have been most widely quoted as being amongst the clearest and strongest examples of the phenomenon. Whilst the validity of other areas in other countries to be called "districts" might sometimes be contested, the eligibility of localities in Italy is undisputed. The special status of the Italian cases, then, justifies particular attention.

It is an aim of the International Institute for Labour Studies to bring to the attention of the public and policy-makers new ideas and developments in the world of industry and labour. The general significance of the industrial district phenomenon and its broader implications and value for those concerned with promoting economically efficient, yet socially worthwhile, economic organisations, remains to be seen. Nevertheless, we hope that the reader will agree with us that a development has occurred which at the very least should be given very careful consideration.

I. What are industrial districts?

Without wishing to pre-empt what follows in the book, we feel it is necessary to give at least a brief description of the nature of industrial districts. This we do with some caution, since, as will be clear to readers of our last section, "Debate", the whole question of definition is not without controversy. Most of the controversy, however, appears to relate to issues outside of Italy. There seems to be broad agreement, at least amongst the contributors to this book, on the basic shape of Italian industrial districts. Below we draw out from what these contributors have written some key characteristics.

The districts are geographically defined productive systems, characterised by a large number of firms that are involved at various stages, and in various ways, in the production of a homogeneous product. A significant feature is that a very high proportion of these firms are small or very small. As Sforzi points out, most of the districts are to be found in North Central and North-Eastern Italy, with different ones specialising in different products, of varying types of complexity and intended end-use. Thus, for example, Sassuolo, in Emilia Romagna, specialises in ceramic tiles; Prato, in Toscana, is known for textiles; shoes are made at Montegranaro in Marche; mechanical engineering is carried out in Cento, in Emilia Romagna; Nogara, in Veneto, specialises in wooden furniture; whilst Canneto sull'Oglio, in Lombardia, makes toys.

A characteristic of the industrial district is that it should be conceived as a social and economic whole. That is to say, there are close inter-relationships between the different social, political and economic spheres, and that the functioning of one, say the economic, is shaped by the functioning and organisation of the others. The success of the districts, then, lies not just in the realm of the "economic". Broader social and institutional aspects are just as important.

Adaptability and innovativeness are hallmarks with a communal capacity to cater for rapidly changing product demands that is heavily dependent on a flexible labour force and flexible productive networks. Some writers (see, for example, Piore and Capecchi) emphasise this character of flexibility when they refer to the industrial district phenomenon as exhibiting traits typically found in the model they call "flexible specialisation", as distinct from more rigid production principles of mass production or "Fordism". Assisting this capacity for adaptability is a highly developed local accumulation of specialised knowledge and skill that is spread throughout the community.

A significant characteristic is that the motor of success has not been the large vertically integrated corporation, with all its internal resources, ability to reap benefits from economies of scale, and market power. On the contrary, organisation and leadership has come from small, often family-owned, businesses linked together by an articulated division of specialisation. As each group of establishments specialising in a particular stage of production or service complements those of others in "the district", there is a kind of "organic" inter-dependency. As a consequence, the whole collectivity of small firms is able to achieve the economies of scale until recently thought to be particular to large corporations, by virtue of the fact that expensive capital equipment can be kept in full use servicing the needs of all district members.

The population of small firms in the industrial district is not just an aggregate of productive units. What makes them more than that is the special systemic way they are organised and the way they relate to one another and their environment. This special kind of organisation is partly captured by the notion of vertical decentralisation referred to above. Also important is the fundamental part played by various forms of inter-firm and communal co-operation.

The importance of inter-firm co-operation is something that is particularly stressed by Sebastiano Brusco, although, as he points out, it is a co-operation blended with competition. At some risk of oversimplification, we can say that Brusco argues that strong competition occurs between firms doing the same thing; co-operation and collaboration, especially over technical innovation and design, takes place between firms doing different things, i.e., at different stages of the production process. The provision of "real" and common services for the small firms are also seen by Brusco as important elements, and increasingly so (see also Brutti and Calistri).

Becattini and Trigilia agree on the significance of co-operation, emphasising in their papers the importance of the local value systems for introducing important elements of cohesion and a willingness to work together to resolve potential clashes of interest.

Whilst the above can be identified as key characteristics defining an ideal type district, it has to be said that despite the commonalities there are also differences. It could be said that just as with large firms, no two industrial districts are exactly alike. The differences, however - in respect of variations in local culture, political allegiances, skill levels, levels of technology, relations between firms and between firms and institutions - appear to be variations in degree or around common themes rather than differences in essence.

II. Policy implications

Pezzini and Brusco argue that policy-makers should not adhere to one single broad economic policy approach for "the small firm". There are different kinds of small firms and different contexts, and therefore there must be different policies adapted accordingly.

A particularly common "broadsweep" approach towards promoting small firm development has been the provision of various kinds of financial incentives or reliefs, such as subsidies, tax exemptions, aid to technological improvement, relaxation of social obligations and so forth. By and large, the object and target of this support has been the individual small firm, with the underlying philosophy being that by helping such units overcome supposed deficiencies in capital and technology they will acquire attributes possessed by larger organisations, and thereby have a better chance of success.

In the light of the experience of industrial districts, this approach might be seen as questionable. The key problem for small firms appears not to be that of being small, but of being isolated. Thus, what might be relevant is not the characteristics and resources of the single small firm but the characteristics of the industrial structure and context in which it is implanted. Consequently, much more emphasis, in this view, should be given to the creation of organisational forms under which the small firm can combine its advantages of flexibility with the support and stability that comes from larger networks. The object should become, then, one of considering the character and quality of inter-firm relationships, networks and community support structures.

Industrial districts would appear to contain the organisational forms that provide the appropriate kind of environment for small firm development. A major question, then, is whether the districts are capable of being the objects of a more general application or replication, or whether they are simply the products of historically or geographically specific processes. Sebastiano Brusco ends his contribution by posing the question of whether institutions successful in promoting industrial districts in the North of Italy could be equally effective in the South. Brutti and Calistri also think that this is an important question; they are clearly of the opinion that there can be a transference and a replication of the success story.

The fact that claims for "districts" have been made in a variety of contexts and countries would seem to support the view that they are not locationally restricted. However, this pre-supposes that all the so-called districts are in fact generically of the same kind. Is the same thing, or variations on the same essential phenomenon, being repeated, or are these very different phenomena that have been inappropriately categorised under the same heading? Ash Amin and Kevin Robins suggest that many of the so-called districts are indeed very different phenomena and these writers are clearly doubtful about possibilities for replicability, especially in view of the very specific historical and social circumstances responsible for success. Michael Storper, on the other hand, argues that many of the districts are similar in respect of crucial aspects, if not in terms of fine details. Amin and Robins, he suggests, fail to recognise that the industrial districts of Northern Italy might be one of a number of possible variations on the industrial district theme, and that there is not only one historical path to the flexible district model. This would imply that if variations were possible then exact replicability might not be a necessary condition for success and that implantation in areas with their own distinct histories could occur.

However, need a policy initiative necessarily start from the assumption that an objective would be to repeat a complete industrial district system? Even if it were to be proved that replicability of the total industrial district experience was impossible, does this mean that there are not still valuable lessons to be learnt which could be put to good use elsewhere? Could certain ideas, like the use of real services extolled by Sebastiano Brusco, not be of policy value regardless of the potential for replicating the total district? Could it be argued that from a policy point of view some characteristics of the industrial district are more important than others? Supposing, for example, that it were to be argued that a particularly valuable achievement would be to create flexible networks within which small firms could be located, without necessarily producing all the other attributes of the industrial district, or indeed necessarily within a restricted geographical area. Would piecemeal initiatives be of any value? Furthermore, given the difficulty of starting from scratch, would they be inevitable?

III. Necessary conditions for industrial districts

The question of replicability takes on a different light if the focus is put not so much on the specific character of social and economic institutions as on the functions that they carry out. The question, then, would be whether the object of a policy initiative should be to identify ways of introducing functional equivalents. Can the conditions said to be necessary for industrial district success be repeated using different social and economic arrangements?

One argument for the appearance internationally of industrial districts could be that functionally equivalent processes have occurred in a number of places; that is to say, in certain localities an appropriate interaction has occurred between local facilitating conditions, and changes in broader economic and social processes at a national or international level, such as the break-up of mass markets, or the appearance of new kinds of technology. To this degree, there has been a process of spontaneous development as, consciously or unconsciously, localities have taken the opportunity to make use of conducive local conditions to meet the challenge of changing broader economic processes. This begs questions concerning the kinds of conditions, both locally and more widely, that are necessary for replicating the industrial district experience elsewhere.

In the case of the Italian experience, a considerable number of conditions have been cited. One important feature of industrial districts appears to be a widespread *entrepreneurial spirit and ability*. In Italy a basis for the necessary entrepreneurial skills has often been thought to lie in a background in *métayage* or peasant farming. Trigilia's paper suggests, however, that other backgrounds might also be appropriate, with many of the entrepreneurs in his research having predominantly manufacturing or commercial experience.

Flexibility is another widely cited condition. It could be that the ability of economic activity to utilise social resources or social structures is becoming more important. This is thought to be especially the case by those who argue that a decline in "Fordism" has been accompanied by an increasing variability and ambiguity of people's roles in economic activity. Thus, in this view, the issue becomes one of maintaining cohesion when roles are changing all the time.

The Italian industrial districts appear to be endowed with social structures that are particularly well suited to the flexible co-ordination of resources. Access to extended family and community resources, for example, are said to have provided the conditions for workers, on the one hand, to adapt to flexible labour requirements, and employers, on the other hand, to have access to a flexible labour source. Close community and kinship ties, furthermore, provide mechanisms for mutual assistance in times of need, as well as funds for establishing new businesses. The way industry is organised provides a particularly adaptable structure for responding to changing market requirements. As Becattini points out, production is less prone to bottlenecks and the "sclerosis" often experienced by large vertically organised enterprises, whilst production and the market may be mediated by the knowledgeable, adaptable activities of the *impannatore* or other similar figures. The flexibility provided by these social organisations appears to be crucial to the success of the districts, but perhaps other kinds of agents and forms, carrying out the same functions, but adapted to different conditions and contexts, might be equally effective elsewhere.

The close community relationships are also thought to play a part, with other cultural and political factors, in preserving local *consensus* and common values, and promoting "social compromise". Agreed standards for the distribution of economic and social benefits, and the curtailing of the excesses of market mechanisms, encourage co-operation, flexibility, and innovation.

The provision of a *local pool of skill* would also seem to be significant. In the past, in many Italian districts large firms seem to have played an important role in this regard. Possibly the policy implication is that large firms should be attracted to areas of underdevelopment. Certainly some mechanism for inducing a rapid growth of skills, capable of application in a variety of contexts and firms, appears necessary.

IV. Labour standards

The kinds of labour standards, working conditions, practices, and wages to be found in industrial districts are crucial questions to be answered. In general, there is a paucity of information on these aspects, and where it does exist it is contradictory and equivocal. On wages, Trigilia says that wage levels in industrial districts are generally underestimated, with local bargaining often pushing rates above nationally agreed standards; this reflects, he argues, another factor which is often undervalued, namely the strength of trade unionism in district areas. Brusco points out in his paper that wages in small firms in industrial districts are comparable *on average* to what large firms pay, although the *spread* of earnings is much greater.

In contrast, Amin and Robins offer a less optimistic view when they point out that in some districts at least there is evidence that development might have occurred on the basis of cheap labour. Brutti and Calistri support this view that "in many cases" there are "intolerable conditions of underpaid labour".

When it comes to evaluating the quality of working in industrial districts, however, simple monetary measures might be insufficient. Psychological and physical conditions come into play. Two attractive features of working in industrial districts that Trigilia reports, are the greater degree of autonomy and space for worker self-management that employment in the small firms permits, and the relatively high degree of social mobility that occurs. Brusco confirms the picture of high mobility, pointing to the frequent changes in status between that of "employer" and that of "employee", whilst Lazerson also notes the benefits of greater autonomy. Becattini suggests that skilled workers find their skills and knowledge better appreciated in the district than elsewhere.

There is also the question of quality of life outside the workplace, the quality of housing, environment, cultural activities, etc. The role of social services might be important as regards their contribution to the local "social wage". Trigilia, for one, thinks that this latter aspect is of particular value.

The diversity of the information we have reflects differences in reality. The truth of the matter appears to be that in Italy, at least, the districts - and Sforzi suggests that there are 61 of them - vary organisationally. It seems reasonable to assume that just as working and social conditions in large firms differ, so they do in industrial districts. Thus, Brutti argues that pay and working conditions in districts can be either more or less than in non-district areas. It seems, therefore, that the contradictory claims might simply be a reflection of different circumstances, such as, for example, the parts played by trade unions or local public policy. Moreover, just as the districts themselves are dynamic and can change, so can conditions for labour. Thus, Brutti and Calistri warn that exploitation in districts is on the increase as firms try to respond to new competitive pressures and that the conditions could deteriorate further unless positive action is taken. Thus, outcomes for labour are highly contingent and this should caution us against making sweeping generalisations.

However, the ambiguities and contradictions might also derive from the limitations of existing conceptual frameworks for capturing adequately processes going on in industrial districts, and for providing a sound basis for making normative judgements. Some people would argue that the principles of social and economic organisation to be found in industrial districts are radically different from those that underpin a mass production model and that therefore new concepts and measurements must be developed before normative judgements can be made as to whether conditions are socially "good" or "bad". In an industrial district there might not be the sharp split between "working" and "non-working" spheres of life that tends to occur in Fordist environments. That is to say that in industrial districts there might be more reason to take into account the whole living experience. Some of the measurements used in a Fordist environment might be redundant. It would follow from this that many of the strategies and objectives pursued by political parties and trade unions concerned with social and employment issues might also be inappropriate.

Flexibility is a key characteristic of the district, and this would appear to be one concept which in itself brings to mind a whole series of relationships, statuses, and experiences which could be eligible for evaluation and measurement. Thus, for example, there is the question of the labour standards enjoyed by the group that Becattini, at least, identifies as crucial for providing the flexibility of the district system, namely (mainly female) part-time and home workers. Is it the case that there is a coincidence of interest between the requirements of the system and the needs or preferences of these workers? Or could it be that the industrial district, and/or some elements in it, thrive at the *expense* of the part-time and home workers? Clearly such questions must be asked in relation to aspects of the household as much as the workplace. If there is a suspicion that an element of labour market segmentation is occurring then analysis must also work at a less aggregated level than "average wages" for the district as a whole. When it comes to flexible contracts, account has also to be taken of degrees of precariousness and pay measured over the aggregate of both non-working and working periods. Further, the intensity of work might also be particularly relevant in a system that is so greatly influenced by the need to meet tight time deadlines.

V. The districts under threat

The districts are living phenomena, and subject to change, and it cannot be said with certainty how they will develop. Many of the contributors refer to new difficulties that have to be faced, which, if not successfully responded to, could result in decline.

Some writers see as a major threat the activities of large firms, and in particular the multinational corporations. A characteristic of the industrial district is that there are many independent, generally small, firms, with no single firm being a strategic centre or "head" for decision making. But can this continue indefinitely? Or will large firms inevitably develop, or enter the district, and swallow the small ones, or at least tend to control them? Certainly, Ash Amin and Kevin Robins warn of the threat that the activities of multinational corporations pose to the independence of small firm districts and urge us to be aware of the limitations of proactive local control. Others, on the other hand, like Michael Storper, see no necessary incompatibility between large firms and industrial districts. It would be premature, says Storper, to assume that the large firm is necessarily the destroyer of the industrial district.

Brutti and Calistri warn of the threat of new international competition and the difficulties districts are experiencing in maintaining efficiency; they warn that action is needed by local authorities and trade unions to prevent districts from degenerating into areas of relative decay and labour exploitation. Trigilia refers to "new types of economies and diseconomies that cannot be easily dealt with at a local level", basically because of problems of scale and through lack of resources, and sees the need for further integration into regional, rather than just local, organisation.

Brusco talks about the need to change the "Industrial District Mark I" into an "Industrial District Mark II", characterised by greater institutional intervention in the provision of "external" communal services.

Becattini sees a problem in the inability to maintain local control over district-specific systems of values which he sees as vital for the working of the districts.

Capecchi and others recognise the problems posed by the ability of the districts to keep pace with the latest methods and technologies, to meet the needs of new markets, and to combat increasing "diseconomies" of an ecological and environmental kind.

Clearly, then, the Italian Districts face serious challenges to their integrity. Inaction would certainly seem to imply a worsening of conditions and vitality. On the other hand, as Michael Storper points out, industrial districts like Prato have faced difficulties before and have adapted. Certainly most of the writers in this book seem to imply that various kinds of intervention and reorganisation can maintain the success story. The future, then, remains open.

2 The idea of the Industrial District: Its genesis[1]

Sebastiano Brusco

The objective of this chapter is not so much to discuss the emergence of industrial districts in Italy, as to present an overview of the way in which the debate on small firms in general has developed in that country over the last 40 years. Thus it narrates the story of how the academic and student communities considered the question of small firms in Italy. It approaches this task by discussing the development of four models, and by highlighting the background factors studied, and the ideas which underlie those factors.

I. The traditional artisan model

The first model considered is that of the *traditional artisan*. The period is the 1950s and early 1960s, when the south of Italy was still fairly underdeveloped and possessed quite a number of small artisan firms producing goods destined to be replaced over the next 20 years by mass-produced goods. Examples are clothing manufacturers, pasta producers, blacksmiths who worked for the production industry, and carpenters of all kinds. These people, who were the last upholders of the old methods of production, were still characterised by low levels of productivity and the use of very labour-intensive techniques. The level of technology in these shops was fairly low, as were the wages. Skills were acquired mainly through apprenticeship and practice. Relations between firms could be described as those of imperfect competition.

During this time, the main discussion of these objects, and of this method of production, was carried out by two authors who are worthy of closer consideration. They are Vera Lutz, who produced important studies on Italian development [Lutz, 1958, 1962], and Graziani [Graziani, 1969, 1972], who wrote two books on the same subject. The discussion on the nature and role of small firms in that period was conducted in terms of a dualism between the North and the South. Lutz's idea was that the North was characterised by large firms which were capital-intensive, efficient, unionised and which paid high wages, and that the South was characterised by small firms, which were labour-intensive, inefficient, non-unionised, and paid very low wages. Thus the small firms were identified as those in which

---

1. This chapter is based on a presentation made at the First Meeting of the Working Group on Industrial Districts, International Institute for Labour Studies, Geneva, July 1988.

production was carried out in an inefficient way using labour-intensive techniques. An implicit assumption in Lutz's work was that large and small firms were found in the same industry, producing the same goods although, in the South, it was a case of producing for specific people ("made-to-measure"), while in the North production was for retail on the national market. According to Lutz the policy implications of this were that the high wages paid in the North prevented Italy from accumulating the capital necessary to transform the small firms in the South. Lutz's general contention was that only large firms were efficient, could afford unionisation, and could pay high wages and that small firms were inevitably inefficient. Her proposal was to lower wages in the North and to standardise the wage structure between the North and the South, and thus acquire the resources necessary for Italian development.

Like Lutz, Graziani also emphasised dualism but based it on a different contention. Graziani's thesis was that while the large firms in the North were open to foreign competition, the small southern firms were not, and were protected by the idiosyncratic consumer tastes of the southern population. Consequently, whilst the northerners' open attitude to foreign competition brought investment, efficiency, unionisation and high wages, in the South investment, technology, unionisation and wages remained low. We must note that here too the assumption was that both the large northern firms and the small southern ones were producing the same goods for the same final market. As we shall see, this assumption changes in later models.

For Graziani the policy implication was to bring large firms to the South in line with his conviction that only large firms would bring high investment and good conditions of work.

This discussion, which took place from around the beginning of the 1950s until the middle 1970s, can be summarised as follows: the South was thought to be characterised by very small, inefficient firms working for the local market; these firms were destroyed during this period by the large firms of the North which were building a national market. Italy did not have a national market for clothes, for ice-cream or for furniture until the middle 1960s. Thus the phenomenon being studied was a backward productive system in the South comprising small firms which were in direct competition with large firms in the North. The idea that the small firms were inefficient and were unable to pay high wages was always stressed.

II. The dependent subcontractor model

The second model I have chosen is the *dependent subcontractor*. The background to this model is the fact that a wave of decentralisation took place in Italy at the end of the 1960s. The degree of vertical integration, as measured by the ratio of value added to sales, decreased substantially in all large firms in Italy. Whole departments of production in large plants were closed down and the activities previously undertaken in-house were handed over to small firms, often situated in the vicinity. Against this background, towards the end of the 1960s, there was considerable collaboration amongst the unions which, at that time, had a hegemonic position in the cultural and intellectual spheres in Italy, as had many academics. The unions and their collaborators carried out a great deal of unpublished research.

We can summarise the discussion which took place in that period by referring to three authors: Massimo Paci [Paci, 1973, 1975], A. Graziani [Graziani, 1975] and myself [Brusco, 1973, 1975]. Continuing the discussion along the same lines there was some debate on the nature of the product of the dependent subcontractor. Paci, who was one of Piore's students, generally maintained, at least at first, that the production of small firms was the same as that of large firms, production being put out by the large firms to the smaller ones on a cyclical basis when demand was very high. (According to Piore's model [Berger and Piore, 1980], when there are ups and downs in production large firms find it convenient to keep the stable production for themselves and to offer the rest to others. This assumes, of course, that the small firms produce the same goods as the large ones.)

Graziani and I maintained that a decentralisation of stages of production was occurring, with the consequence that the production of the large firms was becoming different from that of the small ones. We contended that the large firms sold on the final market - for either consumer or investment goods - while the small firms simply produced intermediate goods - parts and components - for other, larger, units and certainly did not face the final market. Graziani stressed more than I that the stages of production which had been decentralised were the dirtiest, and the ones which had to be conducted under the worst possible conditions.

In the foregoing section we have talked about the product. Let us now discuss the market. In the previous model - the traditional artisan - the small firms worked for the local market. In the present (dependent subcontractor) model, it was agreed that the small firms worked for the national market. Of course the relationship was only an indirect one in that it was a question of small units selling their production to larger ones, which then resold it on the national or international market. However, even though they only worked indirectly for the national market, the small firms were in a competitive system; at least as far as the vertically integrated sector as a whole was concerned they were involved in world competition.

What were the standards of technology, the conditions of work, and the level of wages in small firms? Paci, Graziani and most of the unions maintained that technology and wages were low, that conditions of work were terrible, that there were no career prospects for the workers and no mobility between sectors. The idea was that this system of production was strictly tied to a model of labour market segmentation, in which there was a core of labour in large plants and a periphery elsewhere in the small firms where working conditions were thought to be of a sweat-shop type.

Two points must be noted. The first is that Graziani was proposing more or less the same dualism he had proposed earlier: efficiency versus inefficiency; high wages versus low wages; high technology versus low technology. However, while his earlier idea was of a dualism between North and South, it had now become a dualism between large and small firms. Secondly, a very peculiar feature of Italian research in this period was that the study of industrial organisation and the study of labour economics overlapped considerably. The study of labour market segmentation and the study of how production was conducted became, to a great extent, the same and was conducted by the same people.

The views discussed above were those of Paci and Graziani. My own view was different. I thought that while it was indeed true that many small firms could be characterised as using low technology and paying low wages, nevertheless, there were some small firms that had a technology and an efficiency that was comparable to that found in large ones. It is from this point on that economists began to think that the efficiency of a small firm could be as great as that of a large one, provided the same machines were used. A saying which existed during this period was that "ten lathes under one roof are not more productive than ten lathes under ten roofs", meaning that the lathes in question could be spread all over the territory and still retain their efficiency. This was an innovation. However, I stressed that wages were still low (that is to say, lower than average) even if technology was good. This was another small innovation in the sense that wages no longer appeared to be linked to productivity and that high efficiency and low wages could co-exist.

I feel that the reason why neither Graziani nor Paci saw that small firms could be efficient was simply that they accepted the theory that as the wages were low, efficiency must also be low. That is to say, they derived the level of efficiency from the level of wages instead of looking at efficiency and wages separately.

We have considered the product, the market, technology and the conditions of work. In respect of "skill", it was pointed out that the skills of workers in small firms were very much the same as those in large ones. As regards inter-firm relations, Graziani and Paci both stressed the model of oligopsony, contending that large firms that bought parts and components from small ones squeezed and lowered the small suppliers' profits, thereby engendering low wages. I stressed the fact that, although there was some oligopsony, especially in certain areas like Piedmont, there was also considerable competition.

III. The model of the industrial district Mark I

I shall move on now to the third model - the *industrial district* which I shall call *Mark I*, this being an industrial district without external local government intervention. Later I shall discuss an industrial district Mark II, in which there is considerable government intervention. With regard to the background of the Industrial District Mark I, it grew up in the mid 1970s when a number of industries and towns had become economically successful. The most notable of these were the textile industry in Carpi and Prato, the furniture industry in Brianza and Cascina, and the footwear industry in Vigevano, and even in Puglia. For the first time the Italian machine tool industry was exporting all over Europe. The packaging machines of Bologna were being exported to Japan. This was obviously a time of great expansion which requires a particular label and deserves notice.

Becattini [1979] made one of the most important contributions of this period, applying to these territorially defined productive systems the Marshallian concept of "industrial district" and writing an important article in which he contended that the unit of analysis must change. The idea behind this was that the unit of analysis was no longer a single firm but a cluster of interconnected firms located in a small area.

Let us turn now to the product. What is it? An industrial district may produce anything and, in Italy at least, there are examples of districts producing consumer goods and investment goods, goods which are fairly easy to produce or goods for which production is difficult, using both high and low technology. It is certainly not simply a matter of fashion goods. If we were to schematise the products of firms in an industrial district, we could distinguish three categories. First there are the firms which produce a final product. Up to 30 per cent of firms in a district may have access to the final market. This is the aspect which most impresses the student of the industrial district - i.e. the idea that in some areas there may be up to a thousand firms with less than 20 employees of which 300 have direct access to the final market. Next, there are firms which could be called the "stage-firms" - firms which are involved in one stage of production. For example, in a textile district stage firms would be concerned with just sewing or knitting or weaving or finishing or packaging, etc. It should be stressed that the "stage-firms" are not necessarily engaged in less skilled, less capital-intensive, lower technology activities, but may be engaged in any activity from the dirtiest to the most specialised using the highest technology. There is a third group of firms. These work in a different industry to that which defines the final product of the district but, nevertheless, belong to the same vertically integrated sector as the final firms. For example, in a clothing district there are firms which produce buttons and which, statistically, may belong to the chemical sector; firms which belong to the service sector (such as those involved in leasing or banking); and firms which deal with transport. Although these firms are categorised statistically under different industrial groupings they all work for the clothing industry and belong to the same vertically integrated sector. This idea of paying more attention to the vertically integrated sector than to the industrial sector (statistically defined) is again one put forward by Becattini.

Thus an industrial district is a small area in which, (if we include both dependent and independent workers), there are perhaps 10,000 to 20,000 workers, and around 1,000 to 3,000 firms with fewer than 20 employees. Many of these firms have a direct connection with the final market, others are "stage firms" and, still others, firms of the vertically integrated sector. A district comprises a cluster of firms producing something which is homogeneous in one way or another, positioning themselves differently on the market. Thus, the district could be defined as being a cluster, plus a peculiar relationship amongst firms. One thing that must, of course, be stressed is that this cluster does not have a centre for strategic decision-making. The fact that the firms connected to the final markets are numerous, and independent of one another, prevents the district from having one single head. The market is clearly national *and* international although the "stage-firms" work only indirectly for the international market.

What are the standards of technology, wages and conditions of work? Both Becattini and I have stressed that the standard of technology is good and that these firms use the same technology as large firms [Becattini, 1975, 1978; Brusco, 1975, 1982, 1986; Brusco and Baldassarre, 1983]. I have shown that wages are only slightly lower on average, but that the spread of earnings is much greater than in large plants. A study by Solinas [1982] showed that there is a great deal of mobility between large and small firms, so that one can no longer say that there is a core and a periphery. There is a great deal of interchange. Data published in Italy show that each year an impressive 10 per cent of dependent workers become independent, whilst 7 per cent of independent workers become dependent. Thus, for a variety of reasons, there is a great deal of movement towards independent work away from dependent work and vice-versa.

Skill, and the relations between firms, are areas studied by Sabel who developed a new theory about the way in which the interaction between "final-firms" (i.e. those firms which have access to the final market) and "stage-firms" worked [Sabel, 1982]. Sabel stressed the idea that in this interaction it was possible to introduce (both to use and to produce) a great deal of innovation including incremental innovations and, on several occasions, innovations on the world market. Thus, the skill and the knowledge of the firms in the district are increased by fostering interaction between the skilled workers and small entrepreneurs of the "final-firms" and their subcontractors.

An important feature of industrial districts which must be discussed is the balance between co-operation and competition. I would say that the main form of co-operation is the interaction referred to above, concerning commissioning and subcontracting firms and it is to Sabel's credit that he stressed it substantially. However, there are other forms. In particular, there is co-operation of a type that seeks economies of scale in particular activities - although not in selling or marketing. For example, in respect of book-keeping, a trade association might carry out the function on behalf of many small clients and there is one case where such an association services 60,000 small firms. There are, however, no agreements to fix prices by forming cartels.

Competition occurs among equal firms - i.e. firms working on the same product or the same activity. Thus, there is a great deal of horizontal competition, in the sense that firms which do lathing compete readily with one another. Conversely, there is considerable vertical co-operation in the sense that firms that do lathing are very ready to co-operate with firms that do drilling or planing. Thus, firms which are different are ready to work together, while firms which do the same thing compete strongly against one another.

To conclude this section, I would like to stress that there were other major contributions to the understanding of the district in this period. One was again that of Becattini, who emphasised the role of the cultural background against which the district flourished, and who was perhaps the first to understand that a skill that may appear to be very abundant locally may be scarce on the world market [Becattini, 1975, 1987, 1989; Becattini et al., 1983]. For example, people who have been manufacturing clothes for centuries possess a kind of "clothing" culture and knowledge which is of great economic and productive significance: this is so even though it might not be fully appreciated locally simply because the culture's all-pervasiveness serves to inhibit a detached viewpoint.

Another important contribution was made by Bagnasco and Trigilia, both of whom stressed the significance of interaction between the market and institutions. Bagnasco and Trigilia undertook important studies in which they compared industrial districts in the "red" areas of Emilia Romagna (governed by the Communists) with districts in the "white" areas of Veneto (governed by the Christian Democrats). Their work centered on a consideration of the interaction between the market and institutions - how consensus is created and why it is necessary for the district to flourish - and the interaction between the political arena and the market. It was during this period that Bagnasco defined what he called the Third Italy [Bagnasco, 1977; Bagnasco and Pini, 1981; Bagnasco and Trigilia, 1984, 1985; Trigilia, 1981, 1986].

Finally, it must be noted that very little effort has been made to relate these factors to the main body of economic theory. One attempt was made by Mariti [1980] (who discusses Williamson, Richardson and Roegen - whose work has been presented to the Italian public by Tani [1976]), but this area is one of the least developed.

IV. The model of the industrial district Mark II

I shall now move on to my fourth model, which I shall call the *industrial district Mark II*, meaning that we now have a need for intervention which either did not exist before, or was at least less evident. The underlying contention is that new markets and new technologies have developed since the beginning of the 1980s, posing a problem for both large and small firms.

Large firms have already undergone an important process of restructuring and now small firms in industrial districts are involved in a similar process. Production in an industrial district is carried on as a social process by virtue of a social structure that encourages interaction amongst thousands of people. In order to achieve a capacity for invention and innovation, (referred to by Sabel) it is essential that many people understand the technology with which they work. This, in turn, requires continual informal interaction in cafés and bars and in the street. In this way, new ideas are formed and transmitted. This is very different from what happens in large firms which wish to introduce new technology. In this case, while there is certainly a need for some degree of consensus throughout the firm, it is possible to use a hierarchical process that starts with a decision by the Board of Directors. The very fact that the district has neither a head nor a hierarchical structure, makes a move towards new technology much more difficult. The district is characterised by a sort of strong, heavy inertia. It goes on learning the technology in a deep, personal and creative way, but it is very difficult to move this huge mass of people - not just the dependent workers, but the whole competence of all the people. Therefore, industrial districts must now face the problem of how social districts are to be endowed with the new technologies which are necessary to revive a process of creative growth. It is here that the need for intervention appears.

Some areas in Italy have coped with this problem by giving the firms "real services" rather than financial help. I have tried on many occasions to explain the ideal of real services - the ideal of real versus financial, of offering the firm what they need in kind, instead of offering them money to buy what they need. Perhaps the easiest way to describe "real services" is to give examples. One example is the setting up of a centre for real services in a particular region. The centre collects extensive information on farm equipment in different countries such as the Federal Republic of Germany, France, the United Kingdom and elsewhere on behalf of a cluster of firms producing agricultural equipment. The great difficulty these firms have found in exporting is that the import specifications of different countries change constantly. This is, in fact, a question of non-tariff barriers but it is a fairly difficult obstacle for a small firm to overcome. For example, a given small firm would find it very difficult to get accurate information about developments in Bavaria and may not be able to find out that Bavaria is perhaps stipulating that its railway lines must be no more than 35 cm above the ground. The setting up of an office which would collect this kind of information and pass it on to the people who need it, albeit at a price, would constitute a real service. Another example might be where help is given in bidding for a tender. Again a small firm producing agricultural implements might receive information about the fact that the Nigerian or the Egyptian government requires 500 km of water piping or 100 small tractors. Having received this information the small firm might then need help to get the tender translated and be shown how to put in a potentially successful bid. So it calls upon the assistance of a centre for real services which makes available someone who knows how a tender is made, who has good connections and who might well have worked in the tender office of a large firm in the past.

There are many different kinds of real services. In the textile industry, this might involve the monitoring of the fashion world by a group of sociologists, yarn experts, and fashion designers who predict future fashion trends (different colours, styles and materials, etc.) to artisans preparing viewing collections. Thus, for example, there is an office which, each year, eight months before the start of the season, holds a conference at which artisans can see the styles predicted for the next eight months. This information provides artisans with the inspiration necessary for designing their own collections.

By way of a conclusion, I would like to say that, in some places, real services have certainly been successful in encouraging growth, and have had an important effect in moving districts towards new technology and towards upper segments of the market. However, the problem which now troubles many of us in Italy is whether these internal policy measures which are taken at a local level, could be used in the *south* of Italy to transform clusters of firms into industrial districts. Could a centre for real services be used to this end or could such a centre even induce the growth of real firms where none exist at present?

References

Bagnasco, A. 1977. *Tre Italie: La problematica territoriale dello sviluppo italiano*, Bologna, Il Mulino.

Bagnasco, A.; Pini, R. 1981. *Sviluppo economico e trasformazioni sociopolitiche dei sistemi territoriali ad economia diffusa. Economia e struttura sociale*, Milan, Fondazione Feltrinelli.

Bagnasco, A.; Trigilia, C. (eds.). 1984. *Società e politica nelle aree di piccola impresa: Il caso di Bassano*, Venice, Arsenale Editrice.

---. 1985. *Società e politica nelle aree di piccola impresa: Il caso della Valdelsa*, (IRPET), Milan, Franco Angeli.

Becattini, G. (ed.). 1975. *Lo sviluppo economico della Toscana*, (IRPET), Florence, Le Monnier.

Becattini, G. 1978. "The development of light industry in Tuscany", in *Economic Notes*, No. 2/3.

---. 1979. "Dal 'settore industriale' al 'distretto industriale'. Alcune considerazioni sull'unità d'indagine dell'economia industriale", in *L'industria. Rivista di economia e politica industriale*, No. 1.

---. 1987. "Il distretto industriale Marshalliano: Cronaca di un ritrovamento", in Becattini, G. (ed.): *Mercato e forze locali: Il distretto industriale*, Bologna, Il Mulino.

---. 1989. "Riflessioni sul distretto industriale Marshalliano come concetto socio-economico", in *Stato e mercato*, No. 25 (republished here).

Becattini, G. et al. 1983. "L'industrializzazione diffusa in Toscana: Aspetti economici", in Fuà, G.; Zacchia, C. (eds.): *Industrializzazione senza fratture*, Bologna, Il Mulino.

Berger, S.; Piore, M. 1980. *Dualism and discontinuity in industrial societies*, Cambridge (Mass.), Cambridge University Press.

Brusco, S. 1973. "Prime note per uno studio del lavoro a domicilio in Italia", in *Inchiesta*, No. 10.

---. 1975. "Organizzazione del lavoro e decentramento produttivo nel settore metalmeccanico", in Di Bergami, F.L.M. (ed.): *Sindicato e piccola impresa*, Bari, De Donato.

---. 1982. "Il modello Emilia. Disintegrazione produttiva e integrazione sociale", in *Problemi della Transizione*, No. 5, 1980, translated as "The Emilian model: Productive decentralisation and social integration", in *Cambridge Journal of Economics*, No. 6.

---. 1986. "Small firms and industrial districts: The experience of Italy", in Keeble, D.; Wever, E. (eds.): *New firms and regional development*, London, Croom Helm.

Brusco, S.; Baldassarre, A. 1983. *Struttura e sviluppo in un distretto industriale: La meccanica agricola a Reggio Emilia*, Emilia, CSPMIA.

Graziani, A. 1969. *Lo sviluppo di un'economia aperta*, Naples, ESI.

---. 1972. *L'economia italiana: 1945-1970*, Bologna, Il Mulino.

---. 1975. "Aspetti strutturali dell'economia italiana nell'ultimo decennio", in Graziani, A. (ed.): *Crisi e ristrutturazione nell'economia italiana*, Turin, Einaudi.

Lutz, V. 1958. "Il processo di sviluppo in un sistema economico dualistico", in *Moneta e Credito*.

---. 1962. *Italy. A study in economic development*, Oxford, Oxford University Press.

Mariti, P. 1980. *Sui rapporti tra imprese in una economia industriale moderna*, Milan, Franco Angeli.

Paci, M. 1973. *Mercato del lavoro e classi sociali in Italia*, Bologna, Il Mulino.

---. 1975. "Crisi, ristrutturazione e piccola impresa", in *Inchiesta*, No. 20.

Sabel, C. 1982. *Work and politics*, Cambridge (Mass.), Cambridge University Press.

Solinas, G. 1982. "Labour market segmentation and workers' careers: The case of the Italian knitwear industry", in *Cambridge Journal of Economics*.

Tani, P. 1976. "La rappresentazione analitica del processo di produzione: Alcune premesse teoriche al problema del decentramento", in *Note Economiche*, No. 4-5.

Trigilia, C. 1981. *Sviluppo economico e trasformazioni sociopolitiche dei sistemi territoriali ad economia diffusa: Le subculture politiche territoriali*, Milan, Fondazione Feltrinelli.

---. 1986. *Grandi partiti e piccole imprese*, Bologna, Il Mulino.

3 A history of flexible specialisation and industrial districts in Emilia-Romagna

Vittorio Capecchi

This chapter presents an overview of the historical development of industrialisation in Emilia-Romagna from the beginning of the twentieth century to the present. What makes this history particularly interesting from the point of view of this book is that industrial production in the Emilia-Romagna region is mainly characterised today by a model of flexible specialisation which is very different from the Ford-Taylorist type of organisation. Moreover, it can also be stated that this particular type of flexible production is organised mainly on a basis of industrial districts and urban industrial sub-systems. Consequently, the history of industrial development in Emilia-Romagna is different from that of other regions where industrial production is more generally dominated by companies involved in large batch production and where the presence of industrial districts and urban industrial sub-systems is less evident.

Before the influences that have played a part in Emilia-Romagna's development are described, it is worth defining some of the specific terms which we will use.

I. Flexible specialisation, industrial districts, and urban industrial sub-systems

1. Flexible specialisation

Flexible specialisation refers to a system of producing either investment or consumer goods which can best be characterised by comparing it to a very different, Fordist model of production.[1] The main differences

---

1. The differences between the Fordist model and the flexible specialisation model have been analysed in Piore and Sabel [1984] and Sabel and Zeitlin [1985]. In my analysis of the flexible specialisation model in Emilia-Romagna, I pay more attention to the differences between women and men in social and economic life, to the differences between the informal and formal economy, to the way in which skills are transmitted (in technical schools, in the family, etc.), and to the process of social mobility. In this analysis, I have been strongly influenced by the researches of Adele Pesce. See Capecchi and Pesce [1983]; Capecchi [1987, 1989a, 1989b, 1989c]; Barbagli et al. [1987]; Pesce [1987, 1989].

between the Fordist and flexible specialisation models can be described as follows:

(a) in the Fordist system there is mass production or large batch production, while in the case of flexible specialisation, factories engage in small batch production, producing prototypes and custom-made machinery and/or products;

(b) in the Fordist model the organisation of work is basically Tayloristic, i. e. there is a clear separation between white-collar workers, who are in the minority, and the majority comprising unskilled blue-collar workers. In flexible specialisation, however, the organisation of work is based on a three level co-operation between white-collar workers at the head, skilled workers and unskilled workers;

(c) the key to the system of flexible specialisation is the middle skilled group who come to the factory as professionally skilled workers and, while on the job, increase their professionality with experience. The combination of experience and professional know-how permit these skilled workers to leave the factories and become small independent entrepreneurs. It is clear, therefore, that the flexible specialisation model of industrialisation allows the possibility of social mobility among the working class, a mobility which would not be possible in the Fordist model;

(d) production procedures in the Fordist model are standardised as is the product. The most important element is the price. In flexible specialisation, production procedures require close collaboration between the factory and the client resulting in a custom-made product;

(e) in the Fordist model production takes place in a few big factories, while in the flexible specialisation model production takes place in many small and medium-sized factories organised into industrial districts and urban industrial sub-systems.

2. Industrial districts

When flexible specialisation is organised in a particular way it is said to have developed within the framework of an "industrial district".

If we use Marshall's [Marshall, 1919] definition of an industrial district made known in Italy by Giacomo Becattini[2] then we have an industrial district when:

(a) production is flexible and tries to meet the different needs of clients and, if the client is a wholesaler, is able to make the whole range of the production series for which the wholesaler asks;

---

2. Becattini [1979]. For a more recent discussion on industrial districts, see Becattini [1987, 1989]; Brusco [1989]; Regini and Sabel [1989].

(b) there are many small and very small firms in a given territory which have the same type of flexible production:

(c) among these small, very small or medium-sized firms, some sell their products directly on the market, while others carry out particular processes or produce component parts of a product;

(d) the separation between those firms which sell their products and those which act as sub-suppliers to other firms is not rigid: a small firm can, at a given moment, be a sub-supplier and, at another, a seller;

(e) the relations between firms that sell on the market take the form of an interweaving of competition and co-operation: that means that the firms do not fight one other but try to find market places for new production without having destructive effects within the industrial district;

(f) the zone is so defined because it refers to a very limited geographical area which is specifically characterised by a certain dominant production;

(g) there is a strong interconnection between the district as a production reality and the zone as a mixture of family, political and social life.

On the basis of this definition, it is possible to identify districts in Emilia-Romagna wherein a small town corresponds to a predominant type of production: Carpi, in the province of Modena, for example, is characterised by knitwear clothing production whilst Sassuolo, another town in the province of Modena, is characterised by ceramic tile production.

3. Urban industrial sub-systems

We talk about *urban industrial sub-systems*, however, when there is a situation which has the characteristics of points (a), (b), (c), (d) and (e), but not of (f) and (g). For example in the *city* of Bologna we can identify many industrial sub-systems producing, measuring, packaging and wrapping machines or motorcycles, but not one of these sub-systems characterises the whole productive system of Bologna. Carpi is identified with knitwear but Bologna *is not* identified solely with measuring, packaging and wrapping machine production.

In order to outline the history of flexible specialisation, industrial districts, and urban industrial sub-systems, let us consider three periods: from 1900 to 1950, from 1950 to 1970 and from 1970 to the present.

II. 1900-1950: Social and economic foundations

For the region of Emilia-Romagna, there are seven positive factors present in the years 1900 to 1950 which help to explain the development of flexible specialisation.

1. Socialism in the city and in the country

During the early part of the century female rice workers and male farm hands in Emilia-Romagna became involved in rural struggles. These were so important that between 1904 and 1925 the leadership of the National Federation of Farm Workers was entrusted to a woman from the province of Bologna named Argentina Altabelli. Socialist ideas spread in both the cities and the countryside of Emilia-Romagna with the establishment of the *Camera del Lavoro* (a type of Italian trade union that caters for all workers in a given territory) and the formation of provincial associations of farm labourers. By 1909 [Baldissara, 1987], the Socialists represented 40 per cent of the electorate, and when universal male suffrage was introduced in 1913 four provinces in Emilia-Romagna (Bologna, Ferrara, Reggio Emilia, and Parma) voted Socialist.

The presence of Socialism in rural Emilia-Romagna led to the creation of associations and co-operatives and to the spread of progressive attitudes. This, together with the anarchist and union elements, is one of the most deeply rooted characteristics of the Communist party in Emilia-Romagna and throws light on the direction it took later in the 1950s.

During the 1930s Fascist forces [D'Attore, 1980] tried to create a conflict between the principal components of farm workers, farm-hands and share farmers just as they did in the city between skilled and unskilled workers. However, the resistance movement to Fascism during the Second World War brought about a reconciliation among the greater part of the industrial and agricultural working classes. Consequently, by 1948 Emilia-Romagna was "red" [Galli, 1968] with 52 per cent of votes going to the Communist and Socialist parties as compared to an average of 31 per cent for the rest of Italy.

2. University and università popolari (socialist teaching centres for the working classes)

The University of Bologna [Tega, 1987] concentrated together various disciplines of intellectual knowledge that established an important, fruitful relationship between the social and economic communities in Emilia. This concentration in a "red" province favoured an active role by the intellectual groups who, utilising Socialist aims, tried to spread both scientific and non-scientific culture in the interests of all social levels. As a consequence, in 1901 the Università Popolare Giuseppe Garibaldi, one of the most important of its kind at a national level, was founded in Bologna.

This *università popolare* became the centre of a national movement with Bologna as the seat of the National Federation of Università Popolari, and their activities were organised in the cities of Emilia and the surrounding countryside.

3. A rural area characterised by the presence of small entrepreneurs

During the period from 1900 to 1950, Emilia-Romagna remained a region strongly marked by agriculture. The percentage of the active population in agriculture was 65 per cent in 1901, 61 per cent in 1931 and 52 per cent in 1951 (see table 1), whereas in the rest of Italy the corresponding figures were 62 per cent, 52 per cent and 42 per cent.

Table 1: Breakdown of the population of Emilia-Romagna

	1901	1951	1971	1981
Agricultural employment	64.6	51.8	20.0	13.4
Industrial employment	19.9	25.2	42.6	38.1
Employment in services	15.5	23.0	37.4	48.5
Total	**100.0**	**100.0**	**100.0**	**100.0**
Employment in the engineering industry as a percentage of total industrial employment	14.5	17.0	32.0	41.1

Source: ISTAT.

The composition of the population working in agriculture in the north was very different from that in the south. According to the 1901 census, only 40 per cent of the population working in agriculture in Emilia-Romagna were male or female waged workers (farm-hands or farm labourers); 60 per cent were workers on contract as share farmers (*mezzadri*) or on rented land, or were small farm-owners. Thus, 60 per cent of the population working in agriculture had experience of small farm entrepreneurship.

Another significant factor is that the experience of people in the countryside extended beyond cultivation or animal husbandry to include proto-industrial experience in hemp processing, weaving and straw braiding[3].

4. The presence of industrial and proto-industrial districts

In many small towns of Emilia, which often served as centres of rural areas, industrial and proto-industrial districts were already established during the period 1900-1950, to be continued or adapted during the following period 1950-1970.

For example, in Carpi[4], the work of osier wood shavings and straw braiding for the manufacture of straw hats existed as early as 1500 and, after many ups and downs, at the beginning of the 1900s (in 1904) the Limited Company, *Il Truciolo*, was established in which 30,000 to 40,000 people, mainly women, manufactured straw hats which were sold in many parts of the world, not only Paris, New York and London, but also Manila and Tien-Tsin. It is obvious that this strong marketing network, already existing in this area, made it easier for the Carpi knitwear industry to export during the period 1950-1970.

Similarly, the ceramic tile industry of Sassuolo which also had its roots in the 1500s with the famous Sassuolo potters, experienced a noticeable expansion in the eighteenth and nineteenth centuries. By the beginning of this century Sassuolo ceramics were being exported out of Italy, thanks to the Rubbiani family.

Thus, all the industrial districts of Emilia with an identifiable type of production in the period 1950-1970, could already have been identified as specialised industrial districts as early as 1900-1950.

5. The transmission of technological knowledge by means of technical schools

The most important transfer of knowledge for the industrial development of Emilia-Romagna region has been in the field of mechanics. In Bologna this was facilitated by the work of two intellectuals, the experimental physicist Giovanni Aldini and the economist Luigi Valeriani[5] who, at the end of the eighteenth century and at the beginning of the nineteenth, were inspired by nations like Great Britain and France. During their trips to London and Paris they documented the methods of teaching advanced technology used in these countries.

---

3. The life in rural areas of Emilia-Romagna in 1900-1950 is described in AAVV [1983]; Broccoli [1979; 1988] and Poni [1982].

4. The history of the industrial district of Carpi is described in Cappello and Prandi [1973].

5. The history of Giovanni Aldini and Luigi Valeriani has been described in *Comune di Bologna* [1980].

When they died in 1828 and 1834 respectively, Aldini and Valeriani willed their property to the city of Bologna for the purposes of opening technical schools for the diffusion of mechanical know-how. Consequently, in 1839, the Technical Schools of Bologna were established with the co-operation of the municipal administration, of the University and of the Association of Artisans. In 1878, these schools became the Institute of Arts and Crafts Aldini Valeriani where technical and practical subjects were taught. Other technical school of this type were the Corni Institute in Modena, founded in 1921, and the Alberghetti, founded in Imolo in 1881. All this helps to explain the skill in mechanical design and planning found in this region.

The transfer of know-how in the field of agriculture has also been very important. In this region, intellectuals traditionally helped to develop a more scientifically-based type of agriculture. For example, Antonio Zanelli[6] helped to found a school in Reggio Emilia in 1879 which taught improved agricultural techniques and the principles of scientific breeding, thereby making the rearing of highly prized pigs and cattle possible. After the Second World War, Reggio Emilia became one of the most important centres of swine production.

In the small industrial and proto-industrial districts in this period the transmission of knowledge occurred through apprenticeships, or through schools where specialised workers acted as teachers. In Carpi, women straw braiders taught their techniques on the job and in schools; in Sassuolo the same was done by potters. In the other cities of Emilia, specialised staff taught embroidery, tailoring and sewing. In Bologna, the Elisabetta Sirani Technical School was established by a women workers' association in 1895. The transmission of more complex knowledge was carried out by scholars connected to the university world.

6. An industrial society oriented towards flexible specialisation

In the period 1900-1950, there was limited industrialisation in the region which remained essentially agricultural. However, there were many industrial districts and the beginnings of urban industrial sub-systems in the engineering industry organised on a flexible specialisation basis. In Bologna, for example, between 1900 and 1950 the majority of industries were oriented towards the production of custom-made machinery or in the production of prototypes of automobiles or racing motorcycles.

The two world wars forced many factories in Emilia to manufacture war products but this did not change the characteristics of the predominant production so that, after the wars, production was again oriented towards a plurality of clients and their different needs.

---

6. The history of Antonio Zanelli is in Cafasi [1979].

7. A different power relation between men and women

In all the aspects considered so far, the relationship between men and women is more equal than in other regions; that is to say that in Emilia-Romagna women have had more power than in other regions of Italy [Pesce, 1987; 1989]. They were the initiators of small enterprises in sectors like clothing and ceramics. As regards the engineering industry, women were excluded from technical schools and therefore never participated in machine projects; however, they were present in the management of firms, especially in small firms.

In Emilia women were also present in the unions, in the university and in political parties and participated actively in the resistance against Fascism.

III. 1950-1970: Widespread industrialisation

Of the funds provided by the Marshall Plan after the Second World War for the purchase of industrial equipment, 25 per cent went to industry in Piedmont, 28 per cent in Lombardy and only 0.75 per cent to industry in Emilia-Romagna [Melossi, 1977]. At the same time, on the initiative of the national government, the factories which had been used for the manufacture of arms during the war were either closed down or drastically cut back. In Reggio Emilia the factories which had employed up to 12,000 workers during the war, employed only 700 in 1952; the Ducati factory in Bologna dropped from approximately 6,000-7,000 workers to 1,300 in 1954; Calzoni, another factory in Bologna, went from 1,600 workers to 130; the Cogne factory in Imola dropped from 2,400 to 600 workers. The cut-back of these factories resulted in a loss of business for the smaller firms which carried out work for them.

These difficulties could have led to the emigration of workers and to a slowing down of industrial development in the region. However, things turned out quite differently. This cut-back of specialised engineering workers from the war-time factories is now seen as a positive factor in the dissemination of newer forms of industrial venture. Industrialisation actually underwent a remarkable growth during the 1950-1970 period. This caused the percentage of the active population working in agriculture to drop from 52 per cent to 20 per cent (a difference of minus 32 per cent) and industrial workers to increase from 25 per cent to 43 per cent (or plus 18 per cent), whereas during the same period in the rest of Italy, the variations were less extreme (minus 25 per cent in agriculture and plus 12 per cent in industry) [Barbagli et al., 1987]. During this 20-year period, emigration to other regions and countries was static. There was, however, internal movement from the mountain areas and the smaller centres to the larger cities and towns and to the northern flat lands.

Per capita income increased, as did Emilia-Romagna's share of total Italian exports. The latter rose from 6 per cent in 1963 to 8.4 per cent

[Barbagli et al., 1987] in 1974 with radical changes in the types of goods exported. In the 1950s Emilia-Romagna exported agricultural products and clothing, while in the 1970s exports were primarily made up of machines and mechanical products. The number of employees in the engineering industries as a percentage of total industrial employment (see table 1) rose from 17 per cent in 1951 to 32 per cent in 1971 and to 41 per cent in 1981, the other main sectors being textiles, clothing and food.

There are three factors that helped to influence this development and they can be identified as follows.

1. The construction of a political community in the region

After the Second World War, the Italian Communist and Socialist parties had an absolute majority and governed the Emilia-Romagna region as well as the cities in Emilia.[7] One of the particular characteristics of the Italian Communist party in Emilia, which has differed from that of the Communist parties in France and Spain, is that it has sustained the creation of small businesses and helped salaried workers to become self-employed and create small enterprises. The Communist Party and the Socialist Party have a majority in the labour unions in Emilia-Romagna and also represent the majority in the organisation of small artisan businesses and co-operatives. These associations of artisans and co-operatives, co-ordinated by people belonging to the Communist and Socialist parties, became extremely important centres of economic power, and served as bases for training in business and in the management of small enterprises.

By this means a kind of Communist and Socialist "political community" was formed wherein people of the same political leaning came to be in charge of local and regional government, labour unions, small artisan associations and industries, and firms organised as co-operatives. This "common" management of industrialisation in Emilia-Romagna has had a "common enemy", the national government which, being Christian-Democrat, has traditionally supported the large enterprises of the north and threatened the factories of Emilia.

Women have played an active and recognised role in this community (in contrast with other regions) and the local administrations in Emilia-Romagna have provided many social services such as day-care centres or kindergartens in order to allow women with small children to participate in the working world. In the period 1950-1970, great attention was devoted to social policies (with the help of Catholics in the region), speculation in construction was resisted and small businesses were given support, thereby increasing social mobility as well as improving economic development.

---

7. For a history of a political community of Bologna, see Arbizzani [1961] and AAVV [1988].

2. Gradual agricultural transition

The way in which agriculture was transformed[8] also contributed to a higher standard of living in this region. The drastic fall in the agricultural population did not, in fact, mean an end to agricultural production. There was a change of direction towards capitalistic agriculture which brought about a dramatic increase in productivity per hectare.

The food industry of Emilia-Romagna also became very significant: pasta products were now exported; long-life milk was marketed all over Italy; pork products, such as Parma ham and Bologna mortadella, became better known, whilst Parmesan cheese production from Parma and Reggio Emilia became important; wine was successfully exported along with a whole range of fruit juices.

The majority of farming families did not earn enough to continue with agriculture as their sole activity but did have a large enough income to enable them to leave the agricultural world without too much difficulty.

A process of industrialisation based on the diffusion of middle-sized, small and very small firms came about in rural areas as well as in the towns. Within these rural areas, some of the proto-industrial activities became industrial and the industrial areas within the small towns became increasingly important. In Carpi, for example, the processing of osier shavings to make straw hats evolved into a large number of companies manufacturing knitwear with the first phase characterised by women's work done in the home and then by the establishment of a large number of small and medium-sized companies. The manufacture of ceramic tiles developed in Sassuolo and Fiorano. In the countryside there was the beginning of work connected to the engineering industry.

3. The development of flexible specialisation and the engineering industry

From 1950 to 1970, the industrial development of Emilia occurred primarily in the engineering sector, exports from which exceeded (in monetary terms) those from agriculture and other industries. In the earlier period of 1900-1950, there had only been a few industries characterised by versatile production in towns such as Bologna, Modena and Reggio Emilia. This versatility was used during the two world wars in manufacturing war products that surely contributed to the strengthening of these industries. After the Second World War, this type of know-how, brought about by technical school education and professional training in the firms, was strongly encouraged by a strengthening of market demands, as all the industries producing consumer goods required machinery for the packaging of their products.

Flexible production in Emilia was therefore oriented towards the production of machines for different types of industry and agriculture,

---

8. About this process, see Fuà and Zacchia [1983].

including measuring, packaging and wrapping machines that allowed firms which produce foodstuffs, pharmaceutical products or cigarettes to have custom-made equipment, ranging from cigarette packaging machines, through blistering machines for pharmaceutical products, to packaging and wrapping machines for all types of foodstuffs (cakes, sweets, tea, etc.). A very high market demand and the possibility of undertaking production with limited capital made an extended development possible. This development was of an urban industrial sub-system type and, as a consequence, there was an increase of this type of production in the cities based on medium, small and very small companies (see table 2).

Table 2: Classification of employment in the engineering industry by size of firm*

Size of firm	1927	1937	1951	1961	Size of firm	1971	1981
1-10	52.1	28.6	36.9	37.4	1-9	18.2	22.1
11-100	23.3	16.3	23.1	32.6	10-99	38.7	40.2
101-500	16.8	20.6	21.4	19.7	100-499	25.0	23.0
501+	7.7	34.4	18.6	10.3	500+	17.1	14.7
Total	**100.0**	**100.0**	**100.0**	**100.0**	**Total**	**100.0**	**100.0**

Note: * Excluding repair workshops.
Source: ISTAT.

For example, in the case of the urban industrial sub-system of the packaging industries in Bologna, during the period from 1900 to 1950, packaging machines were produced by only two firms, Acma and Sasib. In the period from 1950 to 1970, the number of firms increased to almost 100 for the production of various machines sold on the market, and to 200-300 supplying special parts and processes to the former.

IV. 1970 to the present

1. Strong competition and new technologies

The dissemination of electronic and computer technology has had enormous repercussions on the industrial system in Emilia-Romagna [Capecchi, 1989c; Brusco, 1989]. There are two closely linked reasons for this: the increased competitiveness of the big multinationals, and the need for a complete reconversion of the mechnical engineering and electrical industries which predominate in the region. The increased competitiveness of large firms is particularly significant. Until recently, the big Fordist-type companies, such as Fiat in Italy, had inflexible production lines; the replacement of one type of machine with another was slow and very costly, whether in terms of time, installation, or work organisation.

Today high technology allows even big engineering firms to change their type of product without particular problems or loss of time. Industrial development in Emilia-Romagna between 1950 and 1970 occurred in a context of competition solely with other European or American small-series industrial producers and without competition from large-scale industry. Today, however, Japanese, American and European multinationals can compete in the production of capital goods in limited series, typical of Emilia-Romagna.

As competition has grown, two problems have arisen: the reconversion of an industry based on groups of small and medium-sized firms, and a generation change. The problems of completely reconverting an industry are of three types: product innovation; innovation in the production process strictly speaking; and innovation in the management and organisation of the different functions of workshops and of work.

Product innovation not only means changing the quality of a type of product (for example inserting electronic components into clothing and packaging machinery in order to improve quality) but also means exploring the possibility of directing a part of industrial production towards new markets. The main problem is that of redirecting a form of industrial production characterised by flexible specialisation and aimed primarily at industry (production of machines for the industrial sector) towards markets currently in expansion (machines and equipment for the social, health, education, banking, commercial and insurance sectors plus all the possible applications of telecommunications and computer technology in urban life). Therefore a change of outlook is needed, and this requires different points of reference with targeted university research, looking at areas of application which are often far beyond the know-how of small entrepreneurs.

Innovation in the area of procedures is a more straightforward matter. It consists mainly of acquiring lines of computer-controlled machines, introducing robotics and the like. However, such innovations require very different worker training, and particular skills in purchasing materials, and in handling the financial problems of modernisation (the very problems that firms which are not well prepared can encounter).

In contrast, innovation in management and organisation is far more complex. Computer-assisted management is only widespread in firms of a certain size (those with over 500 employees and sometimes those with 250 to 500 employees). There is also the problem of reorganising the links between the firms which make up a sub-system. This leads to the standardisation of procedures in order to reduce costs. These are the difficult problems which firms and sub-systems must solve in order to obtain ever tighter links between marketing, programming and production.

There is thus a phase of great technological and managerial change which corresponds to the great social changes taking place at this time. One of the most important changes is the increase, in the younger generations, of the level of education of women reaching higher scholastic levels than that achieved by young males. Women have thus been able to enter tertiary professional activities (today in continual expansion) and top positions in the management of small companies linked to the mechanical industry.

2. Institutional strategies

By the end of the 1980s, the region had experienced an increase of exports, a growth in the gross regional product, and high levels of employment. Significant to this success, and to dealing with current problems of change, are the strategies applied by all the institutions of Emilia-Romagna, including the local and regional administrations, unions, associations of small enterprises, co-operative leagues, industrialists' associations, and the universities.

A. A group of strategies for offering services to firms

In 1974, the region of Emilia-Romagna established a centre called ERVET (Regional Agency for the Economic Evaluation of the Territory) which organised a series of other service centres in the Emilia area according to the type of industrial districts and urban industrial sub-systems. Thus, for example, a ceramics centre was founded in the Sassuolo area, and a footwear centre in San Mauro Pascoli; another, CERMET, has been set up for testing metal materials in Bologna; and in Carpi CITER was established for clothing.

ERVET set up a centralised service to provide information about such matters as patents, and foreign markets, whilst schemes were established with the co-operation of the regional government to help weaker areas in Emilia-Romagna to establish specific vocational training and service centres. Another group of services was offered to the firms by the CNA (National Artisans' Federation) and the Co-operative League, and projects of co-operation between universities and the Confederation of large firms were started.

The point to stress about these undertakings is their *flexibility* - that is, the services offered are quite flexible and are suited to the needs of the various firms in the zones scattered throughout the region. Flexible specialisation of the production system was taken as a model also in the area of services to the firms.

B. Professional training

In Italy, each region is in charge of the way it organises its professional training. This decentralisation has caused lively organisational activity, but only in some regions; in others, such as in southern Italy, there is little activity and the results of professional training are negligible. In a region like Emilia-Romagna, where professional training[9] is well organised, important results are obtained, whether in respect of training for jobs or training on the job.

Also significant is the attention that the municipal administration, the labour unions and the associations of small craft firms give to training for small firms. Public authorities in the various municipalities help in creating projects for easy access to small-scale entrepreneurship. There are

---

9. About professional training in Emilia-Romagna, see Capecchi [1987].

regional laws which help young, innovating firms and courses organised by the CNA to teach entrepreneurs how to manage firms using the new computer and communications technology.

C. The association policy among small firms

A third strategy, aimed at overcoming the big changes that have taken place in Emilia-Romagna, is the policy of setting up small firm associations. Today some changes are occurring in the large industrial districts and in the urban industrial sub-systems because of a growing international dimension whereby lead companies are emerging, becoming multinational, and creating difficulties for smaller firms that are no longer able to supply or produce for them. There is, therefore, a need on the part of small enterprises to form associations in order to address such problems as research, sales and marketing, and these associations which are beginning to form have, in turn, to be flexible to meet varied needs.

V. The past and future of the Emilia "model"

The international attention paid to the Emilia-Romagna industrial system based on flexible specialisation during the years 1950-70 was due not only to the economic success of such a system, but also, and above all, to the blending of a model of economic development with a model of social development. In that period, the spread of industrialisation coincided with a wide process of social mobility from a peasant/working class condition to that of small entrepreneurial activity. The process, moreover, involved both men and women. Women, in fact, who had been excluded from technical schools and who thus had less to do with the engineering industrialisation phase, played a very important part in the dissemination of small entrepreneurship in the clothing sector; not to mention the importance of their role within the framework of the farm or factory family which was a determinant factor in the family paths of social mobility.

The leftist parties, and in particular the Communist party which governed the region, developed not only a political programme of support to small entrepreneurship (as we have already shown), but also a wide-scale programme of social services such as public transport, infant day centres, and low-cost housing districts which provided an opportunity for women to enter the formal economy.

This blending of an economic with a social model was possible, in the first place, because of the democratic dispersion of information and decision-making processes: a person who worked in a firm and wanted to go into business on his own could not only count on a democratic public administration, but also on an unofficial network of contacts and connections with the heads of local governments. This network, quite far removed from the patron-client type of protection common in other regions of Italy at that time, appeared as a true experiment in effective democracy reinforced by the common fight against Fascism and by the widespread Socialist tradition.

The internal contradictions of the political forces and of the people who contributed to the economic and social development of Emilia-Romagna were less noticeable and significant than the external ones. The enemies of the Emilia model were to be found in the central government of centre-right formation led by the Christian-Democratic party which did not help the "red" region of Italy, and in the large industrial companies of northern Italy which received all the support of the central government and whose organisation of work and production were very different: a Ford-Taylorist system as against the flexible specialisation and industrial districts of Emilia, where it was possible to move from a factory wage-earning status to one of small entrepreneurship.

The situation has changed greatly in the last ten years and we now witness an ever-widening division between the economic and social models causing noticeable explosions of internal friction in a way which was unknown in the past. Among these new contradictions, those occurring inside the working world are most noticeable because of the growing internationalisation of the development model and because of a conflict of interests between industrial growth and environmental protection.

The economic successes of Emilia-Romagna have brought about an ever-growing presence of men and women workers from foreign countries (in particular from Senegal and northern Africa) who work in harmful jobs in foundries or in less qualified jobs as household help. Furthermore, the foreign expansion of firms in Emilia is oriented towards those countries in North Africa, Brazil and South-East Asia which have low-cost labour. There is, therefore, a principle of exploitation in respect of foreign labour that was unknown in the predominant industries in Emilia-Romagna during the years 1950-70.

In respect of the environment, the widespread use of chemicals in agriculture both in fertilisers and pesticides has brought about an increase of cancer in farming areas; the unloading of industrial wastes into rivers together with an uncontrolled development of tourist resorts and hotels is helping to destroy the shores and waters of Emilia.

A series of contradictions that were present in the 1950-70 period, are larger and more visible today. For example, the contradiction between women and men was not as pronounced then because the process of social mobility also concerned women and the programme for social services had found women to be the central part of both the economic and social models. Today it is the greater presence of women in the formal economy (the rate of working women in this region is the highest in Italy), as well as their enhanced consciousness due to the spread of feminist movements, that have focussed the conflict between men and women as the latter lay claim to a greater share of political, trade union, economic and cultural power.

These internal conflicts are combined with the presence of populations which have never succeeded in achieving satisfactory social goals; this gives rise to marginalisation and isolation which are very different from the conflicts existing in the period following the Second World War. At that time the degree of interpersonal, family and political solidarity was higher and the social problems as well as the dynamics of economic development were dealt with at the same time.

Finally, the two major leftist parties (the Communist and the Socialist parties) which headed the regional government in Emilia-Romagna after the Second World War are much more divided today. In fact, at present, whilst the Socialist Party is part of the central government in alliance with the Christian-Democratic party, the Communists are in the opposition. Today, the growth of international competition, technological innovation, greater flexibility and the increasing power of large-scale industries present many problems which require the re-thinking of the production system in Emilia. There may be a temptation to solve these problems merely on the technical and economic levels thereby increasing the divergence between the economic and social models. However, another more difficult solution exists which demands that we face the internal contradictions mentioned above, or at least recognise them as the central problem of today's situation.

To proceed in this direction requires a change in attitude: to pay more attention on the social level to those areas of intervention which were traditionally considered technical and economic. For example, attention to the development of new technology in such projects as the Bologna technological and scientific park should not be limited to improving competition and production. The potential offered by the new electronic and computer technologies and communication systems for greater environmental protection, the preservation of health in work areas and in hospitals, improved preventive care, assistance to the handicapped and improvements in the level of social cohesion should also be given careful consideration.

The technological and social challenges to be faced are very complicated and the increase in internal contradictions require simultaneous action on three levels: that of the individual rights of citizens by reducing inequality whilst emphasising the positive differences among people; that of vocational training and scientific research (with the aim of continually increasing the quality and quantity of basic, professional and university training); and finally, that of the new technologies and of the organisation of work, trying, in an international context, to propose what, not long ago, was considered the specific distinction of the Emilia-Romagna region, namely the blending of social and economic development models.

References

AAVV. 1983. *Cultura popolare in Emilia Romagna*, I-VI vol. Milan, Silvana Editore.

AAVV. 1988. *Il sindacato nel bolognese. Le camere del lavoro di Bologna dal 1893 al 1960*, Bologna, Ediesse.

Arbizzani, L. 1961. *Sguardi sull'ultimo secolo, Bologna e la sua provincia 1859-1961*, Bologna, Galileo.

Baldissara, L. 1987. "Le classi dirigenti emiliane fra politiae e poteri locali 1860-1960", in *Italia contemporanea*, No. 167, pp. 65-84.

Barbagli, M. et al. 1987. *La mobilità sociale in Emilia Romagna*, Bologna, Il Mulino.

Becattini, G. 1979. "Dal settore industriale al distretto industriale: alcune considerazioni sull'unità di indagine dell'economia industriale", in *Rivista di economia e politica industriale*, No. 1, pp. 7-21.

Becattini, G. (ed.). 1987. *Mercato e forze sociali: il distretto industriale*, Bologna, Il Mulino.

---. 1989. *Modelli locali di sviluppo*, Bologna, Il Mulino.

Broccoli, A. 1979. *Chiamavano pane il pane*, Bologna, Edagricole.

---. 1988. *Il bello della festa. Storia di donne nel mondo contadino*, Bologna, Clueb.

Brusco, S. 1989, *Piccole imprese e distretti industriali*, Turin, Rosenberg and Sellier.

Cafasi, F. 1979. *Antonio Zanelli. La scuola di zootecnia e caseificio di Reggio Emilia 1879-1979*, Reggio Emilia, Ed. Istituto A. Zanelli.

Capecchi, V. 1987. "Formation professionnelle et petite entreprise; le développement industriel à spécialisation flexible en Emilia Romagna", in *Formation-emploi*, No. 19, pp. 3-18.

---. 1989a. "The informal economy and the development of flexible specialisation in Emilia Romagna", in Portes, A. et al. (eds.): *The informal economy, studies in advanced and less developed countries*, Baltimore, The John Hopkins University Press.

---. 1989b. "Changing patterns of small entrepreneurship", in Strumpel, B. (ed.): *Industrial societies after stagnation of the 1970s*, Berlin, Walter de Gruyter Edition.

---. 1989c. "Petite entreprise et économie locale; la flexibilité productive", in Maruani, M., et al.: *La flexibilité en Italie*, Paris, Syros.

Capecchi, V.; Pesce, A. 1983. "Se la diversità é un valore", in *Inchiesta*, Nos. 59-60, pp.1-37.

Cappello, S.; Prandi, A. 1973. *Carpi, tradizione e sviluppo*, Bologna, Il Mulino.

Comune di Bologna. 1980. *Macchine scuola industria*, Bologna, Il Mulino.

D'Attore, P. 1980. "Una dimensione periferica. Piccola industria, classe operaia e mercato del lavoro in Emilia Romagna 1920-1940", in *Annali Feltrinelli 1979-1980*, Milan, Ed. Feltrinelli.

Fuà, G.; Zacchia, C. (eds.). 1983. *Industrializzazione senza fratture*, Bologna, Il Mulino.

Galli, G. (ed.). 1968. *Il comportamento elettorale in Italia*, Bologna, Il Mulino.

Marshall, A. 1919. *Industry and trade*, London.

Melossi, D. 1977. "Lotta di classe nel piano del lavoro", in AAVV (eds.): *Restaurazione capitalistica e Piano del Lavoro*, Rome, Editrice sindacale italiana.

Pesce, A. 1987. "Trajectoires des femmes dans la famille ouvrière", in *Annales de Vaucresson*, No. 26.

---. 1989. "L'altra Emilia-Romagna", in *Rapporto della Commissione per le pari opportunità*, Bologna, Regione Emilia-Romagna.

Piore, M.J.; Sabel, C. 1984. *The second industrial divide*, New York, Basic Books.

Poni, C. 1982. *Fossi e cavedagne benedicon le campagne*, Bologna, Il Mulino.

Regini, M.; Sabel, C. (eds.). 1989. *Strategie di riaggiustamento industriale*, Bologna, Il Mulino.

Sabel, C.; Zeitlin, J. 1985. "Historical alternatives to mass production: Politics, markets and technology in nineteenth century industrialisation", in *Past and Present*, No.108, pp. 133-176.

Tega, W. (ed.). 1987. *Lo studio e la città. Bologna 1886-1988*, Bologna, Nuova Alfa Editoriale.

4 The Marshallian industrial district as a socio-economic notion[1]

Giacomo Becattini

I. Introduction

The following discussion was conceived initially as a framework for a theory of the industrial district. The objective of such a theory was twofold: first, it aimed at improving the accuracy of, and insights from, empirical studies of contemporary industrialisation; second, it was conceived as a first attempt towards recognising the existing links between the empirical issues of the district, and the main theoretical core of economic thinking - that is, of neoclassical, Marshallian, and Marxian thinking. Such a dual concern causes some sort of "cross-eyed" intellectual view. Whilst one will be forced to a jealous defence of the socio-economic unity of the object of inquiry, in order to stick closely to the "real thing", at the same time one will also be moved to trim and generalise in order to conform as much as possible to the requirements of clarity and symmetry of economic analysis.

In a sense, the result of such a process can only be unsatisfactory, because it will often be misunderstood, whether because some stylisation is needed for a simplified description of reality, or whether because this stylisation is derived from within the theory. However, there are two sides to this. On the one hand, keeping track of concrete phenomena which persist through time - such as that of the district of Prato - gives us some confidence about the "essential coherence" of the stylised phenomenon, since any phenomenon which persists through time is to be assumed to possess some internal logic. On the other hand, retaining a permanent reference to some fragments of existing theories will enable us to grasp the counterfactual implications of the interpretative model, and give a unifying framework to empirical observations which would otherwise remain apart.

These were my initial concerns, which were similar to those of any "applied" economist. However, as the discussion of industrial districts developed, further concerns were added. The fact that a fairly large part of the argument rested on "values", and their interaction with the economic actions which occurred in the period of analysis, made confrontation with what sociologists and other students of society had to say on the matter indispensable. Fortunately, Italian sociologists did not take much persuading,

---

1. The original Italian version of this article appeared, with a few small differences, in *Stato e Mercato*, No. 25, April 1989.

pressed as they were by the succession of events and it would be difficult now to decide whether a greater contribution to the exploration of the "industrial district" has been made by them or by economists. I believe the result to be quite positive. However, its consolidation and extension raises problems which are typical of interdisciplinary discussions on a methodologically ambiguous ground. The additional purpose of these pages is, then, that of offering sociologists a piece of economic reasoning on the district (and around it) which I hope is not incorrect and which I developed in such a way as to give them a support in a form that is as "natural" as I can conceive it, with respect to their analysis. I realise that even though the chapter is wholly dedicated to dialogue, the weight of economic relations is still enormous in comparison to socio-cultural relations and that this weight may be disproportionate. However, I believe that better equilibrium in analysis - if it can be achieved - cannot be reached without the direct contribution of the "non-economists".

II. Characteristics of the district

1. A definition

I define the industrial district as a socio-territorial entity which is characterised by the active presence of both a community of people and a population of firms in one naturally and historically bounded area. In the district, unlike in other environments, such as manufacturing towns, community and firms tend to merge.

The fact that the dominant activity is an industrial one differentiates the industrial district from a generic "economic region". Self-containment and the progressive division of labour which occurs there bring about an increasing surplus of final products that cannot be sold in the district. There follows an ever-increasing problem of placing this surplus on the external - essentially world-wide - market. Such a condition for the survival of the district (the necessity of solving an ever bigger problem of final demand) excludes the possibility of accidental placing of the products of the district on the external market, and requires instead the development of a permanent network of links between the district and its suppliers and clients. Thus, an economic definition of the industrial district which aims at being comprehensive will have to add such a permanent network, and all its interactions with the other elements, to the above-mentioned "local" conditions.

I have freely derived these stylised aspects and problems from the studies that have already been undertaken on industrial districts, and from the very few sketches of theories of the district that I know.

2. The local community

The most important trait of the local community is its relatively homogeneous system of values and views, which is an expression of an ethic of work and activity, of the family, of reciprocity, and of change. To some extent all the main aspects of life are affected by this. The system of values which prevails in the district develops more or less quickly through time, in ways which are still to be explored: it constitutes one of the preliminary requirements for the development of a district, and one of the essential conditions of its reproduction. This does not imply that only one combination of values is compatible with the beginning and the growth of the district, but rather that some combinations are apparently admissible, while others are not. Under no circumstance, however, can the system of values be such as to discourage enterprise or the introduction of technical change. If that were the case, the district could not be an entity which persisted through time, and we would have instead an area of social stagnation.

Parallel to this system of values, a system of institutions and rules must have developed in such a way as to spread those values throughout the district, to support and transmit them through generations. The market, the firm, the family, the church and the school are some of these institutions; but they also include the local authorities, the local structures of political parties and of unions, and many other public and private, economic and political, cultural and charitable, religious and artistic bodies.

For the social metabolism to function with no serious hindrance, the same system of values must, to some extent, pervade the institutions of the district. This will not mean that there will be no clashes of interests between the members of the district, or no perception of such clashes. Rather, they are experienced and defined in similar forms and within a framework of a sort of community-like superior interest which becomes an inner principle for the people of the district as a whole.

All this may look like a description of a "closed community", where people's lives are smothered by a multitude of rules. The industrial district is indeed a place where historical development has induced strong inward constraints to the so-called "natural" behaviour of its individuals. Among these constraints is, for instance, some quantity of "resistance" against unconditional acceptance of values which prevail in the "outside world", and a related tendency to use "double standards" when treating one's own fellow-citizens - even the "new" ones, provided they are "integrated" - rather than "strangers". However, the fact that these values are functional to the kind of economic activity which is carried out and to the consequent economic success, will prevent the members of the district from perceiving such "peculiarities" as limits. Rather, they will be reasons for pride and self-satisfaction. If one considers how the "natural" behaviour in the surrounding world is no less "historically relative" than that which prevails in the district, it will be easily concluded that the question of whether participants in the district are more or less constrained than those outside it is logically unanswerable. All that can be said is that the constraints are different, and that they are perceived and evaluated differently.

Because of the sort of activity performed in the district, life within it is characterised by a continuous exchange of people with the surrounding world - involving both permanent and temporary migrations. In fact, an appropriate supply of the attitudes and abilities required for the continuing development of the district could not occur within a closed population. The community of the district requires fresh blood. However, one must remember that the inflow of individuals from outside brings about problems of social integration which are, *ceteris paribus*, an increasing function of the "cultural distance" between the alien and the native, and of the "power of assimilation" of the district. The persisting success of some Italian districts since the last war is partly explained by their strong capacity of assimilation, and by the fact that - at least at the outset - immigration was a short-distance phenomenon.

3. The population of firms

The term "population of firms" requires some qualification. First, it must be borne in mind that this is not an accidental multiplicity of firms. Each of the many firms which constitute the population tend to specialise in just one phase, or a few phases, of the production processes typical of the district. In short, the district is an instance of a localised realisation of a division of labour, which is neither diluted in the general market, nor concentrated in one firm or in just a few firms. Here the term localisation stands for something other than an accidental concentration in one place of production processes which have been attracted there by pre-existing localising factors. Rather, the firms become rooted in the territory, and this result cannot be conceptualised independently of its historical development.

Hence, it follows that a sufficiently "fine" analysis reveals that the general process of production in a district displays features which are different from those in any other district.

It further follows that any single unit of production which operates within a district is to be considered at one and the same time both as an entity possessing its own history - a history as autonomous as the network of interdependencies allows - which, in principle, is disconnected from its territorial origin, and as a specific cog in a specific district. It is, therefore, incorrect in statistical analysis and in political and economic discussions to group together small firms belonging to industrial districts and small firms operating in other environments. On the basis of this approach the category "small firms" used for the most part in the current debate appears to be an empty one.

The firms of the district belong mainly to the same industrial branch, but the term industrial branch must be defined in an especially broad sense. For instance, in studies on industrial districts the term "textile branch" also includes the machines and the chemical products used in the textile industry, and the various services required by it. In this context, Marshall talked of "main industry" and "auxiliary industry"; other scholars talk of *filières*, or of vertically integrated branches.

If the deep merging between productive activity and the daily life of the district, assumed above, is to occur, it is necessary that the branch be comprehensive enough to provide job opportunities to all sections of the population (the young, the mature, and the elderly, men and women). Or even that the district be "adequately" multi-sectoral. In practice many systems of neighbouring districts, and even some single districts, achieve this condition *to some extent*.

Production processes included in the sector as defined above must be spatially and temporally separable. A continuous production process, whose products could not be transported and stored - such as smelted steel - will not be suitable for the development of the district. In other words, special technical conditions are required, which may allow for the formation of a local network of specialised transactions on phase products.

Among the processes of production which are technically suitable for a district-characterised economic development are those whose products have a final demand which is variable and differentiated in time and space - i.e. neither standardised nor constant.

Definite statements on the dimension of the unit of production of each single phase cannot be made, but it will naturally be assumed that the multiplicity of phases and their increasing decomposition keep optimal technical dimensions fairly small. Strictly speaking this will not exclude even large firms, particularly if one considers that the district produces phase products for the outside world as well. The existence of extremely active competition certainly keeps the phase plant not far from its technical optimum.

Personal relationships - such as kinship between entrepreneurs - between the principals of firms which operate in different phases, are present in the district. The existence of such personal links is indeed an obstacle to the high pliability of socio-economic relations which the district-form requires but, on the other hand, is quite consistent with the existence of deep interactions between community and production processes. Coalitions and agreements of various kinds and importance between firms in the district also occur, but whenever the weight of those which take a financial form increases too much, or the growth of some firm sends it "out of scale", as it were, we are already out of the canonical form of the Marshallian district.

4. Human resources

The ethic of labour and activity which prevails in the district is that everyone must search incessantly for the type of activity and the work allocation which best fit his aspirations and/or abilities. Correspondingly, in such an environment, anyone who does not find work, or who contents himself with something known to be below what he can do, is the target of social stigma. Consequently, moves from one activity to another, however frequent, are not perceived in a socially negative way.

The selection of job positions is especially varied. There is a sort of *continuum*, ranging from home-based work, part-time and waged work, to self-employment and entrepreneurship. Within such a selection of positions, a continuous process of reallocation occurs as an expression of the search for a place which is at the same time more appealing and better suited to the abilities of each person. The nature of the process is sequential, since once a new position is reached, new positions which were out of reach become available and appealing. Does this mean that the districts manage to allocate each individual to the place which suits him best, and/or which he is most eager to occupy? In a sense yes, since a mechanism of penalties and incentives operates towards a convergence between the desired job and the job for which one is objectively best suited. In another sense no, because the dynamic nature of the district - which can only live by growing - assumes a continuous reproduction of the contradiction between that for which one is suited and that to which one aspires.

This inner tendency of the district to constantly reallocate its human resources is one of the conditions for the district's productivity and competitiveness. Powerful "intangible" factors operate here, such as, for example, the pair "hope-dissatisfaction", which become tangible and marketable "in action", and which contribute to that part of the continuous "leavening" of the productivity of the district which is not due to technical progress itself.

The specialisation of the worker - which is sometimes firm-specific and sometimes district-specific - is lost only to a very limited extent, from the point of view of the district, when the worker moves from one firm to another. His specialisation remains part of that "public good" which Marshall labels "industrial atmosphere". When, to quote Marshall, "the secrets of the industry are in the air", the transmission of the skills acquired through the canonical channels (technical schools and factory training), is powerfully integrated by a spontaneous exchange and reorganisation of notions and opinions by "face to face" and "conviviality" relationships which daily life in the district offers with unusual frequency.

An evaluation of a worker's personal and professional qualities, for his most fruitful employment, is much easier for a firm deeply immersed in the community's relations than for an isolated firm or for the firm lost in urban anonymity. The information on a prospective employee available to a firm in the district at a very low cost and with hardly any effort, is much more "revealing" than that which can be gathered elsewhere by means of formal structures. It is reasonable to assume that even the large firm, in spite of all its sophisticated information structures, psychological tests, etc., may be, in some cases, at a disadvantage with respect to the small firm which operates in the district.

Each of the mechanisms described above also works as a factor of attraction to (and retention in) the district of the most able workers. In a very Marshallian way, the most sought-after workers find their ability and experience better acknowledged and appreciated in the district than elsewhere, and thus tend to concentrate and remain in it.

The other category of agents which is quite typical of the industrial district is the one I would label by the somewhat pretentious expression of "pure entrepreneurs". As far as I know, the closest concrete approximation to this ideal-type is the *impannatori* in Prato. The ideal pure entrepreneur operates as follows: on the one hand, he follows with utmost care the events on the world market which concern the products of the district; on the other, he continuously improves his own knowledge of the district as a production and socio-cultural entity. His special function lies in translating all the capabilities which are latent in the historical heritage of the district into products that can be sold in that market. For him the industrial district is a sort of pliable capital, capable of producing many different things within a range (that is typical of the branch as defined above). His main "immobilisation" consists in the fact that he knows only one district and, possibly, its appendages.

How does the pure entrepreneur come to know his own district? He does not own any plant or factory, and does not employ workers, other than a few close collaborators. His only fixed capital is a warehouse for sorting raw materials - which he buys himself - and final products. On the basis of an evaluation of the trends of external markets, he, and his customary phase producers and collaborators, shape a "product project", which usually includes a whole range of products. Having surveyed the prospective success of the product on the market, he will ask some of the phase producers he is in touch with - not necessarily always the same ones - the conditions under which they are prepared to transform raw materials and the "project" into the final product. It so happens that, bit by bit, the pure entrepreneur acquires an ever closer knowledge of the economic and social structure, and hence of the productive capacity, of the district.

A special danger for the district is the progressive tendency towards a loss of the "roots" of and a "cosmopolitisation" of its pure entrepreneurs. Once the entrepreneur has organised his network of clients in the world market, he will pay increasing attention to a comparison between the growth of profits he can expect from a further improvement of his knowledge of the district, and the growth he thinks he can derive from new areas of production. If he proceeds along this road, he will turn from being a sort of pure agent for the district to a pure intermediator. As - and to the extent that - his link with the district becomes looser, and the link with the final consumers of the product stronger, he becomes a "Buying Office".

To complete the picture, the existence of a large base of homeworkers and part-time workers must be kept in mind. These categories are the link between the system of firms and the system of families; that is, between production activity proper and the daily life of the district. These so-called secondary activities also take a deeply different meaning when performed in the context of a well-functioning district. Suffice it to consider that, with full employment, home-based and part-time work are instruments for increasing income beyond the "necessities".

These activities play an essential and two-fold role: on the one hand, they partially absorb external fluctuations by means of internal adjustments in the time budget of the individuals and of the families, thereby dampening the effects of the economic cycle on the basic industrial structure of the district; on the other, they breed and regenerate the recruits of small entrepreneurs.

5. The market

In spite of the intense competition within and between districts, the market that suits the ideal world of the industrial district is not a large, homogeneous, agglomeration of buyers (or sellers) who are indifferent to places of production (or consumption), and who are only interested in prices of raw materials, machines, goods and services, whose quality is given and well-known. In the market of the industrial district, on the contrary, the information carried by the price is greatly insufficient for choice. Hence the need to produce and supply a good deal of further information. This means that (a) the process of the so-called marketing of the final product is not a marginal addition to the transformation activity of the district but that the two match each other fully; (b) that the orderly functioning of the markets internal to the districts constrains the district itself - regarded as a system of values and institutions - with reference to its shape and evolution.

If we consider the industrial district as a special term, and not as a mere indicator of geographical origin, there must not then only be a specialised and well-established network of economic agents who deal with supplying the inputs and placing the products of the district on their final markets, but also an "image" of the district which is separated both from that of the single firms in it, and from that of the other districts. In other words, the "representative commodity" of each particular district must be distinguishable from similar commodities by some special characteristics of its own, regarding either its average qualitative standards (raw materials, technical treatments, etc.), or some accessory conditions of the transactions (timing of the deliveries, homogeneity of the batches, etc.). In short, there must be something behind the unifying symbol (e.g. the ceramic tiles of Sassuolo) which is truly relevant for choice.

As the district is also a big purchaser of raw materials, a substantial number of specialised buyers will normally concentrate in it. This creates opportunities for profit-making from the sale of raw materials, opportunities that are additional to those derived from the production activities of the district. This circumstance contributes to the promotion of economies of scale in the district, by creating an increasing differential in favour of larger and more dynamic districts. The links with the markets which supply raw materials or instrumental goods may turn out to be expedient also for the sale of goods produced in the district.

The origin and the development of an industrial district is therefore not simply the "local" result of a matching of some socio-cultural traits of a community (a system of values, attitudes, and institutions), of historical and natural characteristics of a geographical area (orography, communication networks and junctions, forms of settlements, etc.), and of technical characteristics of the production process (decomposable processes, short series, etc.), but also the result of a process of dynamic interaction (a virtuous circle) between division-integration of labour in the district, a broadening of the market for its products, and the formation of a permanent linking network between the districts and the external markets. Each element feeds back into the other, though not automatically, since the mechanism of expansion for each given district hits the dual constraints of the distribution of income, and the maximum proportion a sector can achieve - with respect to "basic needs" - for any given level of income on the world market. Of course, the share of sales taken by district and non-district firms which happen to satisfy some basic need whilst pursuing their profits is, of course, not unlimited. That share grows and shrinks following the laws of the overall development of the market. This, very succinctly, is the background of the competition between districts and non-district firms. The study of these macrodynamic features of the districts has yet to start, but clues and theories already exist with reference to industrialised countries and branches, and thus can be adapted to the purpose.

6. Competition and co-operation

From what has been said about the labour market, one could infer that the population of the district undergoes a sort of ruthless and incessant Hobbesian struggle of all against all; but this is true only in the sense that everyone struggles incessantly to improve his own and his family's position, and that nobody can rest on economic solutions which are considerably inferior to those which prevail in the markets outside the district. If, on the other hand, life in the district consisted of a struggle of all against all, with no sort of solidarity among the local fighters, where any momentary weakness is implacably punished, and any temporary disadvantage becomes fatal, then such uncertainty would prevail that anyone who may temporarily be a loser would never try again. In fact the industrial district requires that the game of competition may start again, and whoever respects the rules of that community and loses a match, may have a chance to participate in the next one.

A mechanism that increases capital liquidity in a structure - such as the district - which is characterised by firms with legal forms which may not allow for easy access to the financial market, and which eases the decision to stay in business, is the market for secondhand machines. If the small entrepreneur could in no way sell - without heavy losses - a machine that no longer suits him, the effect would be to slow down the acquisition of new machinery - and thus the introduction of technical progress - and, more generally, the spirit of enterprise. Within the broad spectrum of production needs and intensities of utilisation of machines, which is typical of the district, a machine which is unsuitable for one person may turn out to be profitable for another. When this sort of situation occurs frequently, a local market of secondhand machines tends to develop and it allows for a potentially optimal distribution of the existing set of machines (new and old) and promotes an adventurous spirit.

Of the written and unwritten rules which everyone knows and almost everyone respects, and which shape competition in the district, some concern the behaviour which results in the determination of the normal prices of the goods and services which are most frequently exchanged in the district: in particular, phase products and the most typical specialised services. These "local" prices are strictly linked to the corresponding prices in the national and international market, from whose influence they cannot escape; but they are also affected by local demand and supply conditions and, most importantly, by the stabilising influence of local institutions, such as associations among phase producers, and the local customs. They form, then, a strange hybrid between administered and market prices. Some business contingency might suggest to the entrepreneurs to cut wages, or to the workers to halt production activities suddenly, but, given a long-term experience which somehow becomes an internalised rule of behaviour of the agents of the district, and part of customs and institutions, very often such contingent opportunities are turned down. As a result, local prices of these goods and services fluctuate less than external prices and create a kind of local sub-system of prices. This gives everyone some assurance of stability of incomes, production costs, and marketing connections, which is far greater than that enjoyed by agents who operate in completely "open" markets.

From the point of view of its overall performance, the industrial district combines, then, a very active kind of competitive behaviour on the part of its individuals, with a semi-conscious and semi-voluntary co-operation among them, resulting from the special way in which the socio-cultural system permeates and structures the market in the district.

7. An adaptive system

A comparison - albeit quick and succinct - between this form of production organisation, where phase inefficiencies are continuously challenged from within and from without, and the features of the vertically integrated firm, may help us understand something more of the economic logic of the district.

An efficient control of any given phase of production in the large firm - whether private or public - is notoriously hindered by tendencies towards company sclerosis. The "social machine" of the district, on the other hand, seems to be built for the purpose of that control. The systematic and pervasive contrast of interests between all the agents in the district adapts itself quickly and accurately to the ever-changing shape of the production organisation, and operates a kind of automatic efficiency control of each single phase. As we said, this situation does not induce the strain that it would do elsewhere, due to the system of values which prevails in the district.

8. Technological change

Another important characteristic of the functioning of the industrial district is the way technological progress is introduced. In a world of agents whose main capital is "human", (i. e. made up of past experience), technical change greatly impairs the value of that capital. Hence there is strong resistance to its introduction. However, on the other side of the coin, what makes the introduction of technical progress in the large firm especially traumatic and causes resistance, is the fact that it appears to be the result of decisions made by a small number of people, on the basis of calculations which remain incomprehensible to the workers and which are made without consulting them or taking their interests, demands and expectations into any account. In the district, on the contrary, the introduction of technological progress is a social process which is achieved gradually through a process of self-awareness on the part of all segments of the industry and strata of the population.

If one adds to this the fact that the system of values and attitudes which prevails in the district - and which is more or less shared by all strata of the population - includes pride in being up-to-date technologically, then any "painful" decision, such as that of a reorganisation necessitated by the outbreak of technical novelties, appears in a more positive psychological light: i. e. as measures to achieve a better future. The introduction of technological progress is, therefore, perceived neither as a decision to be suffered, nor as an external pressure, but rather as an opportunity to defend an already acquired position. Unlike other forms of production organisation, an industrial district in working order is not necessarily condemned to technological backwardness.

9. A local credit system

One of the best known disadvantages of small firms as compared to large ones is that of more difficult access to credit. Given the crucial relevance of credit for continuous development - an essential component of the notion of the district - one may wonder how such a development could be realised by a population of small firms in the face of the well-known hostility of the credit system. To some extent, what is of help here is what could be defined as the "theory of the local bank". The local bank is an organism born and bred in the district, that is very closely linked with local entrepreneurs (and often with other local social and political lobbies), and deeply involved in local life, which it knows in detail, and to which it gives direction to a considerable extent. An institution of this sort can give a much greater weight to the personal qualities of whoever demands credit, and to the specific prospects of a given investment, than can a bank which is less well rooted in the local environment. Hence, there is an extra "thrust" to accumulation in the district, whatever forms - usually short-term - the credit may take.

The typical credit philosophy of the local bank must obviously be practised in perfect honesty if it is to work. If the managers of the bank give credit to their friends, without taking into account the economic conditions of the operation, the extra thrust turns into a serious danger for the district. The structure of the district is a very dense network of business interdependencies, to such an extent that a problematic role played by the local bank induces a chain of negative effects, all highly concentrated in the district. The very structure which keeps inside the district the multiple effects on income and employment generated by the extra credit fed into the system also retains in the district the chain of negative effects resulting from bad management by the local bank.

10. Sources of dynamism

The dynamic and self-reproducing nature of the district consists of a continuous comparison between the cost of performing any given operation inside the firm and the cost of having it done outside; given a pressing and implacable external competition, this comparison paces the life of any economic agent in the district. It should be noted here that it is not a matter of a generic comparison between doing and buying, but a specific comparison between doing and having done and, in the latter case, a matter of who or with whom, where, when, and how. It should also be noted that this is almost always "doing together". The comparison, then, always involves above all, the district but in all cases it has as its points of reference - invisible, but always present - what is done (and how) outside the district.

This comparison is made on the basis of a view of costs which is grounded in the culture of the district, and which thus does not necessarily correspond to those prevailing in other social environments. In other words, the borderline between what is considered and what is not considered a cost depends on those same historical and cultural factors which define the identity of the district. The pervading comparison between doing and buying and, as a consequence, the explicit or implicit, direct and indirect reduction of a large number of features of daily life to a monetary measure, makes the district an ideal place to which to apply Marshallian economic analysis.

In apparent contrast to what has been said above, the decision to put out or keep in some given phase of a given process of production is never "purely economic". When, for example, a firm decides to put some given phase out, it gives up direct control over the production process and over the workers involved in it, and contents itself with the indirect control allowed by the market, which is of a different, and much weaker, kind. If the firm that has the phase production performed outside remained the only buyer for the phase producer so created, then, in practical terms, the difference in the power of control would not be very great; but if the phase producer starts to sell to more than one buyer, inside and even outside the district, then the power of control of the head firm vanishes rapidly. When two historical trends meet - such as a diffuse desire amongst the local population to set up one's own business, and some kind of indifference by the entrepreneurs to the effects of their economic decisions in terms of local social control over the form of the organisation of production - the process of disintegration may become cumulative. If the entrepreneurs follow the solutions which offer the highest revenues in a strict economic sense and take no interest in the local political, social, and cultural equilibrium - believing, perhaps that they are sufficiently covered by the national or international equilibria - then the process of disintegration may converge towards the "canonical" form of the industrial district.

11. Consciousness, class and locality

Urged by ever-changing endogenous relationships (the relationships between local culture, society and economy), and exogenous ones (effects on the district of external markets, society and culture), the organisation of production and the social structure fluctuate continuously between more or less capitalistic forms (in terms of share of work in the form of waged labour, of greater or lesser vertical integration, of greater or lesser economic and financial concentration, of a more or less "Fordist" or "neo-handicraft" nature of the organisation of the process of production, etc.). In loose correspondence with these "structural" fluctuations, one can assume the appearance of contrasting impulses, at one time in the direction of "class" self-awareness, at another in the direction of "localistic" self-awareness. What cannot take shape, due to the lack of the essential condition is, of course, that "firm identification" which is typical of the areas where the large firm dominates. In the district the centre of gravity of this feeling of belonging is supposed to be that "sense of belonging" to the local industrial community, perceived as the objective basis of the fortunes of the individual and the family, which we have seen to be an essential component of the district.

As possible boundaries of the fluctuation sketched here in a speculative fashion one could imagine, on the one hand, a complete vertical integration of the process in one or only a few firms, which can absorb both pure and phase entrepreneurs (and possibly cause the disappearance of home-based work and external services to production); outcomes of this sort will presumably tend to generate a polarisation and, correspondingly, a social and territorial separation between classes and strata.

One could postulate, in contrast, a disintegration - let us call it "post-modern" - of the process of production, which in the end makes all transformation phases "in the factory" disappear and ends in a situation of great economic fluidity and social mobility. Under this hypothesis, we arrive at a sort of "mercantile community", where a myriad of micro-units of production - whether of individuals or families - each one possessing all its own means of production, is directly co-ordinated by a large and open group of pure entrepreneurs. In this form, factory and waged labour disappear completely. In both cases, however, we are out of the canonical form of the Marshallian industrial district.

The canonical form of the Marshallian district may be thought of as an intermediate case between these extremes. Here the "capitalistic core" of the industrial operations carried out in the factory is immersed in a medium of social relationships, which are functional to that "core", but which are susceptible of evolution in many directions.

III. Future developments of the district

The fact that the district remains "open" to different possible evolutions is due to an uneasy matching of the socio-cultural and the strictly economic components both inside the district and in its relations with the rest of the world. What appears to be most difficult to guarantee is the continuous correspondence - in a changing environment - between socio-cultural, technical, productive and market conditions, since the philosophy of life which prevails in the district is an especially complex variable which, in today's and, presumably, tomorrow's world, cannot be locally controlled. If we observe the existing districts, we already notice signs of disintegration amongst the institutional systems and the systems of values behind them.

Two clear signs of difficulties of adaptation of the industrial district to the fluctuations of external conditions would be the growth of the level of explicit unemployment and a changing ratio between births and deaths of firms. If the expectations of the opinion leaders among pure and phase entrepreneurs include a reasonably short depression, then only a move from explicit employment to the world of part-time and home-based work will appear, together with a poorer ratio between firm births and deaths, which will be more or less serious for the different phases but still greater than unity for many of them. As long as the basis of long-term expectations remains positive, external fluctuations - due to the special structure of the district - cause less than proportional fluctuations in the incomes of the "representative family" of the district, and in the overall amount of work carried out and of goods produced in the district as a whole.

If, on the other hand, opinion-leader entrepreneurs begin to anticipate difficulties which are not temporary, then the ratio between births and deaths falls under the unity and much underemployment and hidden unemployment takes the form of explicit unemployment. Beyond a certain threshold, firm bankruptcies start a chain reaction and those workers amongst the most sought after, who have lost employment, begin to migrate away from the district, possibly towards other districts or towards large firms. When this happens, the wealth of experiences and production capacity accumulated in the course of time (the real "productive basis" of the district) begins to vanish and, consequently, both the system of values and the network of local institutions begin to break down.

Note:

I have reluctantly agreed to the publication of these still very incomplete and "speculative" reflections on the industrial district. As a matter of fact, they form part of a kind of loose *framework* of ideas that I use for seminars which I give in Florence and elsewhere and which I alter every day, as it were, in relation to literature and research and also to discussions with my collaborators in Florence (Marco Bellandi, Gabi Dei Ottati, and Fabio Sforzi), or with my customary interlocutors on "districtism", both Italian and non-Italian. The very broad nature of these intellectual interactions, and the chronically provisional one of the text, have made me resist thus far the idea of publishing, at this stage and in this form. (On the other hand, I must point out that some partial, and naturally different, anticipations of this *framework*, have appeared here and there, mainly as a by-product of the seminars I mentioned above.) If I eventually allowed myself to be persuaded to present in a fairly systematic form my - or rather "our" - reflections at their current stage, it is because I realised that the issue being extremely delicate and manifold, its analysis requires the concurrent contribution of more than one tradition of research and analytic instrumentation. The plexus of social phenomena which - in the wake of Marshall - we have agreed to call an industrial district, is the meeting and crossing point of processes which are traditionally proper to economic studies, such as the functioning of the market and of capitalistic accumulation, or processes which are proper to sociological studies, such as socialisation and the development and disintegration of social institutions, and of processes which remain on the border between the two disciplines, such as the social division of labour, and the organisation of the process of production.

The study of industrial districts originally began - Marshall witnesses - in the area of economic studies, but soon moved towards that of extra-economic studies, albeit with many limits and much clumsiness: think of the Marshallian idea of the "industrial atmosphere". But, already in the last century, crucial contributions to the deciphering of this jigsaw puzzle also came from the sociological side. Think of Tonnies' analysis on *Gemeinschaft* and *Gesellschaft*. What does not seem to take off, on the other hand, is an integration of the two strands of research and reflection (certainly unsurprising given the paths the two disciplines have taken). But for all those who are convinced, as I am, that the common object of studies - man in society - should overcome the divergence of methods, the synergies between sociologists and economists still appear to be too limited and discontinuous. I believe, indeed, that the fact that the phenomenon of the industrial district is either studied with an interdisciplinary perspective, or else we miss it, is a rare opportunity for a growth of social thought in its whole. This is my aim in offering these incomplete pages: a possible catalyst for discussions between economists and sociologists (and other categories of social scholars as well), in the hope that this may help all of us to understand each other, and what happens in the world, better.

5 Work, labour and action: Work experience in a system of flexible production

Michael J. Piore

Introduction

Over the last three years, the International Institute for Labour Studies has been examining the changing size distribution of firms in industrial economies. At the heart of the Institute's work is a set of commissioned studies reviewing the evolution of small businesses in nine countries. The studies collected both quantitative evidence and qualitative material, drawn largely from case studies of industrial regions where small business has been particularly prominent. They confirm the general impression of policy-makers and practitioners that in all of these countries there has been a trend, since the 1970s, toward smaller business units. These trends represent a reversal of those of earlier postwar decades, which in some countries can be traced back to the nineteenth century, toward large business units [Sengenberger and Loveman, 1987]. Most surprising, however, is the finding that many small businesses - or at least the industrial districts which are constituted by them - exhibit a dynamism in the creation of new products and in the evolution of productive technology which we conventionally associated with large corporate organisations. The technical dynamism of industrial districts is especially prominent in Central Italy but it can be found in all of the countries studied.

A parallel development is occurring in the corporate sector. The belief is spreading within a number of firms that have been historically organised in a tight vertically integrated, hierarchical structure that the decentralisation of power and responsibility along lines which resemble that of the industrial district will reinvigorate them and enable them to compete more effectively in the world market. A great many of these major corporate enterprises have begun to move in this direction.

As Sabel and I argued in *The second industrial divide*, conventional theories of industrial development do not provide an adequate understanding of trends of this kind [Piore and Sabel, 1984]. The theory of mass production, as developed out of the work of Smith, Marx, Taylor and Ford, fails to account for the technical dynamism of small firms in industrial districts or of the newly decentralised corporate structure. That dynamism is captured by the neoclassical competitive market model or, at least, the Austrian variant which emphasises the role of the innovating entrepreneur. But the importance which this model places on the independence and the social isolation of the business firm, and on the intensity of the competitive pressures of the market place, fails to capture the heavy emphasis upon the role of co-operation and community which one finds in every single ethnographic study of industrial districts and in the corporate enterprises which are being used by big business as models for their reforms. Sabel and I attempted to think of these developments as a turn toward the craftwork of the nineteenth century but the kind of co-operation among individuals and firms which one observes is not really consistent with the image which craftsmanship entails. The division of labour does not respect the old crafts jurisdictions. New jurisdictions consistent with modern technology are conceivable but not as obvious nor as compelling as a meaningful analogy to a craft organisation would seem to require.

This chapter is offered as a contribution towards an alternative analytical perspective which does capture the characteristics of the newly emergent forms of industrial organisation. For this purpose it draws heavily upon a set of philosophical categories developed by Hannah Arendt in *The human condition* [Arendt, 1958]. It tries to show not only how these categories help us to capture the salient organisational features of these districts, but also the basic difference in the perspective which they suggest from that in which we conventionally view these phenomena; and to indicate what that difference in perspective suggests about the problem of establishing and maintaining structures of this kind through public policy.

The chapter is divided as follows. In the first section, I draw up a list of stylised facts which seem to characterise dynamic industrial districts and their analogues in the emergent forms of decentralised corporate structures. In the second section, I introduce Arendt's categories. The third section discusses the implications of the categories for an understanding of the stylised facts. A final section then considers the implications for public policy.

I. The "facts"

1. The characteristics of industrial districts

There is now a large and growing case study literature on industrial districts. Virtually all of these studies have been conceived and executed to examine a set of expectations formed by theories of mass production and the large hierarchical corporate enterprise which has been its most characteristic institutional form. The studies are thus implicitly comparative, and they suggest a list of factors which distinguish the institutions of these districts either from the large business enterprise or from institutions associated with technologically stagnant small firms, in a manner consistent with the expectations of mass production. The stagnant areas which serve as a point of comparison are often other industrialised areas or the dynamic area itself at an earlier or later moment in its history. Together, the studies suggest a list of what may be taken to be the salient features of industrial districts, what economists would call the stylised facts which any organisation theory is called upon to explain.[1]

A certain amount of caution must be exercised in interpreting this list. Because the studies are all conceived in reaction to the dominant theory, they virtually never compare one of these dynamic districts with another. There is thus really no way of knowing whether the studies are at all comparable in the sense that they are studying the same, or even similar, things. Moreover, the dominant organisational models against which the authors are reacting are seldom made explicit. As a result, one cannot even guarantee that there is a fixed point of comparison. Nonetheless, so many items reappear in one case study after another, that it is very difficult to believe that there is not a single, general process at work in all of them and, hence, that while the list which they suggest may be incomplete, and some particular items on it questionable, it can nonetheless serve as a point of departure for the erection of an alternative analytical framework.

At the top of the list are the two factors which we have emphasised above: the technological dynamism of the districts and the combination within them of the apparently contradictory traits of competition and co-operation. Technological dynamism is an essential criteria whilst the peculiar combination of competition and co-operation figures prominently in virtually every single study on the list, most of which were conceived independently without prior knowledge of other studies of similar areas.

A third characteristic of virtually all of the districts is the fact that they are characterised as embedded within the "culture", the "social structure", or the "community". These terms are not analytically equivalent, and we shall argue below that the distinction among them is important in understanding how these districts actually operate, but the distinction is not made in the studies themselves. Many of the studies emphasise the importance of the family structure, or of the structures of political parties (particularly the Communist Party in Central Italy) and of the church. One French language study of North African districts coined the term *ethno-industrialisation* to characterise the process [Bouchara, 1987]. The correct English translation of ethno is anthropological, but the term ethno-industrialisation itself could be applied as an English word to districts in the United States, many of which are embedded in the social structure of immigrant groups with common ethnic origins. Even the high tech districts of Silicon valley and Route 128 are described as embedded in a culture derived from the universities and the social or communal structure associated with them. Giacomo Becattini characterises the historical emergence of industrial districts in Central Italy as a "*thickening* of industrial and *social* interdependencies in a certain place" [Becattini, 1987, p. 5]. Another metaphor which is sometimes used is one which likens an "industrial district" to a language community: the members share a common mode of discourse about the productive process.

1. This list draws primarily upon the country studies prepared for the New Industrial Organisation Programme of the International Institute for Labour Studies. Additional references can be found in the bibliography.

Fourth on a list of characteristics of industrial districts which emerges in case studies is the idea of these districts as *networks*. The term appears repeatedly in study after study as a way of characterising the relationship which prevails among producing units. In attempts of social psychologists and organisational theorists to formalise their observations, the term refers to a specific body of formal theory. But it seems to arise in most studies as an essentially descriptive term, a metaphor drawn from patterns of telephone communication or transportation which link together households in a city. As such it is designed to capture the contrast between relationships in an industrial district and the strict line of authority and communication in the hierarchical corporation. But it also suggests a richness of communication which escapes the directness and simplicity of the price signals in a competitive market where communication is also lateral and multidirectional. Both qualities are implicit in Becattini's phrase just quoted "a *'thickening'* of industrial and social *interdependencies*" (emphasis added) [Becattini, 1987]. The network idea thus implies not only that there is a great deal of lateral communication and that information flows in many different directions at once but that lines cross cut each other and that communications are multifaceted and complex.

The fifth characteristic of the industrial districts studied is the spontaneous and unpredictable character of success and failure. People do not seem to be able to plan, or even to approach their problems in a fully systematic or rational (or at least controlled) way. Instead, they try a number of different things, some of which "work" and some of which do not. This is especially true of changes in the product, where the market seems to select the winners and losers. But it is also true of innovations in productive technique. The linguistic metaphor appears here again: innovation in an industrial district is like the changes in a language over time. The result of the unpredictable nature of innovation is the phenomenon, which gives rise to the emphasis on the combination of competition and co-operation in the literature, whereby difficulties in maintaining markets continually force competitors to turn around and shift to subcontracting relationships with one another, thereby allowing firms to retain sufficient capacity to meet new demands when they occur. But it also gives rise to frequent bankruptcies, and the result, in a number of districts ranging from traditional garments to high tech silicon valleys, is that bankruptcy is not considered a catastrophic event and has little impact upon an individual's reputation or capacity to engage in business in the future.

Closely connected to the spontaneity and unpredictability of the evolution of the districts is what is frequently described as the amoeba-like quality of their evolution.[2] The patterns of change in the array of products and in the techniques of production tend to evolve continuously. The set of things being done thus seems to expand and contract around the perimeter. This is often contrasted to the discontinuous leaps which occur from one generation of products to another in mass production. It is closely

2. On this point, see especially Ken-ichi Imai [1985] and Imai et al. [1985].

associated in the literature with two other traits of the process of production and innovation.

It is associated first with what Becattini calls the "bottom up" approach to innovation. Both changes in production technology and in the product itself arise either in the shop or in collaboration with the shop. Second the shop itself is open. Producers visit each others' firms and freely discuss their production problems with one another, comparing notes and ultimately sharing innovations.

The openness of the shop deserves special emphasis. It is one of the aspects of co-operation or community which seems so contradictory to the competitive spirit which one also observes among these small firms. It is as if there are no trade secrets. This, it should be said, is not a universal trait. In the high fashion garment industry, as in New York, during the design process, in the period before the big week in which the new collections are presented to buyers the industry is highly secretive, and the carts carrying garments in the streets of mid-town Manhattan are covered to hide the products. It is only after the buyers leave that the shops open up to one another. But in the vast majority of such districts, even this period of secrecy seems to be rare. Raveyre and Saglio [1984], in their study of Oyonnax, for example, associate the openness of the shop and the pace and frequency with which people visit one another with periods of dynamism. And this openness is very prominent in the dynamic industrial districts of Central Italy. One of the characteristics of Italian fashion production in a number of these districts is that they copy designs in the fashion centres of Europe, and there is a good deal of openness and exchange among firms about the copying process and how to reproduce in production a certain feature of a new design which has been photographed at some fashion fair but never physically examined.

2. Public policy

Finally, on the list of stylised facts about industrial districts, one would like to include the role of public policy in their creation and maintenance. Unfortunately, however, the material in the case studies on this question is extremely diffuse. It seems to resist the kind of concise summary which would lend itself to inclusion in a list of this kind. In many studies, in fact, public policy is not explicitly addressed. The focus is on the economies, and even more upon the social structures of the districts, and the public authority is not much in evidence. This could reflect the interests of the researchers but it reveals, we shall argue, something about public policy as well. Public policy in these districts does not, it seems, lend itself to the vocabulary and analytical categories in which it is conventionally discussed. Indeed, one might say that this is the principal "fact" about public policy in industrial districts: *It is too diffuse to be characterised in terms of conventional categories of discourse and analysis.*[3]

Be that as it may, however, it certainly complicates the task of summarising the public policy conclusions, which we will nonetheless attempt to do in a series of observations and remarks, as follows.

A. The provision of particular services

A first set of observations concerns the role of public authorities in the provision of particular services. It is possible to draw up a list of particular services which successful industrial districts need and which are not provided by the firms themselves. This list differentiates this form of production from mass production, where the firm provides the services itself because it is able to capture internally an economic return for doing so. The most important of these services appears to be twofold: research and development, and training and education. But in a number of areas, public or co-operative authorities also provide financial services, marketing, material purchasing services, managerial consulting services, as well as common eating facilities, medical care, and the like, which in Italy a number of small firms often share within a single industrial park. And, in some areas, one or another phase of the production process in which there is a special economy of scale might be performed communally as well. A further paradox to be noted is that many of these services, most particularly training but also medical services and the canteen, are in the competitive market model paid for directly by employees, and it is not at all clear why this does not seem to happen in industrial districts.

A list of services does not, however, go very far in characterising public policy because while services are sometimes provided by the government authority, usually at the regional or municipal level, they are all just as often provided by some other communal organisation or institution: the trade union, a business association, a collective agreement between the union and an employers' association, some form of co-operative venture, or, more rarely, by a religious group or a political party. Moreover, the division of labour among these different organisational forms does not have an obvious pattern. Not only does it vary from one district to another but it also varies within any given district in the sense that some of the services on the list are provided in one way and some in another.

The list of services, moreover, is in no way sufficient to guarantee the success of an area as a dynamic industrial district. The recent vogue of state and local economic development policy in the United States has, for example, succeeded in generating virtually every item on this, or any

3. To go beyond this essentially negative characterisation, one has to examine what the conventions in public policy discussions are and where it is that the policies of industrial districts depart from them. Conventional discussions attempt to identify which set of instruments is appropriate to a particular set of goals. In the present case, one might take an economically dynamic community of small firms as the goal, and then look for the instruments by identifying both the presence of public authorities in the operation of the districts and the institutions over which those authorities exercise some control.

conceivable list, without anything like a comparable success in generating industrial districts, to the point where one is led to wonder whether the preoccupation with a list of functional prerequisites may not actually be a source of the problem which these policies face.

B. Rules and standards of behaviour

A second set of observations concerns the rules and standards of behaviour which govern the operation of these communities. In a sense these are laws or quasi laws. The process through which they are created and enforced and through which disputes about them are adjudicated constitute the classic legislative, administrative and judicial functions of government. Here again, however, the roles and the rule-making processes are not readily understood, at least in so far as we attempt to encompass them within accustomed analytical categories. Thus, for example, virtually every study suggests that there must be a set of rules and their chief function is to curtail the kind of exploitation among members of the community which would foreclose co-operation among them. This is generally perceived as a set of limits upon competition and phrased in terms of restraints upon wage competition, procedures for distributing demand which ensure the full employment of the communities' resources or the sharing of the burden of unemployment, and the like. Here, as in the case of community services, one can probably generate a list. Because both the services and the rules impose burdens upon the community as a whole, it appears that the community must have a perimeter which defines membership, and hence limits access to its members. The definition and the maintenance of that perimeter might be taken as a second functional requirement of the policy-making body.

On the other hand, the way in which these rules emerge and the level at which they are understood and enforced is something which is not easy to delimit and understand. It is illustrated by two points which emerged in a discussion of the country reports at the International Institute for Labour Studies. First, there was a discussion of rules limiting competition, and promoting co-operation. Conventional economic jargon has increasingly talked of the issues at stake here in terms of "opportunism" or "the free rider problem". Much of academic theory is concerned with a range of institutional structures and devices which overcome the incentive of individuals to cheat the community when it is to their personal advantage to do so, even though they also have an interest in the survival of the community as a whole. A typical example is one of whether an individual will voluntarily pay union dues. The conclusion of the discussion group was that such models were not appropriate to the understanding of industrial districts because allegiance to them existed at such a profound level that problems of opportunism never arose: once the members of a community had posed the problem in those terms, it was argued, and begun to look for solutions of the kind which neoclassical economic theory was increasingly seeking to offer, it was already too late; the problem had become too severe to be overcome. The extension of this point, however, seems to imply that industrial districts of this kind could be found but they could not be made, that the rules which hold them together exist at a level much more fundamental (or subconscious) than that at which public policy operates.

But here a second point made at the meeting seemed to contradict the first. Charles Sabel argued, from his studies of the German textile machinery industry, that one could identify a historical process through which such communities were made and the process was more or less conscious; that it involved a chain of concrete material conflicts between the different groups and individuals which came to compose the community, and that the characteristic of each conflict was that the parties came to see in it a choice between their own immediate interest and that of the survival of the community as a whole, and were led to compromise in order to preserve the community. In other words, there were in fact a series of critical rule-making episodes, where the conflict between the community and particular interests became explicit and were compromised so as to preserve community. These conflicts, incidentally, were between an organised employer group and groups of workers. This may be important because the group might have had a stronger sense of community and interest in it than any individual member. The precise role of the group is one to which we will return below for it is not clear what necessary roles groups, as opposed to individuals, otherwise have in such a world.

C. *Political leadership*

The final point about the policy making process which seems to emerge in these studies concerns the nature of the political leadership itself and its activities. Here again, information is scarce but the one study which focuses on this process explicitly suggests that the major part of the leadership's time seems to be spent as mediators in disputes, a point which seems to fit with the preceding observation about conflict and compromise [Ritaine, 1987]. A subsidiary observation in Central Italy stresses another point: the active leadership of business organisations seems to be drawn from the ranks of small firms themselves and seems to be able to compete in terms of interest and prestige with the management of businesses as an activity; this is so even though the knowledge and skills required to perform the offices of the business organisations effectively would enable one to run one's own business.[4]

3. Corporate reform and decentralisation[5]

The analogue among large business organisations to the dynamic industrial districts of small firms is the decentralised corporate structure. Here there is no case study literature comparable to that on industrial districts which would enable us to abstract a list of stylised facts. As we have already noted, many companies initially structured in accordance with

---

4. On the relationship between political and economic leadership, see also Geertz [1963].

5. See Piore [1989].

the principles of mass production have been seeking new organisational forms. This is true in virtually all of the major industrial countries, although since most of the organisations involved are in some sense multinational, it is not obvious that the nation-state is a relevant unit for assessing the dimensions of the trend.

The reforms in corporate structure generally have a common starting point: they are all seeking to move away from a tightly integrated, hierarchical organisation with a strict internal division of labour based on function and product line. They all tend to describe the new forms they are seeking in terms of a decentralisation of power and authority. But it is not at all clear that the structures which are encompassed by this general rubric are the same, or even similar. Indeed, even within the same organisation, considerable confusion and outright conflict is masked by the use of a single terminology by managers who actually have very different visions of how the reforms should proceed. Moreover, while there is something of a literature on what an effective "decentralised" company might look like, there is virtually nothing about the actual process of moving from an original hierarchical structure to one or another of the decentralised models. The vast majority of corporations in the western industrial world, to the extent that they are not still highly centralised, are in fact still in the midst of that process.

What one might take as the analogue to the case studies of industrial districts as a source of stylised facts is the literature on the Japanese company, since most western companies think of what they are doing as moving toward the Japanese model. This approach is not as straightforward as it appears on the surface: it is possible to abstract more than one picture of the Japanese company from the literature, and this is only in part because Japan, like most industrial countries, has a number of different companies. For the debate about corporate structure in the West, Japan often serves as a black box into which each protagonist has inserted his or her own vision. Still the literature does yield a composite set of characteristics which distinguish Japanese business organisations from their Western counterparts organised in accordance with notions of mass production, in much the same way that the case study literature yields a composite picture of industrial districts [Clark, 1979; Imai et al. 1985; Watanabe, 1970].

Firstly, like the industrial districts, the Japanese firm is a co-operative organisational structure. A great deal of emphasis is placed upon team work, in production and in managerial decision-making. And the Japanese have developed close co-operative, or collaborative, relationships with their subcontractors and customers as well. Many - although not by any means all - of the latter are treated as equal partners in a way which much more closely resembles the relationship among firms in an industrial district than that among the subcontractors of the mass production corporation. Secondly, the literature on Japan places enormous emphasis on the social structure of the Japanese company. The company and its structure are often analogised to the family, and it is sometimes argued that the family serves as a model for Japanese business structure and even that the company becomes a surrogate family for its employees. Certainly, the terms social and community appear as often in descriptions of the Japanese company and its relationship to its own collaborators as in the literature on industrial districts.

Thirdly, the network, both as a metaphor and, to a lesser extent, a theory of organisation, is also prominent in the Japanese literature. There is a great deal of lateral communication which cross-cuts what in a typical mass production company would be distinct hierarchical divisions, product lines, and different managerial hierarchies, although this happens in Japan in part because there are no functional divisions or technical and professional specialities in the sense that these exist, say, in the United States of America. The lack of functional and professional categories within the Japanese company makes different parts of the company open to one another in a similar way to what occurs between the small shops of the industrial districts.

The amoeba metaphor, which we used to describe technological change in industrial districts, is actually drawn from the Japanese literature [Imai, 1985; Imai et al., 1985]. The Japanese company is said to be much better at innovating around the edge of an existing technology than in making big discontinuous leaps from one technology to another. The older literature attributes this to the fact that Japan has not invested as heavily in research and development as have Western firms and, thus, it tends to adapt and then perfect developments pioneered in the West. In more recent work, however, there is a tendency to attribute this to the organisational structure itself, to the team concept and to the notions of community and collaboration through which the company is managed. The idea is that all of these elements act as a centripetal force which forestalls big departures and radical breaks with what already exists. The logical extension of this line of reasoning would, it should be noted, exclude any kind of technological change at all, but, since Japanese companies have hardly been stagnant, this is not an issue which the literature is forced to address, and it does not. But the source of dynamism in the communitarian structures is a puzzle which should be flagged and we will return to it below.

One influential school of Japanese management links all of these characteristics to Zen and sees the contrast between Japanese and Western companies in terms of the differences between Zen and the Western philosophical schools. This, as we shall see below, is not as far-fetched as it may initially appear. The theme of Zen introduces notions of spontaneity and unpredictability which, it will be recalled, is another characteristic which emerges in the case study literature on industrial districts.

The set of themes about public policy, which we explored in the discussion of industrial districts, arises in the context of corporate organisation, not in discussions of Japan but in discussions of the decentralisation of authority within Western firms. As power is dispersed to lower levels of the organisation, and those lower levels are in turn encouraged to develop new collaborative arrangements with outsiders, what is left of the corporation as an organisational unit? Since so few Western companies have decentralised to the point where this becomes a real issue, the literature yields virtually no answers. But speculation follows the lines which are pursued in the discussion of industrial districts: the role of corporate headquarters might be to provide a set of particular services to its decentralised divisions, or to promulgate and enforce standards of behaviour, or to define and police the boundaries between the internal and external world. But the attempts to specify exactly why these need to be done by a central authority, or how the central authority should do them, encounter the same problems in the theory of the decentralised corporation as they do in the theory of the industrial district.

II. Hannah Arendt and the human condition. How might one attempt to understand these stylised facts?

Of the frameworks which have been developed for the analysis of work and production, the one which seems most useful in this regard is that suggested by Hannah Arendt in *The human condition* [Arendt, 1958, 1963; Young-Bruehl, 1982]. Her categories of analysis are, strictly speaking, philosophic. They are not empirically derived, nor are they grounded in an analytical (or theoretical) structure. On the other hand, they do have a certain empirical basis. They are based upon a historical view of the actual structure of the ancient Greek city-states, from which the philosophical tradition in which they are grounded derives, and they have been moulded in the light of modern analytical structures, particularly those deriving from Marx, and the contemporary understanding of the evolution of work and the productive structure in modern times.

1. Realms of activity

Arendt distinguishes between three modes of productive activity: *labour*, *work* and *action*. Work and labour involve the relationship between man and the physical world. The distinction between them rests essentially upon the durability of the product. The product of work is permanent. It achieves a durable place in the world in the sense that it outlives the creator, the workman and, in that specific sense, achieves an existence which is independent. Because the product is durable, man is able to attain through work a certain kind of immortality. By contrast, *labour* in ancient Greece, was an activity associated with the biological process and was designed to ensure basic needs or, more literally, human survival. By extension, therefore, it is closely associated with consumption; it often does not usually yield in and of itself an independently identifiable physical product. When it does, that product has only an ephemeral existence. Arendt relates this distinction to the epistemological distinction between the words *labour* and *work*, a distinction which exists, she asserts, in every language but which has been generally lost in common usage. It continues nonetheless in certain specific usages. The original distinction, and the distinction she wants to make between the two as types of productive activity, is captured by the fact that we speak of the birth process as labour and of an artistic creation as a *work* of art. The words *Arbeit* and *Werk* are used in the same way in German; *travail* and *oeuvre* in French.

Arendt's third category of activity is *action*. Action, unlike labour and work, involves a relationship among men. It is the activity through which men reveal themselves to other men, and through which they achieve meaning as individuals. For Arendt, as for the Greeks from whom she draws her understanding, action was the most noble of the three activities. Although not synonymous with speech, Arendt's concept of action involves a discourse among men. Speech and action depend on human plurality, "The twofold character of equality and distinction". If men were not equal they would be completely unable to understand one another; at the same time, if men were not distinct, they would need neither to speak nor to act in order to reveal themselves to one another. Thus, action needs a community of equal men to provide, as it were, the context for their actions. Arendt sees action as a basically political activity, and although she gives virtually no specific examples of it, she leads us to think of action as the political activity of the citizens of the city-state.

Because it is through action that people define themselves as men and women, action is, for Arendt, an end in itself. But each action is also part of a process through which people come to exist in the world and give meaning to their lives. For Arendt, the sequence of actions of an individual over his or her life constitute a story, and it is through that story, remembered and retold in the community of men and women within which those actions occur, that individuals achieve immortality and overcome the biological processes. In this sense, action is also a means, and thus it becomes a means and an end at once.

Because actions take place within a community of differentiated men and women and involve interaction among them, because in effect one person's actions lead other persons to act in their turn, the consequences of action are unpredictable. The story of one's life which emerges in the process of action is thus not a creation but a revelation of self, a self one cannot control and which one does not even know except through action in the community of men and women.

Thus, action is like work in the sense that it gives a person a kind of immortality. It is like work also in that action, or the story of action which is an individual's life, has a beginning and an end. Labour, in contrast, is caught up in the biological processes, and is thus a continual repetition of activity in an endless process, to produce a product that disappears in the act of creation. But action is like labour and unlike work, in that it is not a means toward an end but an end in itself, and it achieves its ultimate meaning as an element in a *process*. The notion of a strong distinction between means and ends, and of an activity which is defined clearly by an output, namely the work which is produced, rather than in terms of a process, is peculiar to work; not to labour and not to action.

A final distinction which Arendt makes is between action and contemplation. In a sense, contemplation might be thought of as a fourth realm of human activity. Contemplation is contrasted to action in the sense that it involves the individual's withdrawal into him or herself and, thus, away from the community of men and women among whom action occurs. It involves a kind of self-definition which, for Arendt, is a contradiction in terms. But it is closely linked to work, in the sense that work involves the construction of a mental image which the production process then tries to recreate in the world. It is this deliberate attempt to reproduce the image that robs work of the spontaneity which characterises action.

Work occurs in isolation: it is only the end product which is presented to other people. The workman works alone. Action takes place in a community of men and women. The activity of labour is often performed among other persons but the people among whom it is performed are undifferentiated; it does not depend on their differentiation in the way that action does - indeed in many activities it is their essential sameness and the harmony which this permits among their separate activities which is critical.

In ancient Greece, labour was an activity of women and slaves performed within the household; work was the activity of the craftsman and the artist; action was the political activity of the Greek citizen in the civic life of the city-state. In modern times, Arendt argues, the craftsman's work has been reduced to labour through mass production. What was once politics has been reduced to technical decisions made by policy-makers, and carried out by bureaucrats, so that it too becomes labour. Action has disappeared as a realm of human activity. To the extent that we retain a refuge from labour in modern times, it is by divorcing contemplation from work, to which it was linked in ancient times, and making it into a separate realm of activity. We thus survive in an age of mass production by withdrawing into ourselves, cutting ourselves off from other people and losing our capacity to act.

In the notion that work has been reduced to labour through mass production, Arendt follows Marx, and this assertion, and its analytical implications, are essentially coincident with the theory of mass production as developed by Marx and later by Taylor and Ford. Most efforts to understand the phenomenon of industrial districts, and what Sabel and I have called flexible specialisation, have defined it as a return toward craft production or, in Arendt's terms, work. From this point of view, the important insight of *The human condition* is the third realm of action. We shall argue below that flexible specialisation is best understood in terms of this third realm. In order to develop this insight and assess its implications for economic and social structures, we need, however, to draw on a second aspect of Arendt's analysis - the way in which these activities were embedded in the social organisation of the Greek city-state.

2. The public and the private realms

The ancient Greek city-state made a very sharp distinction between the private and the public realms. The private realm pertained to the household. Its role was to assure those activities which were central to the maintenance and continuation of life, to the biological reproduction, or the biological necessities of continued human existence. It was a realm to which women and slaves were confined, and its activity was labour. The public realm pertained to politics and the citizen. It was conceived as the realm within which individuals achieved meaning in their lives. The basic activity of the public realm was action. Because it was only possible to give meaning to one's life after one's basic biological needs for maintenance and survival had been met, citizenship was possible only for those who controlled a private realm large enough to free them from labour. Arendt presents this idea in terms of Marx's concept of surplus value: the labour of the household in ancient Greece produced a surplus which was sufficient not only to support those within it but also to sustain the citizen, who did not labour but devoted himself to action in the public sphere. The need of this surplus to sustain public life was in ancient Greece the justification both of private property (and slavery) and the limitation of the rights of citizenship to those with property. The priority of action over labour was clearly indicated in Greek thought by the status given to citizenship and the public realm; but it was also understood that biological necessity took priority over public activity and that the labour of the private realm was the indispensable prerequisite for public action.

Craftsmen played an ambiguous role in this structure. The activity of the craftsman's work took place in the private realm, but it was directed toward the public realm, where it achieved its meaning and, through its durability, gave to its creator the kind of immortality achieved by citizens through politics in action. But the public realm of the craftsman was really the market place, not the political forum. The immortality achieved by the craftsmen through work was, moreover, different from that achieved by the citizen through action because the objects produced by the craftsman became dissociated from the person, and the individuality of the person was lost in a way which could not happen through the actions of citizens. There is a further problem in the role of the craftsman in the structure of Greek life which Arendt does not mention but which is very important for an understanding of industrial districts: in so far as the craftsman lived off the proceeds of his craft, the public realm of the market place achieved a role in biological survival which the public realm of the forum did not have.

III. Productive activity as action in flexible specialisation

To accept Adam Smith's pin factory as prototypical of production in the modern age is virtually to accept the notion that economic development through mass production has been a transformation of production from work to labour.[6] The introduction of the category of action permits us to think

6. This leads us to see flexible specialisation as a reversal of the classic development process, a movement backward toward craftsmanship. But this is not surprising since the distinction which Arendt makes between them is drawn as much from classical economics as from acient Greece, the social structure of which, as we have just seen, hinged much more on the distinction between labour and action than on that between labour and work.

of flexible specialisation, not as a reversal at all but as a forward movement toward a transition to some third form of the production process. We can now think of production as it occurs in dynamic industrial districts and decentralised corporate structures as *action*.

What might it mean to think of production as a form of action? It means that the production process becomes for the people who participate within it a public space like the political forum of ancient Greece, that they see that space as a realm in which they reveal themselves to one another as individuals.

The central activity which occurs in that space must, therefore, not be the creation of physical goods, nor even the improvement of the instruments which are used in production, but the discourse which surrounds the production process, and the opportunity which that discourse provides for each person to reveal him or herself as an individual to his or her interlocutors and collaborators. To say that production is basically an occasion for the discourse is not to say that people only talk to one another. The process could well - does in fact - involve physical acts of constructing and changing instruments of production and using them to actually produce goods and services. But it is always the act of doing these in collaboration and interaction with others which is central, because that collaboration and interaction is the characteristic of action. And since production is the occasion for discourse, and it is the discourse which matters, the subject matter can move as easily toward marketing, or the distribution of productive activity among firms, to compensation or to the politics of the industrial district as toward production itself without threatening the essential quality of the process; indeed by extending the realm of discourse - and, hence, action - that quality might actually be enhanced.

Certain characteristics of the districts, which otherwise appear irrelevant or even contradictory, become self-evident once production is conceived as the arena of action. The openness of the production process, and of the innovations in the instruments of production, becomes almost a prerequisite for their existence. If production is to serve as an arena of discourse and a stage for action, the interlocutors and the audience obviously have to be allowed to enter the theatre. Similarly, the apparent ease with which people move from production to the politics of the organisation of production - the fact that businessmen are so willing and able to become spokesmen for and organisers of the business community - is a reflection that both production and politics are for them essentially the same thing.

The paradox - which is so central in every characterisation of these districts - of competition and co-operation, also dissolves. Both competition and co-operation lose their meaning. They are terms of reference in a model in which production is a means, and the ends which it serves are the product which can be sold in the market for income. They imply a district the members of which are ultimately motivated by profit. Each individual is a potential competitor because his or her sales threaten the profit which any other member can obtain. Co-operation can only be understood by the ultimate need of the individual for the help of the other members and of the district as a whole, if profit is to be earned at all. It is paradoxical because it is hard to understand how the drive for individual profit can be made consistent with the need for collaboration or, conversely, how the possibility of regular collaboration can be sustained over time in the face of the constant temptation offered by the market to compete.

But, once one sees the industrial district as essentially a forum for action, it becomes clear that what is involved is not competition and co-operation at all. We have mistaken competition for the individual's attempt through action to differentiate him or herself. What appear to be his or her collaborators or co-operators in the market model are really interlocutors in the discourse through which the differentiation of the individual occurs and the audience for the story of a life which actions create. Or, to put it in a somewhat different way, what we have seen as co-operation is the quality of equality without which the discourse would be impossible and the differentiation achieved through it meaningless.

In much the same way, the problem of opportunism - a preoccupation which infuses the new economics of industrial organisation - also dissolves. That problem too derives from the model in which activity is a means toward the end of individual income. It is generated by the conflict between one of the means (collaboration through community) and the ends; or, as Marx might have put it, between the collective nature of the means and the private nature of the ends. Thus, the view that once the problem is conceived as one of opportunism it is too late to solve it, takes on a new meaning. It is not that individuals in the community need to suppress opportunism at a subconscious level. It is not, in other words, an issue of internalising social restraints. It is, rather, a question of how one conceives of and understands the process itself. If one conceives of production as a realm of action, the other members of the community cannot ever be dispensed with without making one's acts meaningless.

This new conception clearly forces us to rethink the idea that what is peculiar about these industrial districts is that the economic structure is embedded in the social structure. Or, rather, it suggests that we must disentangle a set of concepts which are used interchangeably in the literature, i.e. society, community, and culture. The critical concept in Arendt's view of action - and by extension the understanding of industrial districts - is the notion of a community of equals. Only within such a community can one differentiate one's self. If the other members of the community are not like one, they cannot appreciate one's differences. Arendt also believes that such a community must be relatively small - small enough for its members to see and know one another as persons. This rules out large aggregates such as national or international communities, and explains why we are looking at relatively limited and contained geographic areas. It also suggests why traditional societies, where such contained areas are relatively common, i.e. relative to modern society, might be particularly hospitable to the development of such districts.

But community in this sense is not synonymous with either society or culture. The community does not necessarily coincide with the society and production does not need to be embedded within the social structure. Some social structures might be compatible with community, moreover, and others might not. The Greek social structure generated such communities and maintained them by creating a category of *citizens*, who were equal, but whom the rest of the social structure, in which individuals were very unequal, laboured to sustain. But one could well imagine some societies, particularly some traditional societies, where people are so highly differentiated that it would be impossible to create a community of equals as Arendt understands that term.

Similarly, the society or its culture (here one probably ought to speak of "culture", not "society") might or might not value *action* enough to generate a dynamic productive realm even if it is capable of sustaining a community in which action could occur. Arendt herself claims that the Christian culture curtailed action by its other-worldly orientation and the effect which this had in turning individuals in upon themselves. And, in the modern age, Arendt seems to feel that the value which the culture places upon contemplation is a threat to action. Again, one is led to wonder how many traditional cultures have a stance vis-à-vis the world which is hospitable to action.

What about the inherited industrial culture? What is the relationship between the social structure of these industrial communities and those of the economic systems committed to mass production? Arendt sees a deep conflict between the social structure of a community of action as we have just defined it and that of modern industrial society. She argues that the effect of modernisation through mass production has been to merge personalised communities of the kind which might have constituted a theatre of action into a vast impersonal social space in which individuals are not only equal but also, at least in their public lives, all alike. To the extent that we retain our individuality, she argues, the dominant Christian ethic has led us to turn away from one another and withdraw into ourselves. Were the modern world the world of competitive economic theory, this characterisation might be true. The market economy which that theory envisages works effectively only if individuals are in fact totally isolated from one another and both society and community are replaced by the impersonal price system. But, as Arendt herself recognises, the modern world has been organised by mass production, not by a competitive market. And here the imperatives of the economic system for the social structure are not so clear. In the realm of production, at least, they are very stringent and demanding but also extremely limited, and the individual is left substantial space outside the production sphere to organise his or her life in accord with other principles. It is possible that the requirements of standardisation of consumption under such a system are such as to leave little room for individuality in the rest of life as well. In the 1950s, when Arendt was writing, it certainly seemed that way to many observers. That perception was no doubt what led Foucault [1979] to see the panopticon as the prototypical institution of modern life, and Arendt herself argues in *The human condition* that the capacity for action has been removed from modern life. But this is not nearly as evident today. One can argue that it is precisely the desire of people for products which permits them to differentiate themselves through consumption which has created a space in the market place for the expansion of industrial districts. And if the culture has permitted us to reassert our capacity for action in consumption, then it would not seem to constitute an insurmountable constraint upon our capacity to reassert it in the sphere of production as well.

The capacity of modern society to regenerate a public sphere is also suggested by the tendency, during modern revolutionary periods, for a form of government which Arendt calls "councils" to spring up spontaneously. Arendt asserts that this is a universal feature of revolutionary periods in the nineteenth and twentieth century. In the modern revolutions, there is invariably a period in which these local councils compete with political parties as a locus of politics and as a governance structure. Arendt views the councils as a public sphere and the activity which occurs within them as fundamentally equivalent to the political life of the citizens of ancient Greece [Arendt, 1963].

Whether or not one accepts Arendt's claim that such councils constitute the embryos of a truly revolutionary governance structure - a claim which in any case would be very difficult to substantiate - any student of labour history will recognise the generality of the phenomenon which she describes in the labour struggles within modern industry. Examples include not only the Paris communes of 1848 and 1870, the soviets, from which the modern Russian state somewhat disingenuously draws its name, the *Rate* in post World War I Germany, and the councils of the Hungarian uprising of 1956; all of which Arendt uses as examples to develop her argument. But numerous examples can be drawn from the relatively brief period of modern history since her manuscript on the subject was first published: the factory councils of France in May, 1968 and in Italy in the hot autumn of 1969; the councils in the Iranian factories after the fall of the Shah; as well as more isolated incidents of worker plant occupations and management such as the celebrated Lipp watch factory in France.

The global political significance of these councils is the challenge which they pose to the power of the nation-state and the parties which govern it, and a series of specific policies which the councils advocate, in opposition to those of the State or the parties, on economic and social issues. The challenge on economic issues is often understood in purely technical terms: a romantic and misguided populism, as opposed to the realism of the professional economists, engineers, and planners. The social issues are more often understood as technically legitimate, albeit highly partisan, disagreements over the distribution of income.

But for those within the factory councils themselves, the issues focus as much on the organisation of the production process as on the conduct of business. The workers seem to be not only demanding, but, through the councils, actually engaging in, the management of the business. Their ability to do this effectively, on a continuing basis, is almost universally discounted by external observers. Indeed, "disparaged" is probably a better term to characterise the views of outsiders about the managerial ambitions of these revolutionary worker councils. Even Arendt, who seems to advocate the council system for the governance of the State as the only alternative to what she views as the mass politics of the modern age, takes this view with respect to their attempts to manage the productive process. "No doubt", she argues, "managerial talent should not be lacking in people of working-class origins; the trouble was merely that the workers' councils existing were the worst possible organs for its detection. For the men whom they trusted and chose from their own midst were selected according to political criteria... but the qualities of the statesman or the political man and the qualities of the manager or the administrator are not the same... The councils in the factories brought an element of action into the management of things and this indeed could not but create chaos" [Arendt, 1963, pp. 278-279].

And yet anyone with actual factory experience will recognise in these remarks a technocratic view of the production process which corresponds little with the realities of shop floor life. The theory of mass production, in which each operation is engineered precisely to dove-tail with the preceding and succeeding operations on the line, and where the chief requirement for the smooth flow of the process is that the workers follow instructions to the letter, is a theoretical ideal which is virtually never realised in practice. The reality is that the production process actually depends on a variety of ad hoc innovations, in procedure and in the physical design of equipment, introduced gradually over time, beginning on the day the engineer tries to set up the new equipment on the shop floor and continuing, long after the engineer has moved on to the next project, through a collaboration of the worker with his or her supervisor, and with the maintenance craftsmen. The fact that this occurs is what makes the ultimate collective weapon in all bureaucratic organisations, the *grève du zèle* (i.e. work to rule), so effective. What differentiates mass production from craft production in this regard is thus not the absence of worker discretion and, hence, the need for their active co-operation and engagement, but the narrowness of limits in which this discretion is allowed to occur. Ultimately, those limits are technical: the production operation is as the theory suggests, highly fragmented, and the pieces do have to fit back together as a whole. But the technical limits are not as stringent as the theory of mass production would have it, and, as the engineers, whose power and self-image derive from that theory and who, therefore, have an ideological commitment to it, would like to believe. While management generally recognises the need for the adaptions which the workers make in the blueprint designs, they tend to place narrower limits upon the freedom and ability to make their ad hoc alterations than is consistent with productive efficiency. Hence the felt experience of the mass production worker is that of a frustrated craftsman, and the initial effects of factory councils, in which workers are freed to pursue the backlog of ideas which management has repressed, is to increase productive efficiency. This undoubtedly is the source of the halo effect which accompanies the introduction of worker suggestions plans, even in factories where the revolutionary moment which generates the council system is so remote as to be truly inconceivable. If factory council management ultimately results in chaos, as Arendt asserts, it is because the workers push their efforts to redesign the production system beyond the ideological restraints upon their initiatives into the realm where the true technical constraints, which underlie that ideology, become binding.

It is not, however, so clear that the chaos does in fact result from the council system, or, if it does, that it is inevitable. The electric impact of the Lipp factory occupation in France in the 1970s upon the intellectual and business elites, it was explained to me by a personal aid to the Minister of

Finance at the time, was due to the ability of the worker-run factory to operate efficienctly enough to demonstrate its viability in the face of the business decision, based on technical engineering studies and the operating experience of the factory managed by elite engineers, that it could not be profitably run. The situations under which factory councils arise in a widespread way in a revolutionary moment are so generally chaotic that it would be impossible to pinpoint the source of business problems, especially in a regime of mass production where efficiency depends so heavily upon the stability of the business environment.

In any case, what limits the effectiveness of individual workers in mass production is the fact that the product is frozen in such a way that every operation of the production process is tightly constrained by all of the other operations. Once the product is allowed to vary, these constraints are relieved. And while any single worker might still not possess the skill or knowledge to manage alone, he or she certainly has something to contribute as part of a team; and teams composed, if not exclusively of workers, at least of the full range of personnel previously assigned to the shop, might well be able to manage a factory. This is indeed the lesson of experiments in corporate decentralisation as well as the industrial districts. Under these circumstances, it is precisely the skills of politics which are required to manage the factory. The full passage of Arendt quoted above with parts omitted reads as follows: "[The] men whom they [the workers] trusted and chose from their own midst were selected according to political criteria, for their trustworthiness, their personal integrity, their capacity for judgement, often for their physical courage. The same men, entirely capable of acting in a political capacity, were bound to fail if entrusted with the management of a factory or other administrative duties. For the qualities of the statesman or the political man, and the qualities of the manager or the administrator are not the same, and they are seldom to be found in the same individual: the one is supposed to know how to deal with men in the field of human relations, whose principle is freedom, and the other must know how to manage things and people in the sphere of life whose principle is necessity" [Arendt, 1963]. The point is that on this score, Arendt is wrong. She was probably wrong even in the age of mass production. But she is definitely wrong in the age of industrial districts, decentralised corporations, and flexible specialisation. Management, as innumerable managerial textbooks are at pains to point out, is now about human relations. And that is what Arendt calls political (the textbooks would probably be better if they recognised this last point). Thus, to the extent that the council system is, as Arendt argues, a universal of the modern age, a form of governance and organisation which emerges spontaneously in every revolutionary moment of our era, there is certainly the capacity in modern culture to generate industrial districts. These are not, in other words, forms of human activity for which we must draw upon the leftovers of premodern social structures to build.

IV. Public policy and industrial districts

What does this ultimately suggest, then, about the "public policy problem" of creating and sustaining districts of this kind? It suggests that the problem may be divided into two distinct components. The first is the problem of how to generate a concern with action. The second is what would be called, in Arendt's terminology, the problem of labour.

About the first problem, there seems to be very little which can be said either from theory or from the case study material. But it is obvious that if one adopts the framework of analysis which we have been developing, it becomes a central problem for further study.

A good deal more can be said, analytically at least, about the second problem. Relative to the social structures of mass production, flexible specialisation involves an inversion of ends and means. Whereas in mass production, the production process is a means for the attainment of income, it becomes in flexible specialisation an end unto itself, or rather the action which occurs in the realm of production becomes an end in itself. But since action, while it gives meaning to people's lives, does not ensure survival, communities which are organised for action need some other means of ensuring it. This is exactly the problem upon which Hannah Arendt focused in the ancient Greek city-state: in Greece, it was resolved through the *labour* of women and slaves in the private sphere. In the industrial districts of the case study literature, it is solved by selling the output of the production process in the market to obtain income, income which can in turn be converted into the means of survival. Thus, these districts invert the relationship between income and production which prevails in mass production: income becomes the means and production is the end. But, because it is the production which generates the income, the relationship becomes extremely complex. Production is not just an end, it is also a means to the end. The balancing of these two purposes, so to speak, of the production process becomes a central problem which the industrial district has to solve. The analytical question is thus: how is it possible to ensure that production serves as an effective means for the community's survival without having the members of the community become so preoccupied with income that action, which makes the community dynamic in the first place, loses its centrality in the community value system? One can suggest some clues to how this problem might be investigated. Obviously, the conflict is less if the community has secure sources of income through, for example, the welfare state, a minimum of subcontracts from larger producers, or a monopoly position such as the craft-guilds enjoyed in the medieval world. But none of these measures would seem to completely dissolve the paradox, particularly if the community were at all conscious of the need to maintain its guarantees or became concerned with their extension.

The paradox is reinforced if one begins to think about industrial districts as a so-called policy problem, because according to the way that such a policy problem is presented, the industrial districts are of value precisely because they are technologically dynamic and generate high income. Our argument has been that they do these things by forgetting income and focussing upon production as a realm of action. And yet this implies that it is the task of the policy maker, who is herself or himself interested in income, to induce the community to forsake an interest in income for action. As suggested earlier, one of the ways this seems to be solved in Central Italy is that the community comes to see the process of creating and maintaining the institutions which ensure survival as a realm of action, in much the same way as production is a realm of action. But whether this is, or could ever be, a general solution to the problem, is doubtful. And thus, ultimately, it, like the value placed upon action in the first place, becomes a central concern of public policy and hence a focus for further research.

What does it imply for the conventional view of public policy in terms of lists of services and the intermediary institutions which provide them, on the one hand, or of rules which govern behaviour, on the other? These old issues remain but they are transformed through this focus on action and the conflict between income and action as opposing goals for production. For example, one becomes interested in the services not only because of the functions they perform from a narrow economic viewpoint but also because of the values which they instill. Do schools, for example, teach skills or do they instill in the students the value of action? And the way in which a service is provided might also become more important because of the impact it has on values than because of the service itself. If the community does not, for example, come to see the provision of these services as a realm of action, perhaps it is better for services to be provided from outside the community by a distant state? Much the same change occurs in the issues surrounding the list of rules. Rules may still be important but now it is not a question of rules which manage the conflict between competition and co-operation or which foreclose opportunities, for these are, as we have seen, no longer issues; but the value which the rules place on action and the way in which action, and not income, is rewarded and sustained.

References

Arendt, Hannah. 1958. *The human condition*, Chicago, The University of Chicago Press.

---. 1963. *On revolution*, New York, The Viking Press.

Becattini, Giacomo. 1987. *Small business development in Italy*, Paper prepared for the New Industrial Organisation Programme of the International Institute for Labour Studies, Spring.

Bouchara, Moncef. 1987. "Industrialisation rampante en Tunisie" in *Economie et Humanisme*, September.

Brusco, Sebastiano. 1982. "The Emilian model: Productive decentralisation and social integration", in *Cambridge Journal of Economics*, No. 6, pp. 167-89.

Clark, Rodney. 1979. *The Japanese company*, New Haven, Yale University Press.

Foucault, Michel. 1979. *Discipline and punish. The birth of the prison*, New York, Vintage Books.

Geertz, C. 1963. *Pedlars and princes, social development and economic modernization in two Indonesian towns*, Chicago, Chicago University Press.

Imai, Ken-ichi. 1985. "Network organisation and incremental innovation in Japan", Institute of Business Research, Hilotsubashi University, Kunitachi, Tokyo Japan, IBR Discussion Paper No. 122, July.

Imai, Ken-ichi et al. 1985. "Managing the new product development process: How Japanese companies learn and unlearn", in K.B. Clark (ed.): *The uneasy alliance*, Cambridge, Harvard Business School Press, pp. 337-375.

Piore, Michael J. 1989. *Corporate reform in American manufacturing and the challenge to economic theory*, Massachusetts Institute of Technology, Department of Economics, Working Paper No. 533, September.

Piore, Michael J.; Sabel, Charles. 1984. *The second industrial divide*, New York, Basic Books.

Puel, H.; Saglio, Jean. 1979. *Concentration industrielle, mutation socio-politique et développement urbain dans les villes moyennes: Oyonnax, formation du capital industriel et transformations urbaines*, Groupe lyonnais de sociologie industrielle, fasc. 1, 173p., June.

Raveyre, M.F.; Saglio, Jean. 1984. "Les systèmes industriels localisés: éléments pour une analyse sociologique des ensembles de P.M.E. industriels", in *Sociologie du Travail*, No. 2, pp. 157-176.

Ritaine, Evelyne. 1987. "Prato ou l'exaspération de la diffusion industrielle", in *Sociologie du Travail*, February, pp. 138-156.

Sengenberger, Werner; Loveman, Gary. 1987. *Smaller units of employment: A synthesis report on industrial reorganisation in industrialised countries*, Geneva, International Institute for Labour Studies, New Industrial Organisation Programme, Discussion Paper No. 3.

Watanabe, Susumu. 1970. "Entrepreneurship in small enterprises in Japanese Manufacturing", in *International Labour Review*, Vol. 102, No. 6, pp. 531-576.

Young-Bruehl, Elizabeth. 1982. *Hannah Arendt. For love of world*, New Haven, Yale University Press.

6 The quantitative importance of Marshallian industrial districts in the Italian economy

Fabio Sforzi

I. Introduction

In the 1980s the development of light industry in North-eastern and Central Italy aroused the interest of both Italian and foreign scholars and laymen, who were attracted by the experience, over the preceding years, of an unusual dynamism and a higher rate of industrial growth than occurred in other parts of the country. Many have recognised in this success the concrete expression of a new regime of flexible accumulation said to typically characterise the current stage of development of advanced capitalist societies. Because industrialisation in these regions has, as a consequence, been viewed as resulting from a crisis of a model based on mass production, recent declines in manufacturing employment in the areas of old and intensive industrialisation in North-western Italy, founded on the company towns of Turin and Milan, and more generally based on large factories organised for production on a large scale, has further served to attract attention.

However, some people, mainly Italians, have developed a slightly different interpretation of light industrialisation based on local economic development. The characteristics of this alternative industrial development were studied and explained in one region, Tuscany, at the end of the 1960s and the beginning of the 1970s [IRPET, 1969; 1975]. From this point on, other studies focusing attention on local economic development contributed to growing awareness among the shrewdest scholars and investigators of the Italian economy that light industrialisation could be said to be an appropriate model for characterising particular localities of Northern and Central Italy, presenting a specific form of development rather than something "peripheral" to that of North-western Italy [Valli, 1986]. This model of light industrialisation can be defined as an organisation of the production process based on single specialised industries, carried out by concentrations made up of many small firms of similar character in particular localities achieving the advantages of large-scale production by external rather than internal economies, with social environments that feature local communities of people adhering to relatively homogeneous systems of values, and with networks of merging urban and rural settlements inside territories united by production and social links [Becattini, 1978].

Before the model of light industrialisation became established, the existence of so-called sectoral distinctions between "more modern", higher technology industries, like mechanical engineering, and "more traditional" labour-intensive ones, such as fashionwear, was assumed to be a key to explaining different spatial patterns of industrial growth. Thus, for a certain period, the successful performance of mechanical engineering in localities of Emilia-Romagna, for example, was viewed as a diffusion of the model of industrialisation dominating North-western Italy, the famous "Industrial Triangle" based on Milan-Turin-Genoa and their surrounding regions of Lombardy, Piedmont and Liguria [King, 1985], thereby neglecting the role played by the particular organisation of the production process and the particular social context found in the areas of mechanical specialisation of North-eastern and Central Italy.

It is no exaggeration to say that in Italy interpretations of economic development have suffered due both to the common use of the North-South division framework, i.e. the Industrial Triangle and the rest of Italy, and the concept of region implicitly assumed, and the related spatial scale used in empirical analysis. Indeed, even "the model of the Three Italies" [Bagnasco, 1977] is empirically based on single administrative regions, although the regional analytical framework used is criticised by the author himself for inadequately distinguishing local features. The negative effects of using the administrative region as the spatial unit of analysis of Italian development are, generally speaking, heavily underestimated. It is not sufficient to recognise that not all the localities belonging to the "Third Italy" are characterised by the same model of industrialisation, or that within the North-west, the "First Italy", there are localities exhibiting similar developmental characteristics to those found in areas of light industrialisation. The problem for empirical investigation is to establish the nature of a spatial unit that is consistent with a definition, both in respect of a theoretical framework and applied analysis.

In general, it can be pointed out that theoretical perspectives - including those based on notions of flexible specialisation and vertical disintegration - neglect the fact that the model of light industrialisation has its own spatial scale. The problem is then compounded when an incongruent administrative region or a single locality, i.e. municipality, is used as the spatial unit of analysis. As a consequence, spatial patterns of light industrialisation based, for example, on an industrial organisation founded merely on flexible accumulation or on vertical disintegration, may be very imprecise and ill-defined, ranging from single isolated localities through industrial quarters within a large town, to a territorially demarcated region where light industrialisation constitutes the dominant characteristic features. Thus, the problem of spatial scale remains an unsolved aspect of the argument and can lead to misunderstandings.

Our opinion is that the spatial pattern suitable for investigating the processes of industrialisation - or indeed socio-economic development in general - is one of local systems, each individual system being interpreted as a "system of interacting localities" and a setting for social and economic interactions.

In Italy, the discarding of both the North-South division and the "Three Italies" as theoretical frameworks of economic development can fruitfully result in an adequate multi-regional view provided that the region is interpreted neither as an economic region nor as a single individual locality but, rather, as a local system. At this stage of the argument, it must be pointed out that the proposition of regional geography based on local systems as an analytical framework for both the theoretical thinking about, and the empirical investigation of, local economies is not designed to "produce as many ad hoc theories as there are local instances" [Harvey, 1985], but to make spatial patterns of different models of industrialisation correspond more closely to both theoretical conceptualisation and empirical requirements.

The basis of this argument about the local system as a unit of investigation for general purposes is that the development occurs locally, that is on a local spatial scale, when an industry and a population have the same spatially-bounded area in common producing systems of social and economic interaction. This happens whether industrial production is organised by individual large factories or by many small businesses of similar character. Both these different forms of industrial organisation interact beneficially with their environment, albeit in different specific ways. What differentiates one from the other is the way in which firms and people are embedded in the division of labour.

II. The Marshallian industrial district as a "system of interacting localities"

In Italy, the concept of industrial district has been formulated and proposed as a category of economic analysis alternative to the industrial sector and the firm and it has been unequivocally defined as a socio-territorial as well as economic concept [Becattini, 1979; Bellandi, 1982]. In other words, space is embedded in the definition, just as the industry of the district is "a system of interacting parts" and the district is an amalgamation of firms and people.

In the district the population of firms - being interdependent parts of the same production process - interacts with the community of people, merging together within a spatially-delimited area to which both belong. The territoriality of the district is nothing but the localised thickening of the network formed by these relations, constituting the area shared in common, and delimiting it.

The industrial district has its own spatial scale defined and delimited with respect to the system of interdependences between congregate firms, and between firms and the community, involving spatially-coherent localities of localised industry and settled population. It is, therefore, a system of localities - i.e. numbers of individual settlements, both places of work and of residence, having relationships between them and implying a high level of interdependence - corresponding to the rationale of a local labour market, that is an area that includes several localities distinguished by a certain concentration of jobs, where the majority of the resident population can find a job - and employees can change their jobs - without changing their place of residence. The main characteristic of such a local labour market is that it is spatially-delimited, and relatively self-contained in the sense that job supply and demand tend to be in equilibrium in respect to the area over which they extend, because the majority of the resident population works within it and employers recruit workers from the constituent localities [Sforzi, 1987].

This geographical "system of interacting localities" corresponding to a local labour market also identifies the time-space pattern of daily life for the resident population where the majority of their social and economic relations take place. If it is true that "now under capitalism, systems of interaction have tended to expand over space and contract over time" [Jonas, 1988], nevertheless recurring interactions related to daily life are still spatially-bounded while the others are occasional and can be interpreted as external to the localised spatial system and relating to the environment with which the system exchanges information, goods and people across its boundaries, the environment being both the surroundings and the "rest of the world".

Marshall, talking about different industrial organisations, introduced a distinction between internal and external economies and pointed out that these last "can often be secured by the concentration of many small businesses of similar character in particular localities: or, as is commonly said, by the localisation of industry" [Marshall, 1920]. These "particular localities" are nothing but industrial districts and they can be conveniently interpreted as local systems endowed with the social, economic and territorial constitutive properties described above differentiating them from other local systems such as those dominated by a large factory. Company-towns, for example, contrast with industrial districts, according to Marshall, because of a different industrial organisation and division of labour. This in Marshallian industrial districts is reflected in a social structure which is particularly characterised by a relatively large number of self-employed people, and by the economic role of the family which is not only a consumer but also a producer.

III. The functional approach to identifying Marshallian industrial districts in the Italian experience

The local systems used to identify Marshallian industrial districts in Italy's territorial economy are the 955 Local Labour Market Areas (LLMAs) defined through the functional regionalisation of 1981 journey-to-work flows (figure 1), connecting places of residence and of work [ISTAT-IRPET, 1986]. Functional regionalisation is understood here not merely as localisation in space, but "as referring to the zoning of time-space in relation to routinised social practices. Thus a place of residence is a locale which is a 'station' for a large cluster of interactions in the course of a typical day" [Giddens, 1985]. Accordingly, the 955 LLMAs represent geographically and

Figure 1. Pattern of local systems in Italy, 1981

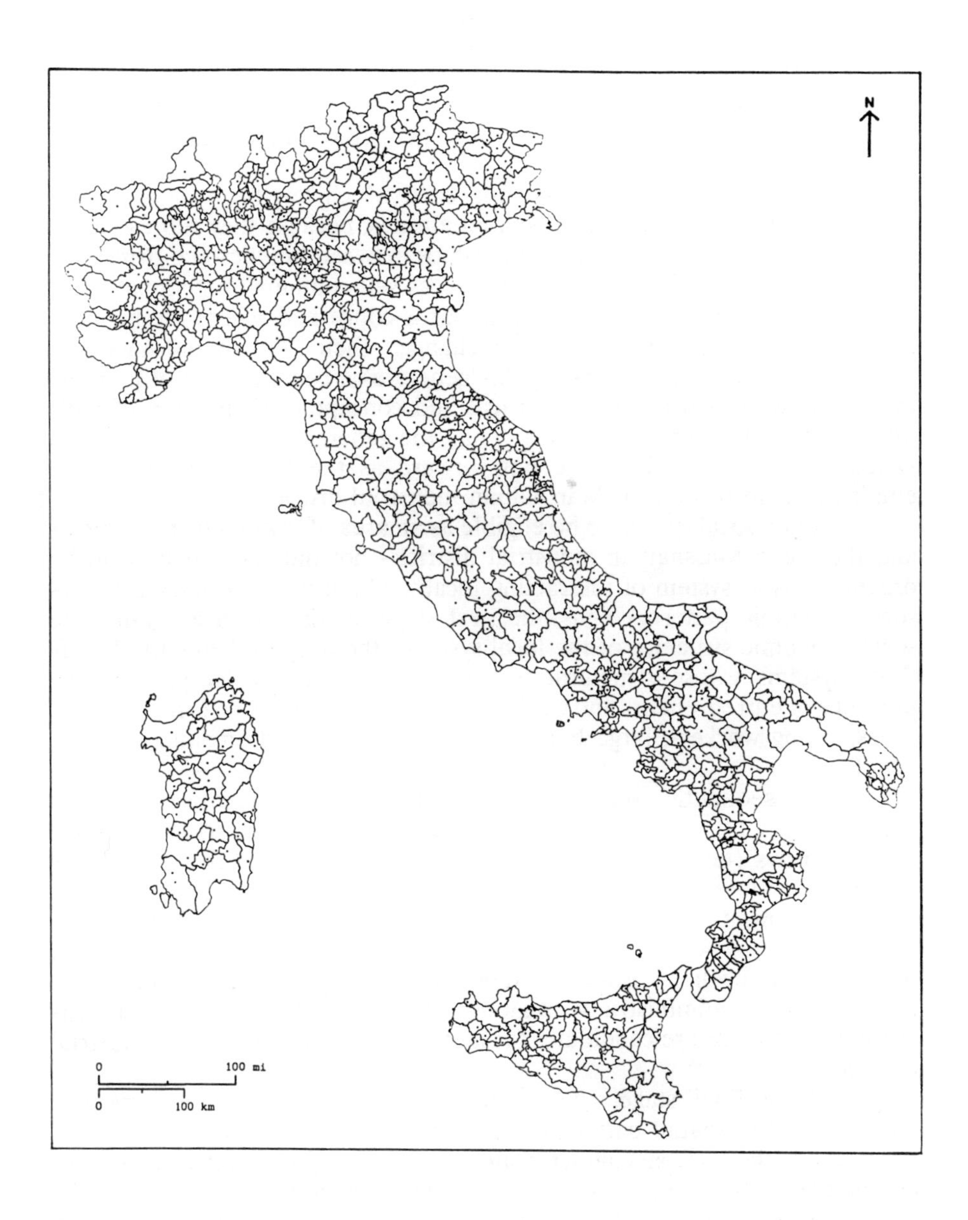

statistically comparable spatial entities and spatially-coherent "systems of interacting localities.

Functional regionalisation provides the key element of a multivariate classification of the 955 LLMAs in order to identify, firstly, which of them show the typical socio-economic characteristic features that distinguish the model of light industrialisation; and, secondly, which of the areas of light industrialisation so identified can then be further distinguished by their dominant manufacturing specialisation as being Marshallian industrial districts.

The multi-stage research approach which has been used [Sforzi, 1987] starts from the LLMAs as spatial entities, because they represent the local systems within which the relationships between families and firms take place. Indeed, they have been identified as self-contained functional areas as far as the supply and demand of labour is concerned, where the majority of the local population can find - or change - their jobs without having to change their place of residence. This generates a complex web of journey-to-work flows which are the empirical and conceptual foundation of daily urban systems [Hägerstrand, 1970]. Thus, the general spatial pattern of local systems (LLMAs) of Italy are put forward as the first element for the empirical identification of Marshallian industrial districts.

For a local system to be eligible as an area of light industrialisation - and then as a Marshallian industrial district - not only does it have to be organised as a "system of interacting localities" but it has to have a typical socio-economic pattern. Thus, the next stage consists in investigating the socio-economic structure of the local systems, the purpose being to identify those systems whose structural features follow a particular pattern: the presence of entrepreneurs and workers in small manufacturing firms, working wives, young workers, large households with elders, and amenities [Sforzi, 1987].

Consequently, the 955 LLMAs have been categorised into 15 different groups of local systems, according to their socio-economic characteristics (table 1). One of these categories fits the socio-economic features mentioned above as typical of the model of light industrialisation. Figure 2 shows the spatial pattern of this category of local systems within Italy, which can be regarded as the spatial pattern of the model of light industrialisation when it is identified by using local systems as suitable spatial units instead of administrative regions. Within this framework of analysis these local systems are candidates for identification as Marshallian industrial districts.

As a final stage, the economic structure of the local systems constituting the spatial pattern of light industrialisation has been analysed according to the sectoral characteristics of their firms, selecting those systems characterised by a dominant manufacturing specialisation.

The outcome of this analysis is the identification of 61 Marshallian industrial districts (DIMs), mainly localised in North-eastern and Central Italy, but also in North-western Italy, with a significant exclusion of Liguria, the sole region almost entirely characterised by large plants in heavy industry. Their location corresponds to a "localised specialisation" within the spatial pattern of light industrialisation (figure 3).

Table 1: A 15-fold classification of local labour market areas, 1981

Category	Denomination(*)	No. of LLMAs	Examples
1	Northern and central urban systems	76	Milano, Firenze
2	Southern urban systems	64	Napoli, Palermo
3	Light industrialisation local systems	161	Carpi, Prato
4	Northern manufacturing local systems	96	Lumezzane, Valdagno
5	Northern commercial local systems	13	Bressanone, Merano
6	Holiday-place local systems	61	Capri, San Remo
7	Northern rural resort local systems	67	Neive, Pievepelago
8	Central resort local systems	91	Abbadia S.Salvatore, Acquapendente
9	Central and island resort local systems	33	Fiuggi, Olbia
10	Island semi-rural local systems	27	Ghilarza, Villamar
11	Southera semi-rural local systems	60	Gibellina, Piazza Armerina
12	Southern rural farm-worker local systems	95	Lamezia Terme, Nusco
13	Southern rural farm-owner local systems	66	Ariano Irpino, Muro Lucano
14	Southern marginal local systems	41	Bovalino, Cetraro
15	Southern deprived local systems	4	Lioni, Santa Margherita Belice

Note: (*)The classification of LLMAs into 15 categories has been developed through a multivariate analysis of 1981 socio-economic census variables. The denomination of each single category corresponds to its regional setting (i.e. northern v. southern), employment status of the resident population (i.e. socio-economic group by class), household composition (i.e. marital status, size of family) and living standards (i.e. education, accommodation, household equipment). For example, Northern and central urban systems are characterised by: high and middle status jobs in manufacturing industry and services, working wives, youths studying, married couples without children, rented dwellings, amenities; Southern urban systems are characterised by: high and middle status jobs in commerce and public administration, large households with children, youths seeking first job, rented dwellings, no amenities; Light industrialisation local systems are characterised by: small entrepreneurs and working class in manufacturing industry, working wives, young workers, large households with elders, amenities; Northern manufacturing local systems are characterised by: employees in manufacturing industry, elders retired from employment, young workers. For a full detailed description, see: Sforzi [1986].

Note: This table is compiled from data discussed in Sforzi [1986].

Figure 2: Pattern of light industrialisation local systems, 1981

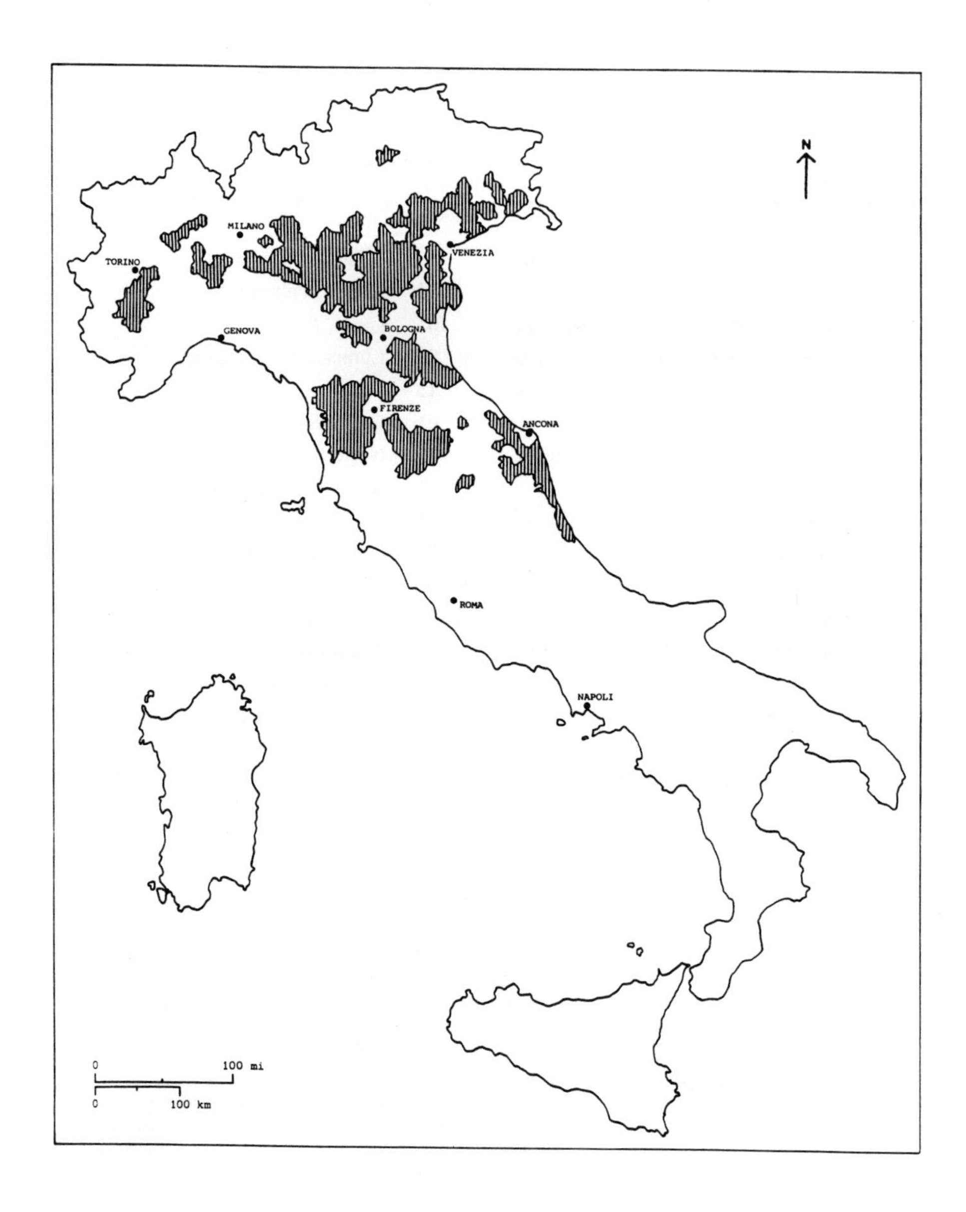

Figure 3: Marshallian industrial districts within the pattern of light industrialisation local systems, 1981

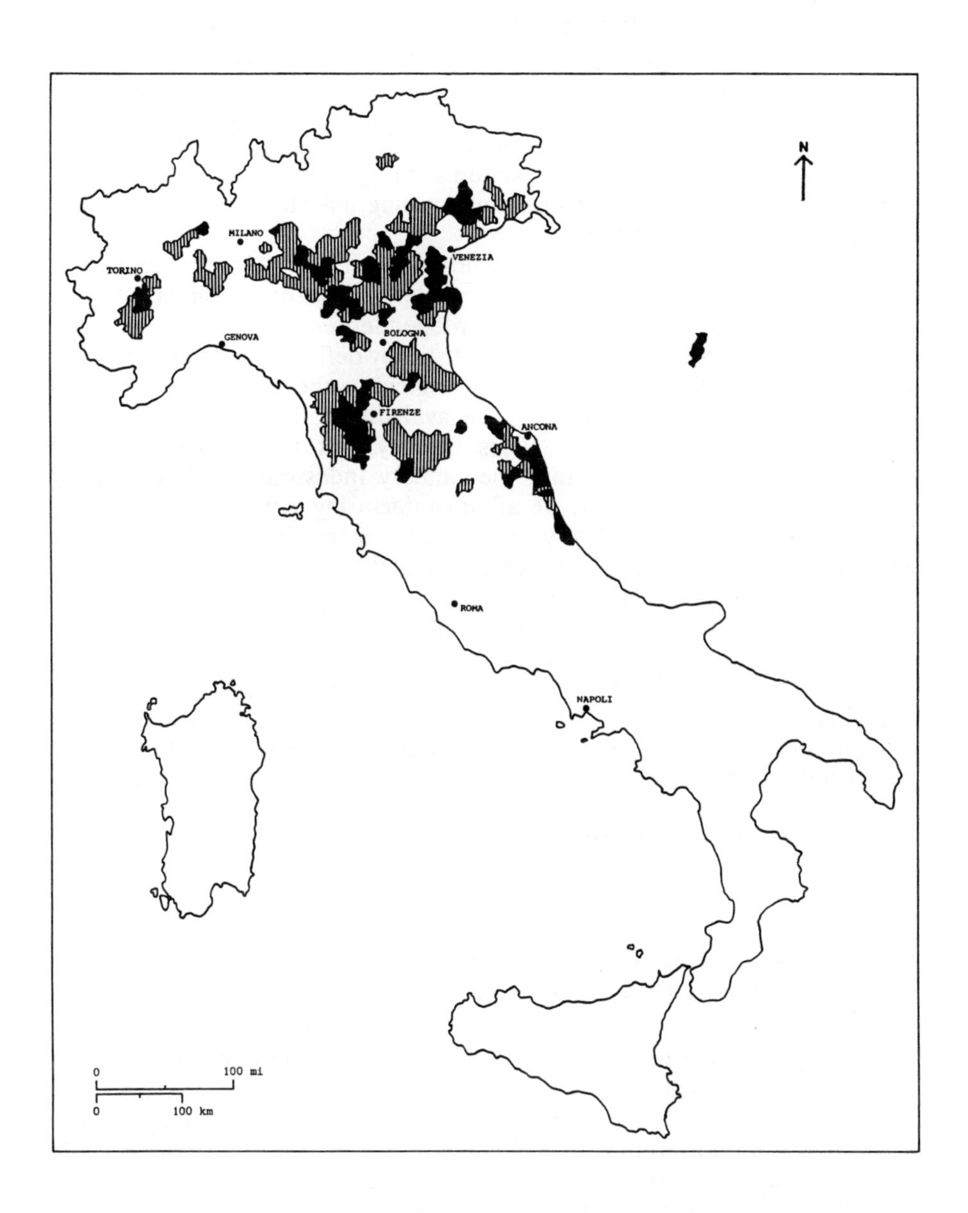

IV. The dominant manufacturing specialisations of Italian Marshallian industrial districts

The majority of Marshallian industrial districts have a dominant manufacturing specialisation in fashionwear industries - i. e. textiles, clothing, footwear, leather goods and tanneries - and wooden furniture; a lower number is dominated by metal goods industries, mechanical and electrical engineering. Then there are districts dominated by ceramic goods, musical instruments and toys. In general, the industries by which different districts are dominated tend to be found in systems of neighbouring districts as shown in figure 4. The employment in manufacturing industries dominating each district is summarised in table 2.

Of course, the industrial structure of each district is also constituted by other manufacturing industries complementary or subsidiary to the dominant one. In fact, the local interdependences of the district do not occur only between phases inside the statistically defined dominant industrial sector, but also with other industries, belonging to other sectors, but involved in the same production process. The available data do not allow us to measure the local interdependences directly, but they provide a good indication. For example, within the tannery industrial districts (tanning accounting for 38.6 per cent of all manufacturing employment in these districts) the footwear industry (being the second industry in terms of employment) employs 27.3 per cent; within the textile industrial districts (textiles employing 73.7 per cent of all manufacturing employment in these districts) the clothing industry (being the second industry in terms of employment) employs 6.7 per cent, while mechanical engineering (being the third) employs 5.4 per cent, of which textile machinery employs 1.7 per cent.

Some industries, and their employees, are more liable to be concentrated in the particular districts they dominate rather than be diffused throughout all the districts as a whole (table 3). Table 4 shows that metal goods and engineering, and leather goods are less concentrated than other industries in the districts they individually dominate.

V. The employment structure of Marshallian Industrial Districts

At the time of the 1981 Industrial Census, the number of jobs in Marshallian industrial districts was 906,009, amounting to 5.4 per cent of a total of 16,883,286 jobs for the whole of Italy. A breakdown of employment according to the different economic divisions shows the contribution made by Marshallian industrial districts to the national total (table 5).

Whereas 5.4 per cent of total employment is localised within DIMs, only 4.3 per cent of the country's resident population lives there (i.e. 2,435,211 people living within DIMs out of 56,335,678 for Italy as a whole).

Figure 4: Marshallian industrial districts, according to dominant manufacturing industries, 1981

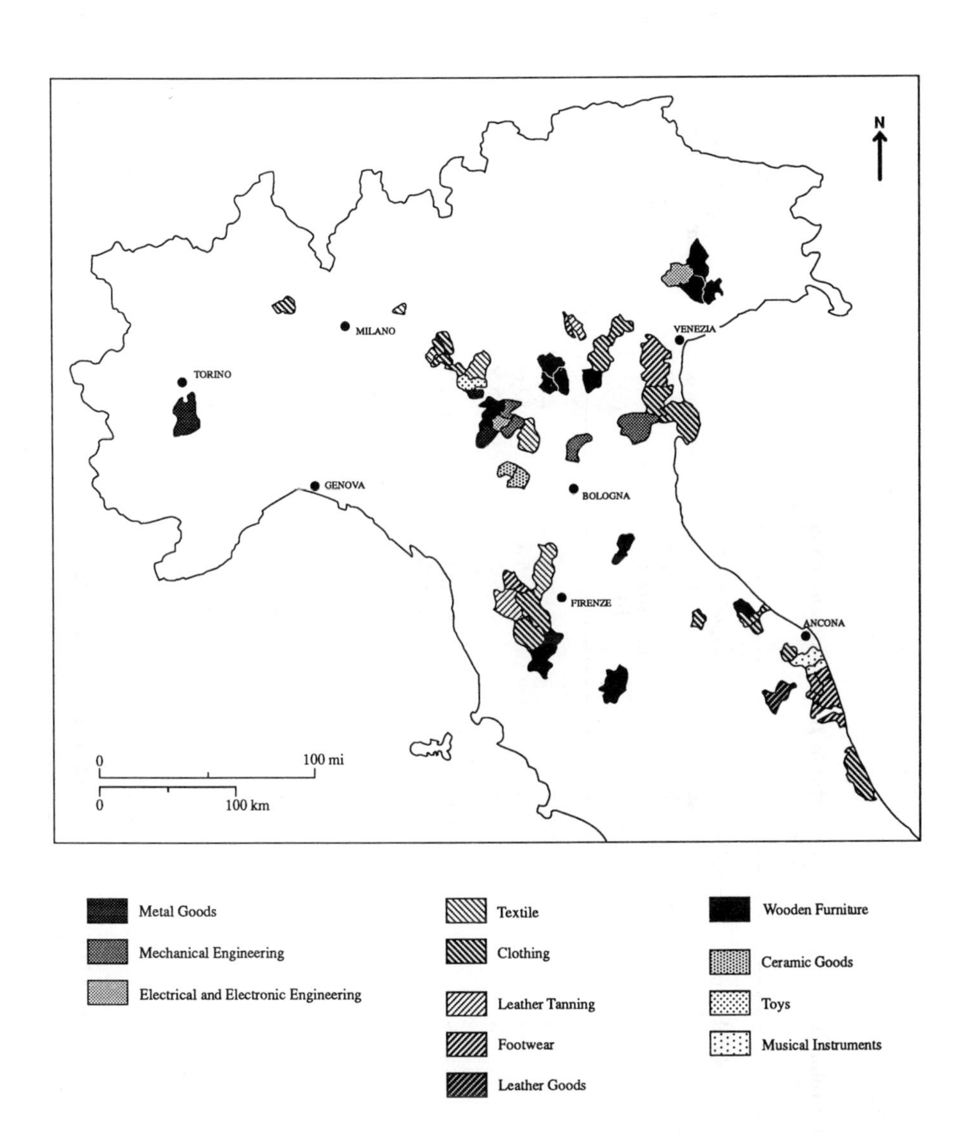

Table 2: Employment of Marshallian Industrial Districts (DIMs) by their dominant manufacturing industries, 1981

Districts by their dominant manufacturing industries	Number of districts	Employment in dominant manufacturing industries (a)	Employment in all manufacturing industries (b)	Total employment (c)	% of employment in dominant manufacturing industries (a/b)	% of employment in all manufacturing industries (b/c)
Metal goods	3	8,005	23,370	42,037	34.3	55.6
Mechanical engineering	4	10,973	28,915	52,665	37.9	54.9
Electrical engineering	3	5,826	23,642	45,662	24.6	51.8
Textiles	5	68,593	93,103	156,070	73.7	59.7
Clothing	16	29,962	88,173	173,373	34.0	50.9
Leather tanning	2	13,721	35,586	56,097	38.6	63.4
Footwear	11	51,303	80,592	149,986	63.7	53.7
Leather goods	1	1,318	3,835	8,083	34.4	47.4
Wooden furniture	12	31,641	66,192	131,274	47.8	50.4
Ceramic goods	2	22,418	36,856	59,563	60.8	61.9
Musical instruments	2	4,162	13,541	25,664	30.7	52.8
Toys and sports goods	1	972	2,800	5,535	34.7	50.6
TOTAL	61	248,894	496,605	906,009	50.1	54.8

Source: The data have been calculated from: ISTAT, *6° Censimento Generale dell'Industria, del Commercio, dei Servizi e dell'Artigianato*, 26 October 1981.

Table 3: Ranked array of employment in dominant manufacturing industries of Marshallian Industrial Districts (DIMs), ranked from highest to lowest, 1981

Dominant manufacturing industries	Employment in dominant manufacturing industries in districts they dominate		Employment in dominant manufacturing industries in all districts	
	Number	Per cent	Number	Per cent
Textiles	68,593	27.6	88,537	21.3
Footwear	51,303	20.6	71,871	17.3
Wooden furniture	31,641	12.7	55,243	13.3
Clothing	29,962	12.0	52,043	12.5
Ceramic goods	22,418	9.0	25,820	6.2
Leather tanning	13,721	5.5	15,379	3.7
Mechanical engineering	10,973	4.4	35,708	8.6
Metal goods	8,005	3.2	41,237	9.9
Electrical engineering	5,826	2.4	19,333	4.6
Musical instruments	4,162	1.7	4,201	1.0
Leather goods	1,318	0.5	5,243	1.2
Toys and sports goods	972	0.4	1,510	0.4
TOTAL	248,894	100.0	416,125	100.0

Source: The data have been calculated from: ISTAT, *6° Censimento Generale dell'Industria, del Commercio, dei Servizi e dell'Artigianato*, 26 October 1981.

Table 4: Employment in dominant manufacturing industries of Marshallian Industrial Districts (DIMs), 1981

Districts by their dominant manufacturing industries	No. of districts	Employment in dominant manufacturing industries in districts they dominate (a)	Employment in dominant manufacturing industries in the rest of districts (b)	Employment in dominant manufacturing industries in all districts (a + b = c)	% of employment by dominant manufacturing industries in districts they dominate (a/c)	% of employment by dominant manufacturing industries in the rest of districts (b/c)
Metal goods	3	8,005	33,232	41,237	19.4	80.6
Mechanical engineering	4	10,973	24,735	35,708	30.7	69.3
Electrical engineering	3	5,826	13,507	19,333	30.1	69.9
Textiles	5	68,593	19,944	88,537	77.5	22.5
Clothing	16	29,962	22,081	52,043	57.6	42.4
Leather tanning	2	13,721	1,658	15,379	89.2	10.8
Footwear	11	51,303	20,568	71,871	71.4	28.6
Leather goods	1	1,318	3,925	5,243	25.1	74.9
Wooden furniture	12	31,641	23,602	55,243	57.3	42.7
Ceramic goods	2	22,418	3,402	25,820	86.8	13.2
Musical instruments	2	4,162	39	4,201	99.1	0.9
Toys and sports goods	1	972	538	1,510	64.4	35.6
TOTAL	61	248,894	167,231	416,125	59.8	40.2

Source: The data have been calculated from: ISTAT, *6° Censimento Generale dell'Industria, del Commercio, dei Servizi e dell'Artigianato*, 26 October 1981.

Table 5: Employment in industries and services for Marshallian Industrial Districts (DIMs) and Italy, 1981

Divisions	DIM (a)	ITALY (b)	% (a/b)	LQ (*)
Agriculture, forestry and fishing	13,066	175,080	7.5	1.39
Energy and water supply industries	4,841	209,366	2.3	0.43
Extraction of minerals	1,483	55,149	2.7	0.50
Manufacturing industries	**496,605**	**5,763,988**	**8.6**	**1.61**
Manufacture of metals, mineral products and chemicals	50,142	841,348	6.0	1.11
Metal goods, engineering and vehicles industries	106,253	2,221,233	4.8	0.89
Other manufacturing industries	340,210	2,701,407	12.6	2.35
Construction	69,753	1,192,398	5.8	1.09
Distribution, hotels and catering; repairs	146,960	3,751,146	3.9	0.73
Transport and communication	29,940	1,148,489	2.6	0.49
Banking, finance, insurance, business services and leasing	27,778	951,016	2.9	0.54
Public administration and other services	115,583	3,636,654	3.2	0.59
TOTAL EMPLOYMENT	906,009	16,883,286	5.4	1.00
Total population	2,435,211	56,335,678	4.3	
Employment rate(**)	37.2	30.0		

Notes: (*) The location quotient (LQ) is defined as: (Eij/Ei)/(Aj/N)
where Eij = employment in industry i in area j
Ei = employment in industry i in nation
Aj = total employment in area j
N = total national employment

(**) Proportion of total population in employment.

Source: The data have been calculated from: ISTAT, *6° Censimento Generale dell'Industria, del Commercio, dei Servizi e dell'Artigianato*, 26 October 1981.

This indicates the proportionally greater importance of DIMs in terms of employment. For manufacturing employment alone, 8.6 per cent of the entire country's manufacturing jobs are located in DIMs.

VI. Comparisons between Marshallian industrial districts and other meaningful local system categories

The above comparisons notwithstanding, for most purposes DIMs should not be directly compared with the country as a whole, an aggregate lacking geographical, economic and statistical meaning, which is moreover clearly out of spatial scale. More suitable for comparison are local system categories distinguished, as in the case of DIMs, by particular sets of social and economic features. Consequently, we have used the 15-fold classification of the 955 LLMAs referred to earlier (table 1) to select four categories of local systems considered to be meaningful for a comparison. One category is that of the local systems of light industrialisation, dominated by small manufacturers, that were used as a basis for identifying Marshallian industrial districts (figure 2). Thus, these systems can be thought of as proto-districts (PROTO), because their social and economic pattern can be seen as the habitat of industrial districts. The other three categories include that of northern and central urban systems (URBAn), dominated by employment in both manufacturing industries and services, the category of southern urban systems (URBAs), dominated by employment mainly in services, and the category of northern manufacturing local systems (INDU), dominated just by employment in manufacturing industries. Figures 5, 6 and 7 show the spatial patterns of these categories of local systems within Italy.

By the above selection (see table 1), categories like "tourist" (holiday-place and resort), "agricultural" (rural and semi-rural) and "backward" (marginal and deprived) local systems are left out. These are grouped to form a single residual category labelleded as "Rest of Italy" (RdI).

Table 6 compares the share of employment in the dominant industries of DIMs for each category of local system as a percentage of the national total. Clearly, the results reflect the different shares of the total employed population within each category of local system, but they also reflect a differential distribution of employment across the country in the district-dominant manufacturing industries. Thus, while jobs in the metal industries and engineering have their highest shares in the northern and central urban systems (URBAn), with more than half the related national employment, in other manufacturing industries, such as tanning, footwear, ceramic goods and musical instruments, the highest shares are in the local systems of light industrialisation (PROTO), and in the Marshallian industrial districts (DIMs).

Figure 5: Pattern of northern and central urban systems, 1981

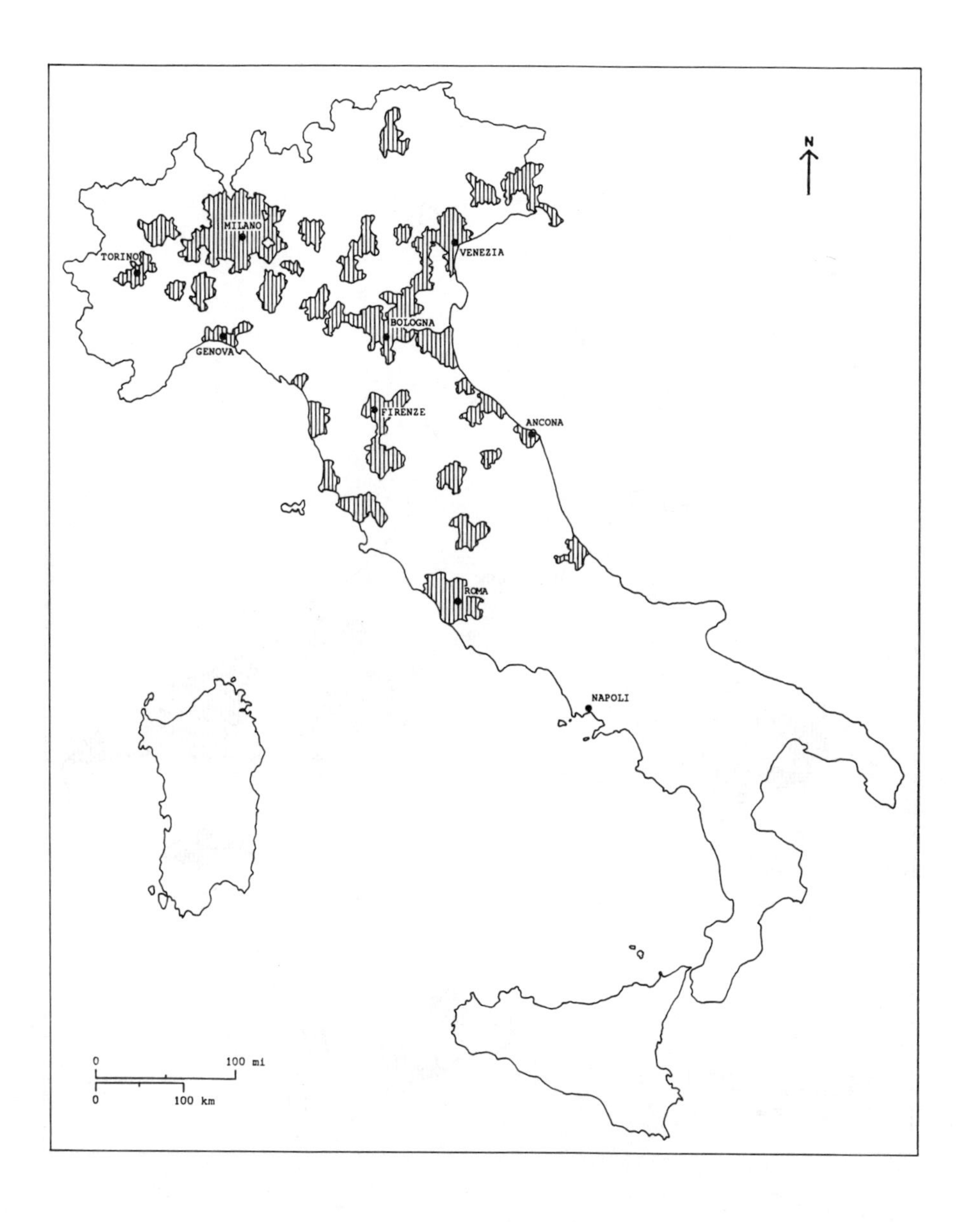

Figure 6: Pattern of southern urban systems, 1982

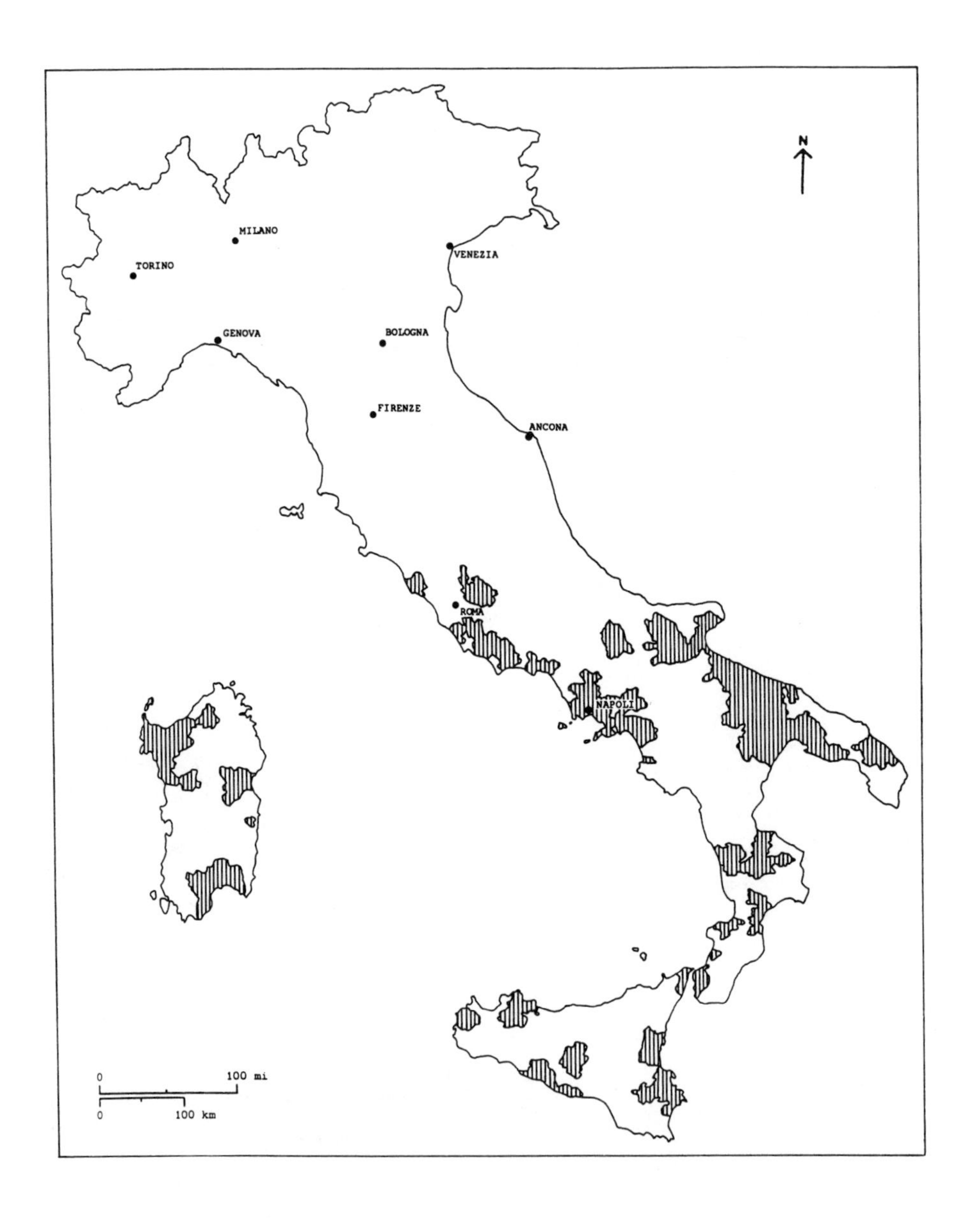

Figure 7: Pattern of northern manufacturing local systems, 1981

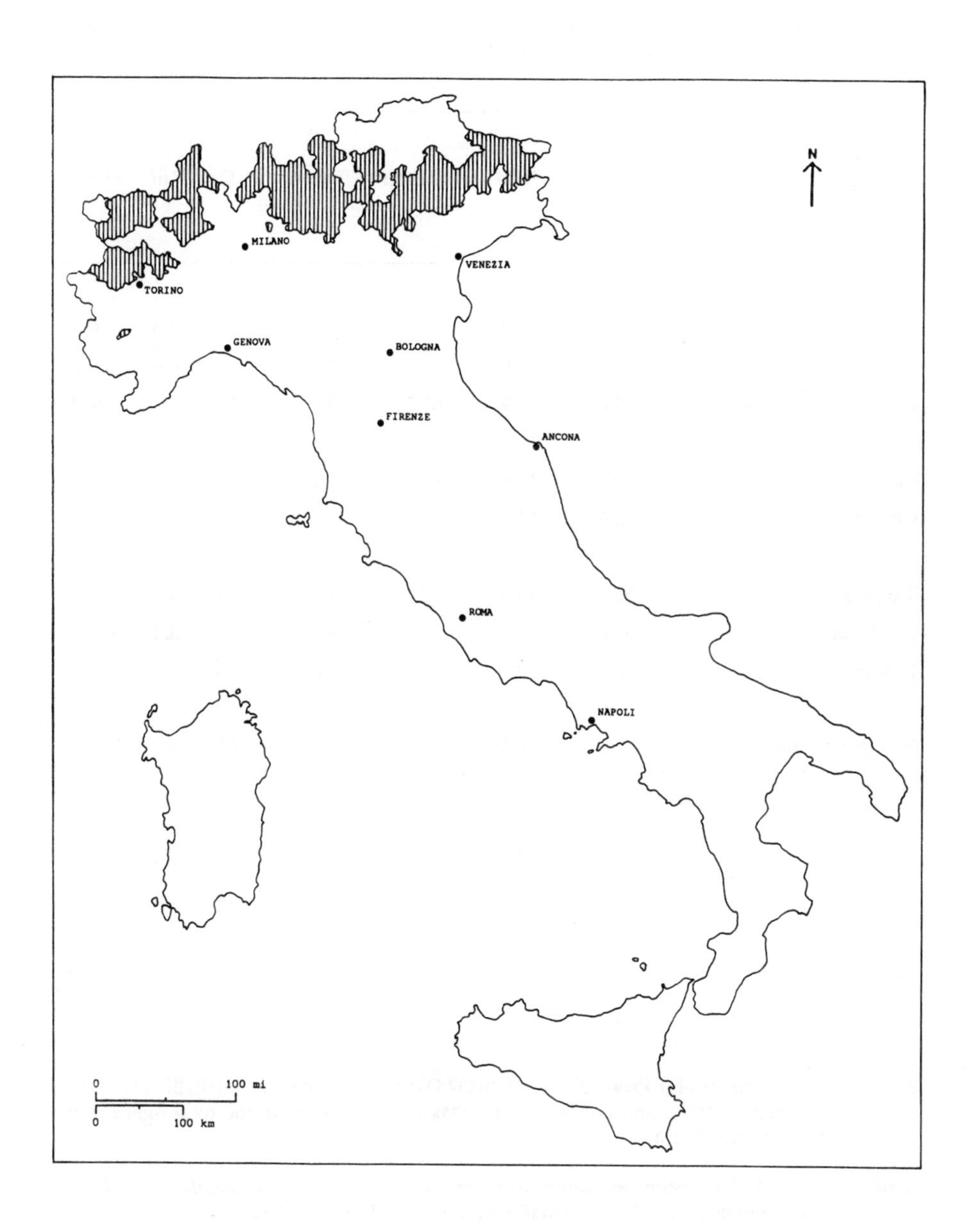

Table 6: Percentage shares of employment in district-dominant manufacturing industries by categories of local systems, 1981

Dominant manufacturing industries	PROTO(*)	**DIM**	URBAn	URBAs	INDU	RdI	ITALY
Metal goods	16.9	**6.0**	48.9	8.5	11.3	14.4	100.0
Mechanical engineering	17.1	**7.0**	60.6	5.2	7.5	9.6	100.0
Electrical engineering	9.6	**3.9**	61.2	13.5	4.8	10.9	100.0
Textiles	30.7	**17.9**	42.3	4.1	14.3	8.7	100.0
Clothing	28.4	**11.5**	37.2	10.6	7.1	16.7	100.0
Tanning	52.7	**43.1**	23.2	4.6	4.8	14.6	100.0
Footwear	57.6	**37.0**	20.0	9.4	1.9	11.1	100.0
Leather goods	25.1	**10.4**	53.7	8.9	2.6	9.7	100.0
Wooden furniture	26.4	**12.2**	38.3	9.8	7.5	18.0	100.0
Ceramic goods	39.0	**26.7**	25.1	7.1	5.3	23.6	100.0
Musical instruments	63.2	**54.5**	25.7	0.6	2.1	8.4	100.0
Toys and sports goods	31.8	**9.4**	48.5	2.1	6.0	11.6	100.0
MANUFACTURING INDUSTRIES	19.5	**8.6**	48.5	10.3	7.1	14.5	100.0

Note: (*) The figures for Proto-districts (PROTO) include those for Marshallian Industrial Districts (DIMs), and the figure of DIMs is not included in the total figure in the right-hand column.

Source: The data have been calculated from: ISTAT, *6° Censimento Generale dell'Industria, del Commercio, dei Servizi e dell'Artigianato*, 26 October 1981.

There are other manufacturing industries, such as the textiles, clothing, wooden furniture, and toys industries, and above all leather goods, whose share of employment is more highly represented in the northern and central urban systems (URBAn) than in proto-districts (PROTO) or in DIMs. While the difference in share of employment for the first four industries is restricted to a range between 8 and 16 percentage points, leather goods score twice as much, indicating the "urban nature" of this industry. The fact that only one district specialises in leather goods production bears out this conclusion. Nevertheless, employment in leather goods is not restricted to a single specialised DIM because the localisation of this industry occurs in other DIMs, dominated by a different manufacturing specialisation where leather goods are a complementary industry.

A hypothesis of different divisions of labour based on whether the organisation of the production process is dominated by either relatively larger integrated industrial firms or small firms specialised in a single or few phases of the same production process should result in different "representative" sizes of establishment in the different categories of local systems. This hypothesis appears to be confirmed if one looks at the average size of establishment in district-dominant manufacturing industries by categories of local systems (table 7). For example, the textile industry has an average size of establishment of 11.7 employees in the northern and central urban systems (URBAn), growing to 19.0 in the northern manufacturing local systems (INDU), while in proto-districts (PROTO), the average size is 5.2 employees, reaching a minimum in DIMs of 4.6, in contrast to the national average of 8.2 On the other hand, there are also industries like leather goods which have the same average size in every category of local systems, except for southern urban systems (URBAs), thus suggesting that for some sectors there are less significant differences in the organisation of the production process.

An appropriate way to test the degree of spatial concentration of district-dominant manufacturing industries is to relate their local employment distribution to national employment by means of a location quotient (LQ) defined for each industry/category pair of local systems.

Examining the DIMs, it can be seen that they show high location quotients in all their dominant manufacturing industries with the exception of metal goods and engineering (table 8). In contrast, non-metallic industries are under-represented in the remaining categories of local systems, except for clothing which is over-represented in southern urban systems (URBAs), wooden furniture in the northern manufacturing local systems (INDU), leather goods in the northern and central urban systems (URBAs) and toys which are equal to the national average location. The textiles industry requires a separate comment because it is over-represented very nearly in the same way both in DIMs and in northern manufacturing local systems (INDU), with a LQ = 2.08 and 2.00, respectively. However, this similarity masks the very different ways of organising the production process, reflected by the variations in average size of textile establishment noted earlier.

Table 7: Average size of establishment in district-dominant manufacturing industries by categories of local systems, 1981

Dominant manufacturing industries	PROTO(*)	**DIM**	URBAn	URBAs	INDU	RdI	ITALY
Metal goods	6.5	**6.7**	8.0	6.0	7.4	4.5	6.7
Mechanical engineering	13.5	**12.6**	16.9	15.3	14.1	13.9	15.6
Electrical engineering	13.0	**12.9**	21.0	36.3	16.6	17.9	20.3
Textiles	5.2	**4.6**	11.7	8.6	19.0	6.1	8.2
Clothing	8.0	**7.7**	5.2	4.0	9.0	4.5	5.6
Tanning	10.6	**9.8**	13.7	7.8	14.1	9.9	11.0
Footwear	9.5	**9.6**	12.4	9.4	11.5	11.0	10.2
Leather goods	5.7	**5.6**	5.7	5.2	5.7	5.7	5.6
Wooden furniture	5.2	**5.8**	4.3	3.0	4.6	2.8	4.0
Ceramic goods	29.7	**50.7**	13.0	11.0	15.2	18.3	18.1
Musical instruments	11.9	**11.1**	8.5	3.1	9.4	5.4	9.7
Toys and sports goods	12.4	**13.4**	9.8	4.9	8.9	10.5	10.3

Note: (*) The figures for Proto-districts (PROTO) include those for Marshallian Industrial Districts (DIMs), and the figure of DIMs is not included in the total figure in the right-hand column.

Source: The data have been calculated from: ISTAT, *6° Censimento Generale dell'Industria, del Commercio, dei Servizi e dell'Artigianato*, 26 October 1981.

Table 8: Local quotients (*) of employment in district-dominant manufacturing industries by categories of local systems, 1981

Dominant manufacturing industries	PROTO(**)	**DIM**	URBAn	URBAs	INDU	RdI
Metal goods	0.87	**0.69**	1.01	0.82	1.59	0.99
Mechanical engineering	0.88	**0.81**	1.25	0.50	1.04	0.66
Electrical engineering	0.49	**0.46**	1.26	1.31	0.67	0.75
Textiles	1.57	**2.08**	0.87	0.40	2.00	0.60
Clothing	1.46	**1.33**	0.77	1.02	0.99	1.15
Tanning	2.71	**5.01**	0.48	0.45	0.68	1.00
Footwear	2.96	**4.29**	0.41	0.91	0.26	0.77
Leather goods	1.29	**1.21**	1.11	0.86	0.37	0.67
Wooden furniture	1.35	**1.42**	0.79	0.95	1.05	1.24
Ceramic goods	2.00	**3.10**	0.52	0.68	0.74	1.62
Musical instruments	3.24	**6.32**	0.53	0.06	0.29	0.58
Toys and sports goods	1.63	**1.10**	1.00	0.21	0.84	0.80

Notes: (*) See Table 5.
(**) The figures for Proto-districts (PROTO) include those for Marshallian Industrial Districts (DIMs).

Source: The data have been calculated from: ISTAT, *6° Censimento Generale dell'Industria, del Commercio, dei Servizi e dell'Artigianato*, 26 October 1981.

The LQs of the three metal and engineering industries indicate they are under-represented in DIMs and in the proto-districts (PROTO), while they are mainly over-represented in the other local systems: all three of them in the northern and central urban systems (URBAn), only electrical engineering in the southern urban systems (URBAs), and metal goods and mechanical engineering in the northern manufacturing local systems (INDU). The final comment is that, at the beginning of the 1980s, metal manufacturing industries showed a marked "urban nature", with the average size of establishment playing an important role in different organisations of the production process amongst the various categories of local systems.

VII. Changes of employment in Marshallian industrial districts during the 1970s

In Italy, a general growth in employment in industry and services took place in the 1970s, increasing by 21.5 per cent between the 1971 and 1981 intercensal period. National employment in services grew more than industrial employment, increasing by 28.5 per cent and 16.4 per cent, respectively. This general growth occurred in different ways throughout the country, with varying degrees of intensity.

Tables 9 and 10 present changes in employment between 1971 and 1981 with regard to categories of local systems and Italy as a whole. It should be noted that, apart from the Rest of Italy (RdI), northern and central urban systems (URBAn) recorded the greatest absolute growth of employment, although at the same time they had the lowest change in percentage terms; the major contribution to the employment growth was associated with services, the increase in manufacturing employment being only modest. The slackening of manufacturing growth in this part of the country - which is noted historically for having the highest level of industrialisation - corresponded to a reduced spatial concentration (table 11). The most convincing explanation for this is the process of "tertiarisation", although the effects of the crisis amongst the large industrial plants particularly prevalent in these areas should also be taken into account. In contrast, in the local systems of light industrialisation (PROTO), changes in manufacturing employment were the main source of job creation, even more than for services. It is not surprising in this context that DIMs registered a similar phenomenon with much greater intensity. Likewise, northern manufacturing local systems (INDU) experienced positive employment changes between 1971 and 1981 for the metal goods, engineering and transport equipment industries.

The growth of employment in southern urban systems (URBAs) was accounted for by services and manufacturing, this last having the highest change rate in Italy after the DIMs and PROTO as a whole.

In the Rest of Italy (RdI), employment change took place in distribution, hotels and catering, that is to say the most traditional service activities, even though manufacturing industry registered a successful performance.

The changes in employment as measured by the location quotient (LQ) confirms a picture of only urban systems having relative over-representation in services, consumer services in the case of the south (URBAs) and producer services for the north and centre (URBAn). In contrast, over-representation of manufacturing industries grew markedly in the local systems of the light industrialisation (PROTO), much more rapidly in DIMs, and only marginally in northern manufacturing local systems (INDU) during the period. It is also worth noting that the Rest of Italy (RdI) showed the highest concentration of employment in commercial and hotel activities.

Focusing attention on the district-dominant manufacturing industries, there was a general growth of employment more or less throughout the categories of local systems, with the exception of northern and central urban systems (URBAn) recording the highest number of declining industries, while those growing had a rate of growth below the national average. The industries in URBAn with a below-average rate of growth included leather goods, in spite of the fact that between 1971 and 1981 it showed a positive rate of growth of 38.1 per cent, being the highest in manufacturing employment in this category of local systems (tables 12 and 13).

Amongst the categories of local systems the fastest change of employment in district-dominant industries was mainly performed by DIMs, where notable changes included leather goods (+147.1 per cent), mechanical engineering (+91.9 per cent) and musical instruments (+78.2 per cent), characterised by rates of growth which were mostly higher than the national average, sometimes by far. The toy industry was the sole declining industry over the period albeit even more markedly so than the national average. In general, employment in fashionwear industries recorded higher rates of growth than other industries. It is worth noting in particular the textile industries of DIMs, because in this category of local systems textiles grew while in the other categories it declined, including in Italy as a whole.

As a result of this pattern of employment changes, between 1971 and 1981 industrialisation became more diffused throughout the country, with DIMs and local systems of light industrialisation (PROTO) recording the fastest rates of growth, this being associated with a more general spatial concentration as measured in table 14 by location quotients.

VIII. Summary and conclusion

This study aimed at examining the distinguishing employment characteristics of the Marshallian industrial districts, and the way in which they changed during the last census decade, but above all at investigating their quantitative importance in the Italian economy. The appropriate development of this task required the definition of suitable local systems

Table 9: Change of employment in industries and services by categories of local systems, 1971-1981

Divisions	PROTO(*)	DIM	URBAn	URBAs	INDU	RdI	ITALY
Agriculture, forestry and fishing	13,889	**4,228**	13,244	7,314	213	28,057	62,717
Energy and water supply industries	3,006	**1,165**	7,223	8,017	-1,087	5,792	22,951
Extraction of minerals	-431	**-171**	45	-696	-1,184	-5,365	-7,631
Manufacturing industries	295,289	**135,675**	40,882	130,774	62,194	179,027	708,166
Manufacture of metals, mineral products and chemicals	18,700	**5,516**	-50,178	12,766	-8,513	23,831	-3,394
Metal goods, engineering and vehicles industries	112,829	**38,621**	111,336	82,708	58,343	101,427	466,643
Other manufacturing industries	163,760	**91,538**	-20,276	35,300	12,364	53,769	244,917
Construction	58,795	**20,314**	34,698	41,759	27,518	91,111	253,881
Distribution, hotels and catering; repairs	82,428	**29,969**	187,401	85,462	23,372	343,690	722,353
Transport and communication	29,589	**10,659**	103,885	47,921	9,477	44,093	234,965
Banking, finance, insurance, business services and leasing	28,770	**10,863**	154,612	39,412	9,699	38,136	270,629
Public administration and other services	8,792	**1,632**	24,861	40,884	6,321	37,885	118,743
TOTAL EMPLOYMENT	520,127	**214,334**	566,851	400,847	136,523	762,426	2,386,774

Note: (*) The figures for Proto-districts (PROTO) include those for Marshallian Industrial Districts (DIMs), and the figure of DIMs is not included in the total figure in the right-hand column.

Source: The data have been calculated from: ISTAT, *5° Censimento Generale dell'Industria e del Commercio*, 25 October 1971 and ISTAT, *6° Censimento Generale dell'Industria, del Commercio, dei Servizi e dell'Artigianato*, 26 October 1981.

Table 10: Change of percentage of employment in industries and services by categories of local systems, 1971-1981

Divisions	PROTO(*)	DIM	URBAn	URBAs	INDU	RdI	ITALY
Agriculture, forestry and fishing	54.4	**47.8**	49.5	42.6	4.5	73.4	55.8
Energy and water supply industries	20.8	**31.7**	8.3	25.9	-9.8	13.4	12.3
Extraction of minerals	-8.0	**-10.3**	0.4	-7.6	-17.4	-17.9	-12.2
Manufacturing industries	35.7	**37.6**	1.5	28.1	17.8	27.1	14.0
Manufacture of metals, mineral products and chemicals	19.0	**12.4**	-11.6	11.6	-14.2	16.7	-0.4
Metal goods, engineering and vehicles industries	62.0	**57.1**	9.5	62.8	54.2	61.6	26.6
Other manufacturing industries	29.9	**36.8**	-1.8	15.8	6.8	15.3	10.0
Construction	42.1	**41.1**	9.1	35.3	43.2	38.6	27.1
Distribution, hotels and catering; repairs	23.1	**25.6**	13.6	17.5	18.0	51.1	23.8
Transport and communication	48.0	**55.3**	20.3	28.1	39.8	30.0	25.7
Banking, finance, insurance, business services and leasing	119.6	**142.3**	64.0	84.1	135.7	88.4	74.6
Public administration and other services	20.7	**10.6**	12.1	54.0	50.9	47.5	28.5
TOTAL EMPLOYMENT	34.7	**36.7**	10.1	28.2	22.4	39.1	21.5

Note: (*) The figures for Proto-districts (PROTO) include those for Marshallian Industrial Districts (DIMs), and the figure of DIMs is not included in the total figure in the right-hand column.

Source: The data have been calculated from: ISTAT, *5° Censimento Generale dell'Industria e del Commercio*, 25 October 1971 and ISTAT, *6° Censimento Generale dell'Industria, del Commercio, dei Servizi e dell'Artigianato*, 26 October 1981.

Table 11: Location quotients (*) of employment in industries and services by categories of local systems, 1971 and 1981

Divisions	PROTO(**)		**DIM**		URBAn		URBAs		INDU		RdI	
	1971	1981	**1971**	**1981**	1971	1981	1971	1981	1971	1981	1971	1981
Agriculture, forestry and fishing	1.68	1.62	**1.49**	**1.39**	0.47	0.50	1.19	0.93	0.76	0.55	1.93	1.86
Energy and water supply industries	0.57	0.60	**0.37**	**0.43**	0.92	0.98	1.29	1.23	1.08	0.93	1.32	1.15
Extraction of minerals	0.63	0.65	**0.50**	**0.50**	0.36	0.46	1.13	1.01	1.98	2.00	2.71	2.19
Manufacturing industries	1.21	1.40	**1.35**	**1.61**	1.08	1.06	0.72	0.69	1.26	1.40	0.74	0.72
Manufacture of metals, mineral products and chemicals	0.86	1.00	**1.00**	**1.11**	1.02	1.00	1.02	0.97	1.29	1.20	0.96	0.97
Metal goods, engineering and vehicles industries	0.77	0.96	**0.73**	**0.89**	1.32	1.26	0.58	0.64	1.11	1.46	0.53	0.59
Other manufacturing industries	1.65	1.90	**1.92**	**2.35**	0.93	0.92	0.71	0.64	1.35	1.41	0.81	0.74
Construction	1.10	1.20	**1.00**	**1.09**	0.80	0.76	0.98	0.89	1.23	1.50	1.43	1.35
Distribution, hotels and catering; repairs	0.87	0.84	**0.73**	**0.73**	0.90	0.92	1.26	1.02	0.78	0.80	1.26	1.33
Transport and communication	0.50	0.57	**0.40**	**0.49**	1.11	1.17	1.45	1.26	0.47	0.57	0.91	0.82
Banking, finance, insurance, business services and leasing	0.49	0.60	**0.40**	**0.54**	1.32	1.37	1.01	0.90	0.36	0.52	0.68	0.63
Public administration and other services	0.76	0.69	**0.70**	**0.59**	0.98	0.95	1.42	1.45	0.54	0.68	1.09	1.08

Notes: (*) See Table 5.
(**) The figures for Proto-districts (PROTO) include those for Marshallian Industrial Districts (DIMs).

Source: The data have been calculated from ISTAT, *5° Censimento Generale dell'Industria e del Commercio*, 25 October 1971 and ISTAT, *6° Censimento Generale dell'Industria, del Commercio, dei Servizi e dell'Artigianato*, 26 October 1981.

Table 12: Change of employment in district-dominant manufacturing industries by categories of local systems, 1971-1981

Dominant manufacturing industries	PROTO(*)	**DIM**	URBAn	URBAs	INDU	RdI	ITALY
Metal goods	36,884	**11,541**	37,162	17,678	30,981	29,350	152,055
Mechanical engineering	39,832	**17,100**	48,608	14,071	12,447	16,430	131,388
Electrical engineering	16,232	**6,157**	24,126	27,183	6,735	18,772	93,048
Textiles	18,181	**13,579**	-42,835	-2,007	-12,988	-7,769	-47,418
Clothing	35,348	**18,190**	-5,329	4,082	6,350	6,104	46,555
Leather tanning	6,000	**5,307**	-709	234	384	2,506	8,415
Footwear	40,745	**31,443**	-1,867	4,749	303	6,728	50,658
Leather goods	6,413	**3,121**	7,480	1,276	606	2,703	18,478
Wooden furniture	19,244	**10,024**	9,151	3,935	6,208	10,996	49,534
Ceramic goods	8,762	**3,067**	1,047	-219	578	6,480	16,648
Musical instruments	2,245	**1,844**	-672	-60	44	76	1,633
Toys and sports goods	-1,130	**-1,100**	-769	105	546	734	-514
MANUFACTURING INDUSTRIES	295,289	**135,675**	40,882	130,774	62,194	179,027	708,166

Note: (*) The figures for Proto-districts (PROTO) include those for Marshallian Industrial Districts (DIMs), and the figure of DIMs is not included in the total figure in the right-hand column.

Source: The data have been calculated from: ISTAT, *5° Censimento Generale dell'Industria e del Commercio*, 25 October 1971 and ISTAT, *6° Censimento Generale dell'Industria, del Commercio, dei Servizi e dell'Artigianato*, 26 October 1981.

Table 13: Change in percentage of employment in district-dominant manufacturing industries by categories of local systems, 1971-1981

Dominant manufacturing industries	PROTO(*)	**DIM**	URBAn	URBAs	INDU	RdI	ITALY
Metal goods	46.0	**38.9**	12.4	42.9	65.4	41.9	28.2
Mechanical engineering	83.2	**91.9**	18.5	112.5	48.2	50.0	34.5
Electrical engineering	52.3	**46.7**	8.7	69.4	40.5	53.9	23.4
Textiles	13.6	**18.1**	-17.0	-9.0	-15.6	-15.4	-8.8
Clothing	37.8	**53.7**	-3.1	9.3	24.5	8.7	11.4
Leather tanning	46.9	**52.7**	-7.9	16.4	28.7	93.4	30.9
Footwear	57.2	**77.8**	-4.6	35.2	9.2	45.2	35.3
Leather goods	102.4	**147.1**	38.1	39.9	85.2	123.3	57.8
Wooden furniture	19.2	**22.2**	5.6	9.8	22.3	15.6	12.3
Ceramic goods	30.3	**13.5**	4.5	-3.1	12.7	39.7	20.8
Musical instruments	85.3	**78.2**	-25.4	-56.1	37.9	13.2	26.9
Toys and sports goods	-18.2	**-42.1**	-9.0	44.7	132.2	65.1	-3.1
MANUFACTURING INDUSTRIES	35.7	37.6	1.5	28.1	17.8	27.1	14.0

Note: (*) The figures for Proto-districts (PROTO) include those for Marshallian Industrial Districts (DIMs), and the figure of DIMs is not included in the total figure in the right-hand column.

Source: The data have been calculated from: ISTAT, *5° Censimento Generale dell'Industria e del Commercio*, 25 October 1971 and ISTAT, *6° Censimento Generale dell'Industria, del Commercio, dei Servizi e dell'Artigianato*, 26 October 1981.

Table 14: Location quotients (*) of employment in district-dominant manufacturing industries by categories of local systems, 1971 and 1981

Dominant manufacturing industries	PROTO(**)		**DIM**		URBAn		URBAs		INDU		RdI	
	1971	1981	**1971**	**1981**	1971	1981	1971	1981	1971	1981	1971	1981
Metal goods	0.91	0.87	**0.77**	**0.69**	1.02	1.01	0.83	0.82	1.27	1.59	1.00	0.99
Mechanical engineering	0.77	0.88	**0.68**	**0.81**	1.26	1.25	0.36	0.50	0.98	1.04	0.66	0.66
Electrical engineering	0.48	0.49	**0.46**	**0.46**	1.27	1.26	1.07	1.31	0.60	0.67	0.67	0.75
Textiles	1.50	1.57	**1.94**	**2.08**	0.85	0.87	0.45	0.40	2.23	2.00	0.72	0.60
Clothing	1.40	1.46	**1.16**	**1.33**	0.79	0.77	1.17	1.02	0.92	0.99	1.31	1.15
Leather tanning	2.87	2.71	**5.18**	**5.01**	0.61	0.48	0.57	0.45	0.71	0.68	0.75	1.00
Footwear	3.03	2.96	**3.94**	**4.29**	0.52	0.41	1.02	0.91	0.33	0.26	0.80	0.77
Leather goods	1.19	1.29	**0.93**	**1.21**	1.13	1.11	1.09	0.86	0.32	0.37	0.53	0.67
Wooden furniture	1.52	1.35	**1.57**	**1.42**	0.75	0.79	1.09	0.95	1.00	1.05	1.34	1.24
Ceramic goods	2.21	2.00	**3.98**	**3.10**	0.53	0.52	0.96	0.68	0.82	0.74	1.56	1.62
Musical instruments	2.64	3.24	**5.43**	**6.32**	0.80	0.53	0.19	0.06	0.28	0.29	0.72	0.58
Toys and sports goods	2.30	1.63	**2.22**	**1.10**	0.95	1.00	0.15	0.21	0.36	0.84	0.52	0.80

Notes: (*) See Table 5.
(**) The figures for Proto-districts (PROTO) include those for Marshallian Industrial Districts (DIMs).

Source: The data have been calculated from ISTAT, *5° Censimento Generale dell'Industria e del Commercio*, 25 October 1971 and ISTAT, *6° Censimento Generale dell'Industria, del Commercio, dei Servizi e dell'Artigianato*, 26 October 1981.

categories to which DIMs could be compared. The spatial patterns of these categories in the Italian territorial economy demonstrated that the interpretation of the territoriality of Italian industrial development can be captured by a framework based neither on a North-South division nor on the Three Italies concept. Rather, in our opinion, it can be better described by assuming a multi-regional framework of interpretation where the concept of region fits that of local system, providing a convenient practical and conceptual tool for examining development problems.

Often an industrial district is thought not to have its own spatial scale but is considered synonymous with a locality, i.e. a town. However, other students of the phenomenon argue that it should not be conceived as being spatially delimited. In fact, in this latter view, the interdependences between firms belonging to an identified industry might cut across localities and be spread over a regional or even a national area. In this study, an attempt has been made to focus attention on this issue. The industrial district, following and developing original Marshallian ideas, should be synthetically defined as a socio-territorial entity characterised by the internal interactions of a system of small manufacturing firms, involved in different phases of the same production process, spatially concentrated, closely linked to the local population and sharing a relatively restricted territory. A full and thorough description of the Marshallian industrial district has been presented in this book by Becattini. Thus, in our opinion, the Marshallian industrial district is a particular form of local system belonging to the model of light industrialisation, as defined in this study.

Although restricted to census data, the type of data analysed here give an indication of the numerical significance of Marshallian industrial districts in the Italian economy. It is worth noting that in 1981 the percentage share of employment in all the dominant manufacturing industries in the districts they dominate accounted for 11.9 per cent of the employment in the country as a whole, corresponding to a location quotient of 2.20. And with the exception of metal goods and mechanical and electrical engineering, DIMs had a higher concentration of jobs in their dominant industries than did any other part of the country. Moreover, Marshallian industrial districts experienced the fastest increase in employment both in manufacturing and in total employment between 1971 and 1981, the figures being 36.7 and 37.6 per cent respectively, far more than the other categories of local systems and the national average.

It is clear that the formulation of industrial and employment policies carried out at the local, regional, and national levels cannot neglect these spatial patterns of high specialisation. The fact that industrial development resulted in spatial patterns of local systems means that the mobilisation of resources to reinforce and promote further diffusion requires more specific locally-orientated policy. At the same time, one should be aware that any economic crisis of an industrial sector in which Marshallian industrial districts dominate would not be a "sectoral crisis" as such but a territorial one, involving a whole range of social, institutional and economic aspects.

References

Bagnasco, A. 1977. *Tre Italie. La problematica territoriale dello sviluppo italiano*, Bologna, Il Mulino.

Becattini, G. 1978. "The development of light industry in Tuscany: An interpretation", in *Economic Notes*, No. 2-3, pp. 107-123.

---. 1979. "Dal settore industriale al distretto industriale. Alcune considerazioni sull'unità d'indagine dell'economia industriale", in *Rivista di Economia e Politica industriale*, No. 1 [reprinted as: "Sectors and/or districts: Some remarks on the conceptual foundations of industrial economics", in Goodman, E. et al. (eds.): *Small firms and industrial districts in Italy*, London, Routledge, 1989, pp. 123-135].

Bellandi, M. 1982. "Il distretto industriale in Alfred Marshall", in *L'Industria*, No. 3 [reprinted as: "The industrial district in Marshall", in Goodman, E. et al. (eds.): *Small firms and industrial districts in Italy*, London, Routledge, 1989, pp. 136-152].

Giddens, A. 1985. "Time, space and regionalisation", in Gregory, D.; Urry, J. (eds.): *Social relations and spatial structures*, London, Macmillan, pp. 265-295.

Hägerstrand, T. 1970. "What about people in Regional Science?", in *Paper of the Regional Science Association*, No. XXIV, pp. 7-21.

Harvey, D. 1985. "The geopolitics of capitalism", in Gregory, D.; Urry, J. (eds.): *Social relations and spatial structures*, London, Macmillan, pp. 128-163.

IRPET. 1969. *Lo sviluppo economico della Toscana: Un'ipotesi di lavoro*, Florence.

IRPET. 1975. *Lo sviluppo economico della Toscana con particolate riguardo all'industrializzazione leggera*, Becattini, G. (ed.), Florence, Guaraldi.

ISTAT-IRPET. 1986. *I mercati locali del lavoro in Italia*, Rome [reprinted by F. Angeli, Milan, 1989].

Jonas, A. 1988. "A new regional geography of localities?", in *Area*, No. 2, pp. 111-119.

King, R. 1985. *The industrial geography of Italy*, London, Croom Helm.

Marshall, A. 1920. *Principles of economics*, Eighth edition, London, Macmillan.

Sforzi, F. 1986. "L'Italia marginale: Una valutazione geografica", Paper presented at the 7th Annual Conference of the RSA Italian Section, Urbino, September 14-17 [reprinted in: Becchi Collidà, A. et al. (eds.): *Aree interne, tutela del territorio e valorizzazione delle risorse*, Milan, F. Angeli, 1989, pp. 203-231].

---. 1987. "L'identificazione spaziale", in Becattini, G. (ed.): *Mercato e forze locali: Il distretto industriale*, Bologna, Il Mulino, pp. 143-167 [reprinted as: "The geography of industrial districts in Italy", in Goodman, E. et al. (eds.): *Small firms and industrial districts in Italy*, London, Routledge, 1989, pp. 153-173].

Valli, V. 1986. *Politica economica. I modelli, gli strumenti, l'economia italiana*, Rome, La Nuova Italia Scientifica.

7 Subcontracting in the Modena knitwear industry

Mark H. Lazerson

I. Introduction

For organisational theory the sun has long set on the putting-out system and other forms of domestic production [Smelser, 1959]. The English industrial revolution, where putting-out became an ever smaller island in a sea of factories, and self-employed domestic workers were swallowed in a tide of proletarianisation, was transformed from a historical episode into a prophecy. Marx's description of this process and his foreboding that the "country that is most developed industrially only shows, to the least developed, the image of its own future" [Marx, 1977, p. 19], were later to be mirrored by his severest critics who insisted that the developmental patterns of all industrial societies were converging [Kerr et al., 1960]. As regards small firms, this linear perception of industrial organisational development from the less to the more complex is beginning to unravel. Historical research demonstrates that nineteenth-century England's early "capitalist growth was rooted in a sub-soil of small-scale enterprise that accompanied the rise of large factories" [Samuel, 1977, p. 8]. France's stubborn attachment to craft production into the early twentieth century is now understood as a better exploitation of its comparative advantages than factory production [O'Brien and Caglar, 1978]. Even in advanced-capitalist societies, craft-type artisanal production today is accorded an important space [Berger, 1980; Sabel, 1982]. Yet, the original verdict on the putting-out system remains uncontested.

In economic history, the very centralisation of production in the factory is connected to the failures of the putting-out system. As the physical distance between managers and workers increased, so did the latter's proclivity to theft, embezzlement, and idleness [Landes, 1969, pp. 56-60]. Accordingly, "the thoughts of employers turned to workshops where the men would be brought together to labour under watchful overseers, and to machines that would solve the shortage of manpower while curbing the insolence and dishonesty of the men" [Landes, 1969, p. 60]. Marxists contend that even in the absence of suitable technologies, factory organisation enhanced surplus extraction by improved discipline and surveillance [Marglin, 1976]. Arguments based on the factory's organisational superiority have also been appropriated by the "new institutional economists" like Oliver Williamson, who insists the factory was simply more efficient, reducing transaction costs imposed by servicing dispersed putting-out stations [Williamson, 1981]. More balanced accounts stress that despite all these organisational drawbacks, putting-out remained a profitable alternative to the factory until technological advances could combine mechanisation with centralisation [Kriedte, 1981, p. 137; Schlumbohm, 1981, p. 109; Jones, 1982].

I do not wish to belabour these explanations for the factory's victory over the putting-out mode two hundred years ago, but rather to question their contemporary relevance. If we are to believe Marglin, the factory's extreme division of labour permitted cheaper female and child labour to replace the skilled-male labour used in the putting-out system [Marglin, 1976]. Its disciplinary system also ensured that workers came to work regularly, instead of working the partial and uncertain week common among cottage workers. But today, putting-out reduces labour costs and permits a division of labour no different from that of the factory. To present-day employers, no longer worried about whether their employees will engage in a full week's work but whether they will have to be paid a full week's wage irrespective of production requirements, the putting-out system offers an attractive alternative to the factory mode of production.

II. The background to the research

1. Knitwear putting-out in Modena

In this chapter I have situated the debate about the putting-out mode within an empirically grounded context, rejecting the abstract approach applied by Williamson [1980, p. 12]. The research focuses on the knitwear industry in the province of Modena, a prosperous agro-industrial area of 600,000 people located in the Emilia-Romagna region of North-Central Italy and governed by the Italian Communist Party. The Modena knitwear industry's 4,291 firms employ approximately 16,000 people (the third-largest industry in the province after mechanical engineering and ceramics) and depend almost exclusively on putting-out. Although putting-out and craft production are traditionally associated with the initial phases of industrialisation [Mendels, 1972], Modena is among Italy's most developed regions. Similar to the putting-out system of earlier times, when merchant-manufacturers provided household labour with raw materials to be transformed into finished or semi-finished products [Landes, 1966, p. 14], knitwear production commences with the manufacturer. The latter designs and produces the first prototypes and obtains initial orders from wholesalers or large retailers. Since he has either limited or no production facilities, he depends on a vast array of highly-specialised subcontractors to transform his materials into a finished product. These knitwear subcontractors contribute only their labour, skill, workplace, and machinery. Weavers transform the manufacturer's yarn into cloth; assemblers cut and sew it into sweaters; and other subcontractors press, inspect, mend and package them. Additional steps, depending upon the requirements of the buyer and the type of material, include the sewing and pre-ironing of the cloth prior to its cutting; the dyeing of the already assembled sweater or the washing of it to

Table 1: Typical sequence in knitwear production (a)

Manufacturers

Design and production of prototypes. Solicit orders from wholesalers and retailers. Buy raw materials to be transformed by subcontractors. Final shipment to buyer.

Subcontractors

1. Weaving	2. Pre-pressing and pre-stitching	3. Embroidery	4. Assembly	5. Fabric treatment	6. Button-making	7. Pressing and ironing	8. Finishing, inspection and packaging
Manufacturer's yarn woven into cloth, according to desired specifications.	If cloth is to be cut it must first be pressed and stitched together in order to lie flat. Homeworkers often used for stitching.	Computer-controlled machinery stitch designs on cloth pieces. Marginal phases of production sent out to illegal homeworkers.	Cloth pieces cut and sewn into garments. Sometimes cutting separate phase. Marginal phases sent out to legal and illegal homeworkers.	Depending upon buyer's requirements and characteristics of cloth, cloth or garments sent for special softening, cleaning or dyeing treatments.	Buttons and buttonholes are added to garments.	Garments are pressed and ironed. Labels usually added. Minor ironing of collars and waist borders sometimes farmed-out to specialised artisans.	Garments are checked for defects, mended, folded and placed in plastic bags. Some manufacturers inspect and package garments themselves to improve quality control. Often this phase is integrated with pressing and ironing.
		3A. Illegal homeworkers Remove excess paper on reverse side of embroidery pattern. Hand embroidery.	**4A. Homeworkers** Cuffs, collars and borders are attached to garment. **4B. Illegal homeworkers** Seams are hand finished.				

(a) Unfinished goods are usually returned to the manufacturer following each production step and then immediately reshipped to the next subcontractor.

soften it and remove excess animal hairs; embroidery; and button-making. Subcontractors themselves sometimes rely on homeworkers. Especially low-paid marginal work is performed by illegal homeworkers who are not registered with the state employment office. Table 1 presents a flow chart describing the actors and the production sequence.

2. Firm topography

Most of the province's 4,291 firms are extremely small, have only one plant, and are owned by artisanal subcontractors. The average size is

Table 2. 20-year change in distribution of Modena knitwear firms by workforce size (a), (b)

size of workforce	1	2	3-5	6-9	10-19	20-49	50-250	Total (c)
1981								
No. of firms	2,145	858	634	308	232	78	36	4,291
%	49.9	19.9	14.7	7.1	5.4	1.8	0.8	100
No. of staff	2,145	1,716	2,339	2,234	2,892	2,337	3,305	16,968
%	12.6	10.1	13.7	13.1	17.0	13.7	19.4	100
1971								
No. of firms	548	410	299	112	92	77	52	1,590
%	34.4	25.7	18.8	7.0	5.7	4.8	3.2	100
No. of staff	548	820	1,085	793	1,237	2,376	4,384	11,243
%	4.9	7.2	9.6	7.5	11.0	21.0	38.9	100
	Employment size of firm (d)							
	1	2	3-5	6-10	11-20	21-50	51-264	Total
1961								
No. of firms	678	259	196	88	53	27	25	1,326
%	51.1	19.5	14.7	6.6	3.9	2.0	1.8	100
No. of staff	678	518	737	678	749	862	2,369	6,591
%	10.2	7.8	11.1	10.2	11.3	13.0	35.9	100

Notes: (a) Workforce includes owners, family members, employees and homeworkers. The knitwear category also includes production of socks and stockings. In 1981, only 4 firms and 59 persons were engaged in this activity.
(b) Sources: ISTAT, 1985, pp. 14-15; ISTAT, 1975, pp. 8-9.
(c) Percentages may add to less than 100 because of rounding errors.
(d) ISTAT, 1984, pp. 20-21. In this earlier census the category "various other textiles not otherwise classified" was used instead of knitwear. Since knitwear constitutes the only measurable textile production in the province, this category is essentially identical to the knitwear category contained in later census reports.

3.93 persons, including owners and family help. Excluding the latter, firm size falls to 2.39 [ISTAT, 1985, pp. 15, 48]. Owners and family help represent 39 per cent of the total work force [ISTAT, 1985, p. 48]. The contribution of large firms (those employing more than 50 persons) to employment has been declining: between 1961 and 1981 their share of the sector's work force dropped from 49 per cent to 33.1 per cent (see table 2). This trend has continued through 1988.[1] In the same period, the proportion of microfirms with five or fewer persons has expanded from 29.1 per cent in 1971 to 36 per cent in 1981. Improved statistical collection and the legalisation of many small artisans account for some of these changes, but the absolute decline in large firms from 32 in 1981 and to 21 in 1988[2] clearly demonstrates a structural shift toward the putting-out mode of production.

Knitwear firms usually comprise only a single plant. Of the 33 firms including more than one plant in 1981, the single largest had three units [ISTAT, 1985, pp. 4, 16-17]. The 89 per cent of the sector's firms that are artisanal are legally limited to a single plant. In Italy, *artisan* is a legal classification granted to those entrepreneurs who own the means of production, are personally engaged in their firm's productive activities, and have no more than 22 in-house employees, including family members [Lazerson, 1988]. Artisans benefit from subsidised loans, special dispensations from labour and social security laws, and other economic incentives.

Artisanal knitwear firms are usually subcontractors engaged solely in production. Their small size is made technically possible because of the extreme division of labour. This point is made clear in table 3, based on membership data provided by the Modena National Confederation of Artisans (CNA), which represents between 50 and 60 per cent of all knitwear firms in Modena. Except for firms specialising in "complete assembly", production firms without employees compose a majority of the industry.

3. The explanation for putting-out

Marketing, technological, and labour-market imperatives in large measure assure the survival and reproduction of small producers and subcontracting. Because of shifting consumer tastes and unpredictable climatic changes that result in a vast number of constantly changing styles, knitwear production is marked by short production runs that preclude large economies of scale. Abrupt cyclical changes are also more common in the knitwear industry than elsewhere, making factories with large amounts of fixed capital and many employees particularly vulnerable during economic downturns [Mariotti and Cainarca, 1986, p. 352]. According to Chandler, these characteristics explain the lack of large-scale integration in the American textile industry [Chandler, 1977].

---

1. Data supplied by Statistical Office of the Modena *Camera di Commercio*, November, 1988.

2. Data from Statistical Office of the Modena *Camera di Commercio*, November, 1988.

Table 3: Number of knitwear artisan firms in the Province of Modena by number of employees and principal phases of production (a)

Production phases	None	1	2-3	4-6	7-10	11+	Total (b)
Weavers	229	29	32	13	3	4	310
%	73.9	9.3	10.3	4.2	1.0	1.3	100
Complete assembly	88	17	26	30	31	32	224
%	39.3	7.6	11.6	13.4	13.8	14.3	100
Partial assembly	267	30	33	24	16	4	374
%	71.3	8.0	8.8	6.4	4.3	1.1	100
Fabric cutting only	33	10	2	1	1	0	47
%	70.2	21.3	4.3	2.1	2.1		100
Finishing, inspection, packaging	73	7	21	4	5	3	113
%	64.6	6.2	18.6	3.5	4.4	2.7	100
Laundry, pressing	166	32	31	25	19	9	282
%	59	11.3	11.0	8.9	6.7	3.2	100
Button making	37	4	6	5	1	2	55
%	67.3	7.3	10.9	9.1	1.8	3.6	100
Embroidery	70	10	18	11	2	5	116
%	60.3	8.6	15.5	9.4	1.7	4.3	100

Notes (a) Percentages may add to less than 100 because of rounding errors.
(b) Data provided by the Modena CNA as of October 1988. The category "employees" includes homeworkers, but excludes family help.

Since the possibilities for automation of the most labour-intensive phases of knitwear production (garment assembly, pressing, inspection, and packaging) are limited, small firms and large firms share similar technologies. Indeed, in knitwear dye-works where capital investment requirements are far greater, firms with fewer than 20 employees are rare. Finally, sharply higher labour costs in the 1970s and increased industrial conflict over health conditions among laundry, pressing, and dye workers intensified the sector's already strong centrifugal tendencies. Manufacturers' strategy of reliance on small artisanal producers allowed the same technology to be employed without any diminution in the economies of scale, reduced costly investment in plant and equipment, and replaced much of the blue-collar workforce with self-employed entrepreneurs.

Despite its functional rationality, the putting-out system depends upon two key, socially determined elements for its existence and continuous reproduction. First, state labour, social, fiscal, and business policies have established the structural conditions that allow large numbers of individuals, most of whom are ex-knitwear workers [ERVET, 1983, p. 32], to operate small firms with minimal organisational resources. Second, many individuals endowed with skills, tight-knit family resources [Pitkin, 1985], and the willingness to sacrifice provide a large reserve of labour available for self-employment.

III. The research

These non-economic considerations dominate my analysis of the putting-out mode based primarily on field research, which I conducted in the province of Modena in the spring and autumn of 1988. In order to understand the organisational structure of the industry, I visited 44 firms (16 manufacturers and 28 subcontractor-artisans) covering every single phase of knitwear production and used open-ended questionnaires to interview their principals. In two cases, I spent several days accompanying knitwear employers during their visits to contractors and subcontractors. I also interviewed eight homeworkers in their homes. Except for three firms located in adjoining provinces, the entire interview sample was based in Modena. Most of the interviews with the subcontractors were arranged by the National Confederation of Artisans (CNA). The Industrial Association of Modena (Confindustria) and the Association of Small Entrepreneurs (API) provided me with access to about half of the manufacturers I interviewed. Other interviews, including all those with homeworkers, were arranged through personal contacts. These interviews were supplemented by continuous discussions with industry and union representatives, principally those of the CNA and the Modena Labour Council (*Camera del Lavoro*), and by statistical data obtained from government, union, and industry sources.

I begin my discussion by demonstrating that the traditional weaknesses of the putting-out system have, today, either been overcome or else represent strengths. I find no empirical proof within the Modena knitwear system for Williamson's claim that the putting-out system is burdened by excessive transaction costs. In the next section, I show how the flexibility of the organisational structure of the putting-out system is in many ways dependent on its social rather than its technical characteristics. This is most evident in the way the law defines the roles and relationships of artisans, homeworkers, and illegal homeworkers.

IV. The putting-out system then and now

1. Theft and embezzlement

If there is one link uniting nearly all accounts of the putting-out system, save that of Bendix [1974, p. 203], it is that embezzlement and dishonesty by workers, especially in the cotton and wool industries, were widespread [Landes, 1969, pp. 56-57]. The dispersed form of production, which physically separated the owners of the material from the producers, meant that workers were able to substitute cheap wool for more expensive wool, wet the wool to distort its weight, work carelessly to increase their piece rates, or just simply steal. Legal measures to halt theft proved futile [Sayles, 1983]. Although Jones concludes that workers' embezzlement was a response to meagre wages and employer abuses [Jones, 1982, pp. 129-132], Williamson points to it as an example of the need to subject human opportunism to strict hierarchical control in order to guarantee efficient economic arrangements [Williamson, 1983]. The relative importance of worker theft is also in dispute. Jones contends that losses due to embezzlement were an insignificant production cost, viewed customarily as part of the wage bargain. But Marglin and Williamson list worker embezzlement as one major reason for the collapse of the putting-out system.

But what about embezzlement in Modena's knitwear production? To put it boldly and simply, according to the manufacturers, theft and misappropriation of their property by artisans and homeworkers are so uncommon that it has no visible effect on their business activities. Nevertheless, most manufacturers take precautions against cheating. They normally weigh and count the woven pieces of cloth upon delivery by weavers, who are traditionally permitted a margin of between 1 and 2.5 per cent for waste and lost material, depending upon the quality of the yarn. If there are any shortfalls they are immediately apparent, for each spool of yarn yields a precise number of cloths. As a further safeguard, some firms engage specialised laboratories to test the cloth's quality and thickness. But there are also manufacturers who own no scales and have neither the time nor personnel to weigh the material; they count only the pieces of cloth. Despite these measures, weavers could still manage to keep some yarn, but the amount would be of inconsequential effect. Opportunities for embezzlement also exist during the assembly phase, when the cloth is cut, leaving considerable waste. But when knitwear contains cashmere or other expensive materials, the yarn is often knitted to approximate the human form to avoid wasteful cutting of the finished cloth. Should high-grade wool be cut, the manufacturer would ordinarily request the subcontractor to sort the waste by colour and return it. Since this increases labour expenses, the subcontractor will usually negotiate to keep some of the waste wool. Today, artisans are normally free to sell the waste, which is often composed of recycled wool and acrylics. The theft of finished garments by workers is equally rare, and if even one or two garments out of two or three thousand were to disappear, manufacturers would not always request reimbursement from the artisan. It should also be remembered that knitwear workers are allowed to buy most garments at cost from the manufacturers. In general, manufacturers eschew expensive and costly controls over their subcontractors because of established relations of trust and confidence developed over a long time, which few artisans would risk undermining.

Where some manufacturers do take precautions against possible artisanal opportunism is in the protection of design secrets and of trademarks. Indeed, preserving the secrets of production has been one explanation for the rise of factories [Chapman, 1967, p. 34]. I did learn of one artisan subjected to civil prosecution after he misappropriated some material, reproduced it, and then used the manufacturer's patterns to make finished garments out of it. To avoid such problems, manufacturers who invest heavily in fashion design almost invariably produce the first prototypes internally, commissioning orders to subcontractors only after the buyers' initial orders have been received. Since many Modena manufacturers invest little in fashion and rework the designs of others, plagiarism does not pose a substantial risk.

2. Employee idleness and quality control

If lack of supervision once encouraged embezzlement, it also impeded manufacturers from controlling how much outworkers worked. Landes says that the manufacturer "had no way of compelling his workers to do a given number of hours of labour; the domestic weaver or craftsman was master of his time, starting and stopping when he desired" [Landes, 1969, p. 58]. This situation reflected the continued importance of subsistence agriculture to rural domestic workers [Sewell, Jr., 1986, p. 50] and the widespread resistance in English society to market culture [Reddy, 1984] and time-based factory discipline [Thompson, 1967].

Today in Modena, material well-being and even social standing are difficult to separate from one's earnings. Nor is agriculture any longer a secondary source of income for most knitwear workers, although it once played an important part in the origins of the Modena putting-out system [Cappello and Prandi, 1973]. If anything, the putting-out system today, unlike that of yesterday, appears to be the choice of those who value work far more than leisure. In one survey, knitwear artisans on average worked 2,428 hours annually, although weavers reported working 2,817 hours [ERVET, 1983, p. 34]. Another study of Modena's knitwear sector concluded artisans "are prepared to be available for long hours, almost without limits, at times even on holidays and Sundays" [Comune di Modena, 1978, p. 83]. In Modena today, it is the factory system with its five-day, forty-hour week that promises some reprieve from work without end.

The absence of supervision has also been blamed for output of poor and uneven quality under the putting-out system. Quality control is a major concern of most Modena manufacturers, for most garments are priced in the middle- to upper-end of the market. A few manufacturers reported that defects among put-out garments were slightly higher than those produced internally. Nevertheless, the costs of defects under putting-out are still lower than under the factory system, for subcontractors, unlike employees, are liable for their own mistakes. Thus, despite the absence of bureaucratic supervision, subcontractors face greater pressures to satisfy the principals' standards than an employee. But it should be understood that this application of agency theory [Alchian and Demsetz, 1972] is subject to clear limits, for if subcontractors are charged for every minor error or made to pay high prices for damaged garments, they will find other customers, disrupting the long-term relations necessary for quality and efficient production. But defects do not normally cause serious contention; otherwise 85 per cent of subcontractors would not have long-term, stable relations with their customers [ERVET, 1983, p.57].

3. Transportation costs

As in the traditional putting-out system, where the product had to be moved from cottage to cottage, transportation plays a crucial role in the organisation of knitwear subcontracting. Knitwear lends itself to frequent movements, for it is light and relatively immune from damage during transport. Whereas in eighteenth-century England it was the manufacturers' responsibility to move the goods from one station to the next, in Modena it is the custom that subcontractors move the unfinished garments to and from the manufacturers' warehouses after each manufacturing step. Subcontractors' transportation costs are a function of their size, organisational structure, and proximity to customers. Transportation costs normally vary from 2 to 10 per cent of their total expenses. But even if all transportation costs are eventually absorbed by the manufacturer, they amount to no more than 0.6 to 3 per cent of total expenses, based on estimates that subcontractors' labour costs represent approximately 30 per cent of a manufacturers' total expenses [Bursi, 1987, 1989].[3]

In contrast to the English putting-out system, which grew up in an area physically distinct from the factory [Jones, 1983, p. 65], 90 per cent of all Modena knitwear firms are located in three townships, all situated within a radius of 25 miles from one another.[4] In Carpi, the second largest city in the province of Modena which accounts for about one-third of all knitwear production and where workshops protrude from the ground floor of hundreds of residential buildings, garments are frequently moved by handcarts from one subcontractor to the next. On the other hand, some firms use subcontractors located in the far south of the country.

---

3. Data provided by the statistical office of the *Camera del Lavoro* of Modena, based on annual company statements filed at the Modena courthouse.

4. Source: *Provincia di Modena*, June, 1987: *L'occupazione dipendente in provincia di Modena*, p. 49.

4. Other transaction costs

Williamson claims that theft, shirking by employees, and high transportation costs raised the transaction costs of the putting-out mode to unacceptable levels [Williamson, 1980; 1983]. He also says that putting-out needs larger buffer inventories to assure constant product-flow because of the long distances between work-stations. But until recently, factories have maintained large inventories to guarantee full utilisation of labour, organised along rigid work schedules [Jones, 1982, pp. 127-129; Sayer, 1986]. In the knitwear sector a just-in-time supply system is used: raw materials are purchased and then consigned to the producer only immediately after the order is received. If serious disruptions prevent a subcontractor from completing the work in time, the manufacturer can almost always find alternative subcontractors. Within a centralised, production-organisation, the facility to jettison and substitute malfunctioning elements rapidly is limited. Thus, even if we accept Williamson's claim that internal hierarchies have greater access than market systems to information, the capacity of the latter to act on information is much greater [Williamson, 1981, p. 559].

One of Williamson's claims requires a longer view to adjudicate. He says that a weak decision-making hierarchy impedes the ability to "recognise and implement system innovations (of process, product or organisational kinds)..." [Williamson, 1980, p. 23]. Indeed, Lazonick says the decline of the English cotton industry can be attributed to its excessive decentralisation, which deprived it of the large integrated producers capable of providing the costly equipment needed to compete with new foreign producers [Lazonick, 1983]. So far, the few significant technological leaps in the knitwear sector such as the application of numerical-control computer technology to weaving, embroidery, and cutting have been rapidly adopted by many small firms. Admittedly, the development and application by foreign competitors of automated equipment requiring massive capital investments could eventually undermine the putting-out model in Modena. But, as the following section demonstrates, the scope for automation and centralisation in the knitwear sector is very narrow.

IV. The actors

1. The manufacturers

Manufacturers, with their dual capacity to design and market a product, dominate the artisan-producers, who in turn now command most of the homeworkers. The sheer number of Modena knitwear manufacturers, however, dilutes the power of any single firm over subcontractors, and makes it impossible for any one to hold monopsonistic power. As of April, 1988, there were 597 industrial manufacturing firms[5], in addition to probably 200 artisanal firms, many of which also have some production capacity and may serve as subcontractors for other manufacturers. Annual sales for manufacturers vary from under one million dollars for artisans, to more than 200 million dollars for firms with international reputations. The heterogeneity of the Modena knitwear sector contrasts sharply with that of the knitwear industry in the Veneto region, where one producer - Benetton - not only dominates production, but pressures subcontractors to work exclusively for it [Belussi, 1987, pp. 28, 32].

In Modena, most knitwear subcontractors normally work for several different manufacturers, in contrast to the extreme dependence of eighteenth-century English cottage weavers and nineteenth-century silk-ribbon weavers upon a single merchant-manufacturer that eventually undermined their autonomy [Mantoux, 1965, pp. 64-65; Aminzade, 1986, p. 405]. Though there are artisans in Modena obliged to work 100 per cent of the time to repay manufacturers for loans or machinery given them to start their businesses, they are few in number. In my interviews, most manufacturers, whether large or small, believed artisanal dependence upon a single manufacturer undermined one of the aims of decentralisation; that is, the separation of knitwear marketing from its production. Artisans also reported that manufacturers often referred them new customers. Within the city of Modena, which accounts for about 10 per cent of all artisanal subcontractors in the province, the 1984 records of the Artisans' Register revealed that only 15.3 per cent of all knitwear artisans had one customer (*Commissione Provinciale per L'Artigianato*, 1987, p. 47). A 1988 survey of 12 per cent of Modena weavers revealed that 60 per cent had from three to five customers and 21 per cent had six or more.[6]

The vast majority of manufacturers depend on subcontracting for all phases of knitwear production. Those manufacturers who adopted subcontracting strategies generally obtained higher profits; those who did not were soon forced to imitate their competitors [Bursi, 1989]. Most manufacturers limit their direct involvement in production to the design and execution of the first prototypes and to the delivery of the finished garments to buyers. Some manufacturers at the upper end of the market, but by no means all, package the finished garments internally in order to supervise quality control directly. Manufacturers who subcontract the design aspects of production are relatively few in number. Some of the larger manufacturers invest large sums in fashion design or else contract with prestigious Paris, Milan, and New York fashion houses. But for many others, one of the owners can usually create a prototype, invariably inspired by someone else's ideas. Theft of ideas is common in an industry that depends on appropriating the creations of others to make *haute couture* accessible to the masses.

---

5. Industrial manufacturing firm data of April, 1988 provided by *Camera del Lavoro* of the Province of Modena.

6. Source: CNA, September, 1988: *Indagine strutturale congiunturale sul comparto della tessitura*, Modena, *Confederazione Nazionale dell'Artigianato*.

2. Fashion-ready design

Manufacturers' ability to produce, unburdened by a productive structure, has led to new marketing strategies in order to better exploit this flexibility. Traditionally, manufacturers receive orders six months before the garments arrive in the shop. Orders are first solicited through displays of large numbers of costly prototypes, either in fashion shows or by sales agents. Thus, in February and March, manufacturers send their orders to subcontractors for the autumn/winter collection. By the time manufacturers are paid for their garments an average of four months has elapsed, imposing upon them large financing costs [Bursi, 1987]. As a result, some of the newer entrants have developed a production strategy known as fashion-ready, a just-in-time strategy that accepts orders from wholesalers and retailers, at the start of, or during, the season for delivery within 20 to 60 days. Prototypes are frequently copied from the current season's designs already selling in the shops. Fashion-ready production sharply cuts not only outlays for costly prototypes and interest charges on orders receivable; it also reduces buyers' inventory costs and the number of unsold garments.

Since fashion-ready production is based on small orders (500 garments would be a large production run compared with 1,000 or 2,000 normally) that must be produced quickly, manufacturers require a local network of contiguous subcontractors. Indeed, for Modena subcontractors, fashion-ready design serves as a defence against cheap Third World imports and low-cost Southern Italian competitors, whose distance from manufacturers excludes them from the market. The diverse productive capabilities of these subcontractors satisfy the technical requirements of hundreds of different production orders that change after each season. No single firm, or even group of firms, could profitably provide the range of machinery and skills necessary for all the different phases of production. As I shall demonstrate in the next part, this flexibility is made possible because small firms are able to realise economies of scale at minimum thresholds, a result of the particular social features of their construction.

VI. Artisans, the embodiment of flexible production

The Emilian model has been presented by Piore and Sabel [1984; Sabel, 1982] as a paradigmatic example of flexible production, based on small craft shops using highly versatile machinery operated by polyvalent operatives. But few knitwear subcontractors, no matter how skilled or advanced their machinery, can always satisfy the myriad tastes of the fashion industry. The knitwear industry's real flexibility is located in its totality rather than in its individual parts and rests upon a social and legal structure that insulates subcontractors from the worst ravages of the market's unpredictability. In the following sub-sections, I detail the elements which contribute to the sector's flexibility.

1. Technological flexibility

During my research, many of the weavers I visited sat idle; their thick-gauged needled looms unsuitable for the finely woven cloth then in demand. The problem reflected the limited adaptability of knitting machines. Not even the most advanced, numerical-controlled looms, manufactured in Japan and costing $150,000, weave yarn of more than one thickness. Any loom can be converted to a different yarn gauge for about one-sixth of its original cost, in addition to $400 in labour charges and two days' lost production for each resetting. Still, there is no guarantee that this new gauge will be useful when fashions change.

Numerical-controlled machinery can also be far less productive than older, traditional and less costly machinery. For example, during the autumn of 1988, weavers with the most advanced, numerical-controlled looms were able to produce the classic sweater model then in demand. But since these machines were not specifically designed for this sweater model, their productivity was far surpassed by traditional mechanical looms capable of knitting only classic sweaters. In most other phases of production, where capital costs are significantly lower, there is more versatility but the number of applications is still limited. In knitwear assembly, where most machines cost an average of $6,000 new, specialised sewing machines that cut and sew fine knitwear are unable to cut and sew heavier knitwear. Nor can seamstresses in small shops, though far more versatile than the pin makers studied by Adam Smith, easily switch from one material to another without sharp drops in productivity. Because of their small size and limited capital, most artisans offer only a modest range of services, even if collectively they are almost always able to meet the exigencies of the market. But, as a result, a large percentage of artisans remains idle for one to two months annually for lack of orders [ERVET, 1983, p. 75].

2. Social flexibility

Artisanal knitwear firms are characterised by heavy dependence on family labour, low overheads, extraordinarily long working hours and less costly labour laws. Some of these advantages depend on the frequent juxtaposition of home and workplace. More than 75 per cent of knitwear artisans locate their workplaces either in the garage or on the ground floor of their homes [ERVET, 1983, p. 22]. Most of the artisanal villages that dot the Modena landscape combine residential and industrial quarters. Thus few artisans pay rent; and special low interest-rate loans for workshops also subsidise their home building costs. The spatial integration of productive and reproductive spheres also permits artisans to rely on the casual labour of family members, particularly women and pensioners. A remarkably high percentage of Italians in the region of Emilia-Romagna live in extended families. According to a random survey of 4,500 households, 26 to 32 per cent of married sons (the frequency positively correlated to age) live in the same house or apartment building with at least one parent [Barbagli et al.,

1986, p. 18]. The assistance of family members, combined with the proximity of home and workplace, eases the burden of the long work days of artisans.

3. Legal inducements

Because of differences in pay, social insurance costs, dismissal protection, and sickness benefits, artisanal firms have lower labour costs than industrial firms.[7] Wages for artisanal and industrial employees in the province of Modena are about equal, though some large industrial companies pay as much as 10 per cent more. But artisanal employees receive less for overtime, weekend, and night work, and if absent from work for illness are reimbursed only from the fourth day, unlike industrial employees who receive 100 per cent of their wage from the first day. Artisanal employees also can be dismissed immediately with only one month's severance pay, unlike industrial firms where dismissals are both more costly and time consuming. Industrial employees are also less likely to be dismissed outright, for a special insurance fund pays them approximately 80 per cent of their take-home pay when temporarily laid off. These benefits are denied to artisanal employees. In addition, owners of small firms who work alongside their employees can closely supervise them, leading to 10 per cent higher productivity than in large firms, according to studies by Benetton [Belussi, 1987, p. 31]. In Modena, unionisation rates of about 30 per cent in knitwear artisanal firms are half those of industrial firms.[8]

3. The preference for self-employed and family labour

A series of social security laws encourages artisans to minimise their use of hired labour by relying on their own and family labour. Artisans are taxed at 26.39 per cent of the employee's gross wage for pension benefits, above the employee's own contribution of 7.5 per cent. But artisans themselves are only assessed 1.3 million lire annually plus 4.5 per cent of declared income. Not surprisingly, their benefits are also lower; a flat 450,000 lire per month regardless of earned income, in contrast to employees, who receive 60 to 80 per cent of their last monthly earnings. Artisans are charged payroll taxes of 14.1 per cent for employees' health, sickness, and maternity insurance, but pay only 6.5 per cent to insure themselves. Although artisans are not insured for income lost due to illness, their maternity benefits are equivalent to those of employees. The segment of artisanal payroll taxes based on earnings is reduced even further by widespread and substantial under-reporting of income by Italy's self-employed. This factor explains why factory workers are the third highest paid

---

7. *Contratto collettivo Nazionale di Lavoro per i lavoratori dipendenti delle imprese artigiane dei settori Tessile, Abbigliamento e Calzaturiero*, 6 June, 1984.

8. Data from *Camera del Lavoro*, Province of Modena, November, 1988.

occupational category according to Italian internal revenue data. In Modena, for example, a typical knitwear employee earned about $12,310 (gross) in 1987, whereas in the same period Modena artisans in the manufacturing sector reported average incomes of only $9,846.[9]

Family members employed in artisanal firms are treated like artisans according to social security and health insurance regulations. The law presumes that any close family members (defined broadly to encompass first cousins, in-laws and their close relatives and great-grandchildren) employed in the 76 per cent of knitwear firms organised as individual companies [ISTAT, 1985, p. 6] are not employees but partners with a right to share in the firms' profits.[10] According to census data, family help constitutes 7 per cent [ISTAT, 1985, p. 48] of all industry personnel. In reality, the percentage is far higher, but government statistics exclude those family helpers who have second jobs, are retired, or have others reasons for hiding their gainful activity. Nevertheless, employers and family help still account for 39 per cent of all those occupied in the knitwear sector according to the official statistics.

The character of market demand also offers artisans an additional motive to prefer family labour to hired labour. The highly cyclical nature of the clothing industry, intensified further by the growth of the fashion-ready sector and its tight production schedules, results in extremely heavy and often unplanned workloads during certain periods of the year. As indicated above, long hours in the industry are common for artisans, yet financial and social reasons restrict overtime work by employees. According to the national artisanal labour contract, a surcharge of 28 per cent is applied to the first four hours of overtime and 35 per cent to any additional hours above those. In practice, however, overtime is traditionally paid off the books because employees want to avoid inclusion in a higher tax bracket and employers want to escape the 40 per cent payroll taxes. But even unburdened by payroll taxes, employers cannot afford unlimited overtime payments since undeclared wage costs are not deductible from gross income. A larger impediment to overtime work is the mostly female work force that in large part is unable to accept extensive and unplanned overtime because of family obligations. For these reasons, an artisan and his family willing to work late into the night, and even on Saturdays and Sundays, often have a greater capacity to fill quickly sudden orders than an artisan completely dependent on hired labour.

---

9. *Gazzetta di Modena*, 5 October, 1988, p. 5.

10. Italian Civil Code, number 230-bis.

4. Homeworkers or artisans?

Homeworkers, a majority of whom are employed by artisans,[11] constitute another essential pillar of flexibility. Organisational differences that separate artisans from homeworkers are often nebulous. Both artisan and homeworker transform the manufacturer's material through a narrow division of labour, with neither one producing or marketing a finished product. Both must strictly follow the precise instructions of the manufacturer as to the garment's design, colour, shape, and texture. Both depend entirely on piece rates and normally own the means of production. Both usually work at home, with women accounting for about 100 per cent of homeworkers and 69 per cent of artisans [ISTAT, 1985, p. 48]. The similarities and differences of the two groups are detailed in table 4.

Until the early 1970s, the regulatory framework that sought to distinguish legally between the two categories had minimal effect, since both operated in the second economy, paying neither taxes nor social security contributions. Only after 1973, when Italy imposed upon producers the obligation to pay value-added tax (VAT) on all goods and services (a measure also intended for income tax purposes), did this situation start to change. Though widespread abuses of VAT payment continue to exist, the law nevertheless pushed subcontractors to register as a business. Homeworkers, who had few economic motives to act similarly, also benefited the same year from a more effective homeworkers' law.[12]

The ease with which the artisanal law[13] [Lazerson, 1988] allows domestic workers, who resemble homeworkers, to register as artisans underscores the critical role of the state in defining and creating social classes. The law distinguishes the two categories most clearly in their relationship to other labour categories. Homeworkers cannot hire employees, and any help they receive from family members must be limited to dependents and be of marginal importance. Employers are required to pay the same payroll taxes for homeworkers as for other employees. Since these rates are based on a minimum daily wage of 31,376 lire ($24), homeworkers must earn at least that amount. Otherwise the relative burden of payroll taxes to the employer rises even further. This factor makes homeworkers a less flexible source of labour than subcontractor artisans, who pay their own social insurance costs. Although artisans without employees always earn as much as a factory employee - and many earn two and three times as much - registered homeworkers usually earn one-third less than a factory employee. Some highly skilled homeworkers, however, earn considerably more than employees [Malagoli and Mengoli, 1979].

---

11. Sources: Ministry of Labour statistics available at the Regional Labour Office of Emilia-Romagna, Bologna and data provided by the Modena CNA.

12. *Le nuove normative per la tutela del lavoro a domicilio*, Law of 18 December 1973, number 877.

13. *La legge quadro per l'artigianato*, Law of 8 August, number 443.

Table 4: Key organisational attributes of subcontractor artisans and homeworkers

	Artisans	Homeworkers
Principal differences		
Right to hire employees or homeworkers	+	-
Place personal wealth at economic risk	+	-
Technical instructions normally provided by work assigner	+-	+-
Right to unlimited assistance by unpaid family members	+	-
Principal similarities		
Income dependent on piece-rates	+	+
Conceive and design work	-	-
Access to market	-	-
Transform manufacturer's material	+	+
Own means of production (includes leasing and renting)	+	+-
Establish own working conditions and work pace	+	+
Workplace located in home	+-	+
Produce semi-finished goods	+	+

Key: + = presence of the defined characteristic
- = absence of the defined characteristic
+- = the defined characteristic varies within the same organisational mode

Inclusion in the Artisans' Register is both a prerequisite to receiving artisanal privileges and differentiates homeworkers and artisans. Under the law, the provincial artisanal commission (CPA) controls eligibility standards for inclusion in the Artisans' Register. In Modena, the CPA is controlled by the National Artisans Confederation (CNA), which is closely affiliated to the Italian Communist Party and to a lesser extent the Socialist Party. Other artisanal associations, trade unions, and public officials are also represented on the CPA. Though court decisions have stated that an artisan should enjoy gross revenues considerably greater than that of an average employee's wage,[14] the only clear standard established by the Modena CPA for applicants who appear to resemble homeworkers is that they own their machinery.[15] In large part, the definition of artisanal status is a political one. Unions believe many artisans are really homeworkers and would like to raise the entrance barriers of the Artisans' Register. But artisanal associations risk losing potential members to associations with less rigid standards, as happened with the CNA of Modena in the early 1970s, if they discourage those with dubious qualifications from enrolling in the CPA. The CNA, however, continues to recommend to artisans that they have at least two customers before initiating their business activity.

The real impediment to homeworkers registering as artisans in the last few years has been the increasing cost of artisanal social contributions, combined with improved enforcement measures by the Modena provincial offices of the national departments of labour and health. More punctilious tax measures have also increased accounting and reporting costs for small firms. Indeed, immediately following an important tax reform in 1985,[16] there was a record drop in the number of knitwear artisanal firms organised as simple individual companies.[17] Although some of these resurfaced as partnerships (a more costly form of business organisation), others may have expanded the underground economy, for the number of registered homeworkers has remained essentially unvaried.

The legal distinction between artisans as entrepreneurs and homeworkers as employees has important organisational effects. State-subsidised artisanal loans of up to $92,000 for plant and equipment allow artisans to develop their productive capacity, though at times the capital requirements of an artisan may be no greater than that of a homeworker. An artisan who inspects, finishes, and packages garments needs no more than $3,000 to establish a home workshop, compared with $1,500 to $4,500 for homeworkers who assemble garments. On the other hand, the many homeworkers who 30 years ago operated small motorised looms [Davolio, 1981-82] have been all but expelled from weaving, unable to afford the far more productive and costly new looms.

Entrepreneurial status also signals that artisans are more committed and amenable to working longer hours than homeworkers. More than 75 per cent of knitwear artisans have chosen their profession out of a desire to be self-employed or to increase their earnings [ERVET, 1983, p. 28]. On the other hand, homeworkers have had their occupational choice imposed upon them by family responsibilities that exclude them from full-time employment [Comune di Modena, 1978]. Thus, artisans normally transport knitwear to

---

14. *Court of Cassazione*, 27 April 1985, number 2750. *Rivista italiana diritto del lavoro*, 1985 (4), pp. 806-809.

15. Based on an interview with Ermanno Gasparini, Vice-President of the Modena Provincia Commission of Artisans and a memorandum of the CPA, *Decisioni e nuovi criteri assunti dalla Commissione Provinciale Artigianato* of November 14, 1977.

16. *La legge Visentini*. Law of February 1985, number 17.

17. Data from Statistical Office, Modena Camera di Commercio.

and from the factory, but homeworkers do not. These organisational differences usually lead manufacturers to entrust artisans with most production responsibilities, even if the latter's labour costs may be slightly higher than those of homeworkers, whose unit labour costs are approximately 35 to 50 per cent less than for in-house employees. A central aim of the homeworkers' law to equalise pay standards between the two groups has never been implemented. Among CNA artisans, 79 per cent of knitwear homeworkers are employed by assembly shops, constituting 40 per cent of all employees in that phase of production.[18] They normally attach collars, cuffs, and waistbands with the use of a circular-sewing machine or else perform other final phases of production that do not interfere with the work flow within the assembly shops. But there are firms that depend on homeworkers to assemble the entire garment after the cloth is cut in the shop. Here, too, there is normally a rigid division of labour. Each homeworker sews only one or two seams before the employer consigns the garments to the next homeworker for the subsequent assembly phase.

5. Illegal homeworkers

Alongside registered homeworkers, there have always existed many unregistered homeworkers, who together with their employers avoid all social contributions and taxes. Their precise numbers are unknown, but they may exceed registered ones, especially in Southern Italy and Veneto, where weak and disorganised unions are unable to pressure provincial and regional authorities to police unregistered homeworkers, and high unemployment creates a large supply of homeworkers [Fondazione Pietro Sevezo, 1986]. In Modena, illegal homework has probably been declining and is now rather limited. Two studies that attempted to survey the universe of all homeworkers in the township of Modena in 1971 and 1977 revealed a notable decline in the number of homeworkers and, more significantly, a sharp rise in their median age [*Commune di Modena*, 1978, pp. 17-27], most probably the results of tight labour market conditions in the Modena economy marked by high wages and a 3.8 per cent unemployment level, a sharp contrast to the national average of 11.9 per cent.[19] Employers who rely extensively on unregistered homeworkers must now seek them in less prosperous surrounding provinces [Solinas, 1982].

Better application of the tax laws in Modena since 1979, enforced by an extensive system of road blocks operated by the national tax police who regularly stop commercial vans and trucks, has also made it more onerous for artisans to depend on unregistered homeworkers. The law requires anyone transporting commercial goods on public roads to possess a waybill listing his tax code and destination, and the number and description

18. Data provided by the Modena CNA, 16 November 1988.

19. Source: *Provincia di Modena Camera di Commercio*, September, 1988. E ELLE No. 3, p. 9.

of the goods being shipped. Though numerous subterfuges have reduced the efficacy of these measures, it is no longer possible in Modena to evade the tax net completely. In addition, employers dependent on unregistered homeworkers are unable to deduct their expenses for income tax purposes. Export-oriented firms, which must produce all official invoices at the time of export, also have few opportunities to evade taxes.

Nevertheless, illegal homework in the knitwear sector continues to attract pensioners and others needing to conceal their extra income from the state, along with unskilled young mothers whose availability for part-time homework excludes them from registered homework, for which employers must pay payroll taxes based on a full day's work. These unregistered homeworkers usually live near the artisans for whom they work, using back roads and passenger cars to avoid the tax police. Most of them, with the exception of a few elderly skilled workers, finish off cuff and collar seams, hand embroider or cut the excess paper-backing from behind embroidery stitched by automated machinery. Because this marginal unmechanised work is extremely slow, employers claim that they cannot afford payroll taxes, even though unregistered homeworkers earn only one-third as much as employees [Comune di Modena, 1978, pp. 70, 72]. Indeed, it is quite normal for an employer with unregistered homeworkers to hire also registered homeworkers for more remunerative forms of work.

VII. The frontiers of subcontracting

Subcontracting strategies are now being applied even by subcontractor-artisans themselves. According to a 1982 industry survey, 28 per cent of artisans subcontracted work to other artisans, up from 16 per cent in 1975 [ERVET, 1983, pp. 60-63]. Since then, subcontracting has certainly increased, though a 1985 tax law[20] (which expired in 1988) that disallowed artisans using the simple accounting method from deducting all of their expenses paid to other artisans has slowed its growth.

Subcontracting by artisans usually takes two forms. In some cases, artisans engage in subcontracting because manufacturers, anxious to reduce transportation costs, entrust them with organising several different production phases.[21] Thus, an artisan with a pressing firm might also be assigned responsibility for dyeing the garment and adding buttons to it. Here, the artisan, like the manufacturer, subcontracts by specialisation. But in other instances, artisans subcontract by capacity to exploit the flexibility engendered by the particular characteristics of the knitwear industry [Nadel, 1989]. In this case, the artisan possesses the production facilities to undertake the task herself but prefers to exploit the existing organisational

20. *La legge Visentini*, Law of February, 1985, number 17.

21. Data provided by the *Centro Dati Abbigliamento* of the Provinces of Modena and Reggio Emilia, *Camera di Commercio di Modena*.

structure for more profitable aspects of production, while farming out less well-paid tasks to even smaller subcontractors. This strategy is also intended to reduce environmental shock if their own contractors cut back production. Artisans can then reabsorb the subcontracted production to preserve their own organisational structure. But by increasing their own stability within the putting-out system they decrease it for others. In fact, some artisans who subcontract seek to discourage family-operated firms from hiring employees by dividing their orders among several smaller artisans rather than relying on a single producer. They fear that if production volumes suddenly dropped, the higher fixed costs of employees would force subcontractors to raise their prices.

Artisans who contemplate dismissing all their employees to then subcontract their work to other artisans in order to increase their profits, are presented with several legal and organisational obstacles. Legally, an artisanal firm must be engaged in production; business activity limited solely to the intermediation of labour between manufacturers and subcontractors is prohibited.[22] Organisationally, artisans who subcontract work that requires neither enormous investments nor great skill could eventually find their own subcontractors dealing directly with the manufacturer. Possession of a productive structure is also essential to convince manufacturers that the artisan can competently and rapidly fill large orders, even if the former know that subcontractors are employed. In a certain sense, the factory has become as much a showroom as a productive centre. Finally, even in the knitwear sector, throughput efficiency requires some centralisation. Thus, for instance, pressers could achieve substantial savings if they hired subcontractors to sew brand labels in garments. But the risk of disruptions in the flow of labelled garments back to the pressing firm, which could interrupt the critical pressing operations, excludes such a strategy.

VIII. Conclusion

Knitwear production with its minimal economies of scale, unstable demand, limited opportunities for throughput efficiencies, and relative imperviousness to automation left the factory vulnerable to the challenge of decentralisation. The same can be said of the clothing and shoe industries, where small-scale production is the dominant form of organisation, not just a specialised niche as in the mechanical engineering sector. Though the application of the putting-out mode will always be circumscribed by the technical characteristics of production, there are no substantial organisational impediments to a highly decentralised, non-bureaucratised production system. With the consolidation of a market economy, the factory is no longer necessary to maintain discipline among the producers, except perhaps in the negative sense that its ubiquitous shadow serves to remind artisans of the

---

22. Law of 23 October 1960, number 1369.

virtues of sacrifice. In addition, many of the organisational advantages of the factory system over parcellised production units have been neutralised, in large measure because of the gains of organised Italian labour in the post-war period. In a somewhat perverse sense, union victories have increased the space available for workers to become entrepreneurs.

The other reality which emerges from this research is the crucial role played by non-economic structures in stimulating economic transactions. An intricately woven legal fabric gives shape and colour to the vast artisanal network in Italy. It favours family labour over hired help; it integrates home and workshop; and it establishes the artisan as a hybrid figure placed between capital and labour. Although the putting-out mode happens to be a most efficient form of economic exchange, it owes its organisational existence to the particular social and political system in which it is embedded. A comparative glance at the clothing industry in the United Kingdom, which is dominated by large manufacturers surrounded by a fringe of sweat-shops, underscores this point [GLC, 1985; Rawsthorn, 1988]. Economic activity and organisational structure are profoundly shaped by non-market forces even if efficient forms of exchange also have their claims [Robins, 1987, p. 77].

Finally, I should ask whether the putting-out mode of production represents a social advance over the factory. To labour process theorists who criticised the capitalist factory for progressively extending managerial control over the labour process at the expense of worker autonomy [Clawson, 1980, p. 116], putting-out demonstrates that capitalistic production can be safely entrusted to small firms hiring no labour. This development should not be seen as just another form of the subordination of labourers to manufacturers, as has been argued in the context of nineteenth-century France [Aminzade, 1986]. Artisans working for multiple customers and owning their workplace and machinery have more autonomy and freedom than the average employee, which probably partly explains their willingness to exchange factory positions for the risks of self-employment. Putting-out, with its large network of independent producers, may offer one alternative to large, hierarchical, bureaucratic organisations that have reduced individual choices.

If putting-out represents a democratic organisational alternative to the large factory, I am less sanguine about the contribution of knitwear production to an advanced industrial society, whether it be organised in small or large units. Its limited skill levels discourage educational attainment; the average education of both employer and employee is between five and eight years. Some of its job tasks test the limits of human endurance; the young girls who begin work on the steam presses at 16 years of age have only five years before physical exhaustion will send them in search of less demanding work. Indeed, the steam-press position silently exacts its toll, at times exposing its young female operators to early sterility. Older homeworkers are sometimes subject to premature cataracts because of the fine needles, threaded by hand, on the special machines used to attach collars and cuffs to sweaters. But if knitwear work itself does not sap the body, its monotonous routines of buttoning and folding sweaters day in and day out often dull the mind.

Note:

Support for this research came initially from a Jean Monnet Fellowship at the European University Institute and later from the Organization of Economic Cooperation and Development's Office on Local Employment Initiatives. Charles Perrow inspired me to write this paper and afterwards helped me with useful comments. The Bignardi families of Cavezzo and Modena assisted me at every turn during my field work, especially Paolo Bignardi, who introduced me to the inner workings of the knitwear industry. Lauro Venturi, Andrea Tosi, Omar Sala and Mario Poltronieri and other representatives of the Modena National Confederation of Artisans (CNA) assisted me throughout the field research; without them most of the interviews with the Modena artisans would never have been granted. Ughetta Gani of the Modena Camera del Lavoro (FILTEA-CGIL) gave generously of her time and made available important data. Representatives of the Modena Association of Small Enterprises (API) and the Modena Industrialists Association (Confindustria) also introduced me to their members.

References

Alchian, Armen; Demsetz, Harold. 1972. "Production, information cost, and economic organization", in *American Economic Review*, pp. 777-795.

Aminzade, Ronald. 1986. "Reinterpreting capitalist industrialisation: A study of nineteenth-century France", in Kaplan, S.; Koep, C.J. (eds.): *Work in France: Representations, meaning, organisation and practice*, Ithaca, Cornell University Press.

Barbagli, Marzio, et al. 1986. *Mobilita sociale in Emilia-Romagna*, Bologna, Regione Emilia-Romagna, Assessorato Lavoro e Formazione Professionale.

Belussi, Fiorenza. 1987. *Benetton: Information technology in production and distribution: A case study of the innovative potential of traditional sectors*, Sussex, University of Sussex Science Policy Research Unit.

Bendix, Reinhard. [1956] 1974. *Work and authority in industry*, Berkeley, University of California Press.

Berger, Suzanne. 1980. "Discontinuity in the politics of industrial society", in Berger, Suzanne; Piore, Michael (eds.): *Dualism and discontinuity in industrial societies*, Cambridge, Cambridge University Press, pp. 132-149.

Bursi, Tiziano. 1987. *Indagine sulle condizioni economico-finanziarie delle imprese Emiliano-romagnole del tessile abbigliento (1982-1986)*, Carpi, CITER.

---. 1989. *Piccola e media impresa e politiche di adattamento: Il distretto della maglieria carpigiana*, Milan, Franco Angeli.

Cappello, Stefania; Prandi, Alfonso. 1973. *Carpi: Tradizione e sviluppo*, Bologna, Il Mulino.

Chandler, Alfred. 1977. *The visible hand: The managerial revolution in American business*, Cambridge, Harvard University Press.

Chapman, S.D. 1967. *The early factory masters - The transition to the factory system in the Midlands textile industry*, Newton Abbot, David & Charles.

Clawson, Dan. 1980. *Bureaucracy and the labor process*, New York, Monthly Review Press.

Commissione Provinciale per l'Artigianato. 1987. *Le imprese artigiane del comune di Modena*, Modena, Commissione Provinciale per l'Artigianato.

Comune di Modena. 1978. *Recenti evoluzione del lavoro a domicilio nei comuni del comprensorio di Modena*, Modena, Dipartimento Interventi Economici, Comune di Modena.

CNA. 1988. *Indagine strutturale congiunturale sul comparto della tessitura*, Modena, Confederazione Nazionale dell'Artigianato.

Davolio, Stefano. 1981-1982. *Carpi: Dal lavoro alla casa dalla casa al lavoro*, "Laurea" thesis, Political Science Faculty, University of Bologna.

ERVET. 1983. *Le aziende artigiane del tessile-abbigliamento in Emilia-Romagna: I comparti della magliera, delle confezioni e della pelletteria*, Bologna, ERVET Regione Emilia-Romagna.

Fondazione Pietro Sevezo. 1986. *Homeworking in Italy*, Brussels, European Economic Community's Employment, Social Affairs and Education Commission.

GLC. 1985. *Strategy for the London clothing industry: A debate*, Economic Policy Group, Strategy Document No. 39, May. London, Greater London Council.

ISTAT. 1964. *Annuario di statistico Italiano: 4th censimento generale dell'industria e del commercio 16 ottobre 1961. Dati sulle caratteristiche strutturale delle imprese e delle unita locale*, Vol. II, No. 36, Provincial Data - Modena, Rome, ISTAT.

---. 1975. *Annuario di statistico Italiano, 5th censimento generale dell'industria e del commercio 25 ottobre 1971. Dati sulle caratteristiche strutturale delle imprese e delle unita locale*, Vol. II. No, 37, Provincial Data - Modena, Rome, ISTAT.

---. 1985. *Annuario di statistico Italiano: 6th censimento generale dell'industria, del commercio, dei servizi e l'artigiano 26 ottobre 1981*, Vol. II - Province of Modena, Rome, ISTAT:

Jones, S.R.H. 1982. "The organisation of work: A historical dimension", in *Journal of Economic Behavior and Organization*, No. 3, pp. 117-137.

---. 1983. "Technology and the organisation of work: A reply", in *Journal of Economic Behavior and Organization*, No. 4, pp. 53-66.

Kerr, Clark, et al., 1960. *Industrialism and industrial man*, Cambridge, Harvard University Press.

Kriedte, Peter. 1981. "Proto-industrialisation between industrialisation and deindustrialisation", in Kriedte, Peter et al. (eds.): *Industrialisation before industrialisation: Rural industry in the genesis of capitalism*, Cambridge, Cambridge University Press, pp. 135-160.

Landes, David. 1969. *The unbound Prometheus: Technological change and industrial development in Western Europe from 1750 to the present*, Cambridge, Cambridge University Press.

--. (ed.) 1966. *The rise of capitalism*, New York, Macmillan.

Lazerson, Mark. 1988. "Organizational growth of small firms: An outcome of markets and hierarchies?", in *American Sociological Review*, No. 53, pp. 330-342.

Lazonick, William. 1983. "Industrial organisation and technological change: The decline of the British cotton industry", in *Business History Review*, No. 57, pp. 195-236.

Malagoli, Werter; Mengoli, Paola. 1979. "Lavoro a domicilio e artigianato nel comparto della maglieria", in *Citta e Regione*, No. 5, pp. 84-92.

Mantoux, Paul [1937] 1965. *The industrial revolution in the eighteenth century: An outline of the beginnings of the modern factory system in England*, New York, Harper and Row.

Marglin, Stephen. 1976. "What do bosses do? The origins and functions of hierarchy in capitalist production", in Gorz. A. (ed.): *The division of labor: The labor process and class struggle modern capitalism*, Sussex, Harvester Press.

Mariotti, Sergio; Cainarca, Giancarlo. 1986. "The evolution of transaction governance in the textile-clothing industry", in *Journal of Economic Behavior and Organization*, No. 7, pp. 351-374.

Marx, Karl. [1867] 1977. *Capital: A critique of political economy*, Vol. 1, London, Lawrence and Wishart.

Mendels, Franklin. 1972. "Proto-industrialization: The first phase of the industrialization process", in *Journal of Economic History*, No. 32, pp. 241-261.

Nadel, Henri. 1989. "Employment growth in French small and medium enterprises: An ambiguous reality", in *The economics of small firms: An international perspective* (forthcoming), Dordrecht, Kluwer.

O'Brien, Patrick; Caglar, Keyder. 1978. *Economic growth in Britain and France 1780-1914: Two paths to the century*, London, George Allen & Unwin.

Piore, Michael; Sabel, Charles. 1984. *The second industrial divide.* New York, Basic Books.

Pitkin, Donald. 1985. *The house that Giacomo built: History of an Italian family 1898-1978*, New York, Cambridge University Press.

Rawsthorn, Alice. 1988. "The vicious circle of the British rag trade", in *Financial Times*, 19 November, p. 6.

Reddy, William. 1984. *The rise of market culture: The textile trade and French society, 1750-1900*, Cambridge, Cambridge University Press.

Robins, James. 1987. "Organizational economics: Notes on the use of transaction-cost theory in the study of organizations", in *Administrative Science Quarterly*, No. 32, pp. 68-86.

Sabel, Charles. 1982. *Work and politics: The division of labor in industry*, New York, Cambridge University Press.

Samuel, Raphael. 1977. "Workshop of the world: Steam power and hand technology in mid-Victorian Britain", in *History Workshop*, No. 3, pp. 6-72.

Sayer, Andrew. 1986. "New developments in manufacturing: The just-in-time system", in *Capital and Class*, No. 30, pp. 43-72.

Sayles, John. 1983. "Embezzlement, industry and the law in England", in Berg, Maxine et al. (eds.): *Manufacturing in town and country before the factory*, Cambridge, Cambridge University Press.

Schlumbohm, Jurgen. 1981. "Relations of productive forces - Crises in proto-industrialization", in Kriedte, Peter et al. (eds.): *Industrialization before industrialization: Rural industry in the genesis of capitalism*, Cambridge, Cambridge University Press.

Sewell, William, Jr. 1986. "Artisans, factory workers and the formation of the French working class, 1789-1848", in Katznelson, Ira; Zolberg, Aristide R. (eds.): *Working class formation: Nineteenth-century patterns in Western Europe and the United States*, Princeton, Princeton University Press.

Smelser, Neil. 1959. *Social change and the industrial revolution*, Chicago, University of Chicago Press.

Solinas, Giovanni. 1982. "Labor market segmentation and workers' careers: The case of the Italian knitwear industry", in *Cambridge Journal of Economics*, No. 6, pp. 331-352.

Thompson, Edward. 1967. "Time, work-discipline, and industrial capitalism", in *Past and Present*, No. 38, pp. 56-97.

Williamson, Oliver. 1980. "The organization of work: A comparative institutional assessment", in *Journal of Economic Behavior and Organization*, No. 1, pp. 5-38.

---. 1981. "The economics of organization: The transaction cost approach", in *American Journal of Sociology*, No. 87, pp. 548-577.

---. 1983. "Technology and the organization of work: A reply to Jones", in *Journal of Economic Behavior and Organization*, No. 4, pp. 57-62.

8 Industrial districts and the unions[1]

Paolo Brutti and Franco Calistri

I. Industrial districts

What are bosses for? What roles do they play in systems of production? Is it possible for employers to play different roles to those found in a mass-production context? Are there alternative viable forms of industrial organisation to that of the mass production model? What implications would such alternatives have for trade union policies?

These are the sorts of questions which anyone who sets out, naively and with no preconceived ideas, to observe the life, and the modes of production inside industrial districts, inevitably asks himself sooner or later. We too have posed these sorts of questions: as the CGIL (*Confederazione Generale Italiana del Lavoro*) we have done so in the context of research which involved large sections of our union and which was concerned with the spread and the characteristics of industrial districts in Italy.[2] In our research we employed the term Areas of New Industrial Development (ANID) which no doubt strained, to some extent, the classical definition of the Marshallian industrial district. Through its use we meant to include in our field of analysis all territorial areas of some size which were characterised by a marked presence of integrated small- and medium-sized firms and in which life was centred around one prevailing *manufacturing* activity. We reached two major conclusions:

(1) there are many such areas in Italy, particularly in the North-Central area of the country, but interesting instances (perhaps "embryonic" districts) are also identifiable in the South - for example in Abruzzo, and Puglia, in the "Sanità" quarter in Naples for bread production, in Sardinia for cork production and developing agro-industrial districts in the areas of Sibari and of Gela in Sicily;

(2) industrial districts are not simply a question of an agglomeration of small- and medium-sized firms located in areas where advantage can be taken of a disadvantaged and ill-protected labour force; that is to

---

1. An Italian version of this article has been published in *Il Ponte*, No. 2, 1989.

2. The research "Aree distrettuali e sistemiche in Italia" and the papers presented to the seminar on the same subject, held in Rome on 9 March 1988, are published in: Garavini, R. et al.: *La quarta Italia - Il lavoro e la politica industriale nei distretti e nelle aree integrate in Italia, a cura di P. Brutti e G. Ricoveri*, Ediesse, Rome, 1988.

say, areas where there is low pay, extensive use of "black" labour, and little protection against environmental and health hazards (although it must be noted that these factors might may well exist, to a greater or lesser extent, in district (as elsewhere). Rather, we were often confronted with systems of firms able to achieve relatively high levels of strategy and autonomy, characterised by a decomposition of phases of production between individual firms, high levels of efficiency and specialisation, well-developed information networks amongst entrepreneurs, and a self-reproducing industrial mentality and atmosphere conducive to the development of new skills and entrepreneurial abilities. We came to define these areas as being like "one single large firm, an ideal model of production efficiency and commercial flexibility, employing a plurality of technologies and modes of utilisation that adapt to different circumstances following the criterion of maximising productivity".[3]

In other words, we perceived clearly that we were confronted with a very complex phenomenon and one that relied on a delicate socio-economic mechanism (to use a somewhat overworked metaphor, we were confronted with the old, classical mechanism of an eighteenth-century clock). We were impressed by the capacity these areas possessed for fully employing different forms of labour flexibility, thereby making it possible for a multiplicity of modes of organisation of labour and production to exist side by side, and by the fact that all this was heavily influenced by particular local cultural characteristics, including a system of values and customs, against which background technology and differing labour force requirements structured the labour market.

In this light, the process by which new technologies are introduced is highly instructive. (It must be noted that these districts are not just areas of labour but of advanced technology as well). Given the peculiar way labour and production are organised, the decision to introduce new technology is not taken at a particular privileged point of the system: this is in fact the model of the large firm. Rather, the decision is participated in, and lived, by the whole social and productive body, be they proprietors or employees of firms, or directors of the local bank. The substitution of one machine for another results from a discussion in which labour is involved; one receives the clear impression that, within these systems of production, workers, including those who receive very low wages, retain a capacity for understanding what is going on, and a feeling for the entirety of the production cycle.

In other words, the massive expropriation of knowledge, and the impossibility for workers to gain an overall view of production (a central feature of the technological revolution taking place in large complex firms) does not occur in industrial districts. Technological innovation does not expropriate labour by force; within the industrial districts, labour retains its central role.

---

3. Ibid., p. 94.

II. A changing picture

The industrial districts are now finding it increasingly difficult to maintain their efficiency and competitiveness, due in particular, to the effects of far-reaching international changes. These include the effects of increased international competition, the impact of technologies of the third industrial revolution, and the renewed interest of large-scale international capital in sectors of production typical of the districts. These are all well-known elements which brevity of presentation does not permit us to treat here. These changed conditions induce strong pressures for innovation at a micro-economic level, in the very structures and strategies of firms. The firm is pushed in the direction of a rapid process of transformation into a financial and tertiary structure, characterised by the following patterns of operation:

(a) an increased differentiation between control and managing functions;

(b) a greater weight for marketing and product policies;

(c) the introduction of sophisticated services in relation to production management and marketing;

(d) new forms of financial supply.

As a consequence of such transformations, the management of the firm becomes increasingly complex and professional; success and profits depend increasingly on non-productive factors. Even while they maintain their pecularities, firms in industrial districts cannot escape these general processes of reorganisation. However, our research indicates that so far they have only reacted to changing developments using old methods: everywhere production specialisation and fragmentation is accompanied by increased exploitation. Hence a qualitative jump is strongly needed. If this does not occur, the industrial districts will continue, but their importance will be reduced as they threaten to transform into areas of relative decay, with the possibility of a migration of brains and profits. The districts would be left as areas of exploitation with people struggling to survive.

III. The response of the unions

It is quite evident that these first considerations of the nature and characteristics of the industrial districts reveal the existence of very complex problems for the unions. How should we be present in these areas where labour has such a central presence but where the workers' material conditions are often poor? The classical union strategies and their bargaining instruments, appear to be very inadequate. The unions have, for a long time, accepted the idea that the sorts of socio-economic systems found in these districts were pre-capitalistic industrial relics, destined to be "modernised" in the natural development of the economy.

However, once it has been realised that these areas are not marginal, since they house a large part of Italian manufacturing employment, it is clear that not "seeing" this reality has increasing consequences for trade union self-exclusion and loss of representation.

It becomes necessary to define strategies of intervention which are tuned to these areas; that is to say intervention policies specifically for the districts, and not simply generically addressed to small- and medium-sized firms. The unions need to design strategies aimed at strengthening and developing the districts at the same time as introducing procedures and well-defined rules to preserve the rights of workers: strategies which are able to envisage a new industrial policy for labour. What might be the cornerstones or guiding lines of such a policy?

1. Decentralised intervention

One first question concerns the need for an industrial policy adapted to the territory, one involving a new division of powers and areas of intervention between central government and local authorities.

In the past, local authorities have played a crucial role in the formation, strengthening and growth of industrial districts. It is now a question of a massive decentralisation to the regions of an important part of industrial policy, permitting a co-ordinated and well-targeted use of resources. We have in mind a specific well-defined model, which in our view is suitable for intervention in socio-productive systems like the districts. This is the model of integrated area plans.[4]

A key point of such a plan would be intervention in the areas of training and real services, enabling improvements to be made at the weak points of the district systems. Such weak points might include:

- poor ability to adapt to changing market requirements requiring improvements in management, product standardisation, better timing of deliveries, quality standards, and market intelligence;
- inadequate product design and marketing systems: their realisation requires complex Research and Development structures, and at least a medium period planning capacity, with the back-up of substantial financial resources;
- a growing requirement for applied research activities with long-term perspectives, something not within the reach of small- and medium-sized firms;

---

4. Such intervention is not unknown to the regions: recall the practice of IMP -Integrated Mediterranean Projects - or the new procedures for intervention to utilise EEC structural funds: the Social European Fund, the European Fund for Regional Development, and the Structural Fund for Agriculture Intervention.

- an inadequate capacity for a constant up-dating of skills, requiring interventionist methods and practices that the districts largely lack;
- a lack of knowledge of the newest and most sophisticated techniques of financial sourcing;
- difficulties in confronting obsolescence inherent in quickly-changing process technology.

Within this context, the central government must be requested to provide a legal framework which recognises the peculiarities of the industrial district (a legislation for the district), and clearly distinguishes intervention in the district from generic intervention in favour of small-and medium-sized firms.

2. Intervention on labour issues

Another question concerns labour, where the unions and their bargaining policies are directly involved. As was noted earlier, among the reasons for the successful growth of the districts in recent years is their ability to make full use of different forms of labour flexibility. Such ability has made and still makes possible the existence of a multiplicity of modes of organising labour operating under a range of individual and social conditions.

This leads in many cases to intolerable conditions of underpaid labour, breaches of labour contracts, and abnormal forms of labour relations. We do not believe that this should or need be the rule. How then is it possible to guide a process of growth in the districts, without damaging the endurance and equilibria of the structure of production? How is it possible to develop fully the many opportunities for differentiation and flexibility without falling inevitably into the practice of underpayment, of black, hidden and illegal labour?

What must the main lines of this intervention be? It is necessary first to effect a far-reaching reform of the way the system of social security is financed. The financing takes the form of a levy on firms that rises according to the number of people employed. Thus, the fact that the industries of the districts are highly labour-intensive means that they bear a greater weight of social security contributions than do production activities employing a lower proportion of labour. Consequently, the present structure of contributions is nothing less than a tax on labour; it gives a financial advantage to firms which subcontract operations with a greater content of labour, and it brings about a net transfer of resources to firms with a greater productivity per employee. It is not surprising that the firms which bear the burden of this system practise widespread evasion of contributions, and resort to "hidden" forms of "employment" such as the guise of self-employment.

A change to a system of contributions based on value added, that the CGIL suggests, would lower the cost of labour, and would, at the same time, improve the ratio between gross and net wage. Moreover, a system based on value added would be better suited to a discriminatory rebate policy which could be used as an instrument to provide incentives for the creation of new districts, in the areas of the South, for example (we will return later to the issue of the industrialisation of the South).

A second guiding line for a policy of labour intervention concerns questions of mobility and flexibility, and hence the need for their regulation. We have already emphasised that the district requires a labour force that is closely linked to a differentiated job structure, a labour force that has a mobile and adaptable nature. To encourage this, there must be large investments in training, and incentives must be provided to encourage the acquisition of skills through inter-firm movement. This process can be helped by institutionalising income protection against variations resulting from carrying out different work activities. This implies changes in the unemployment benefits system.

Another issue to be faced in the districts concerns the relation between remuneration and productivity. Tying remuneration to productivity can only be realised first by individual territorial contract bargaining and then by further bargaining at the level of the individual firm. It is in all cases necessary to base these different stages of contracting on new procedures and powers, which allow the workers to acquire quantitative and qualitative data concerning firm and district production trends. This appears to require legislation to support the unions' rights to contract, in order to allow for territorially determined systems of remuneration to develop independently of national ones.

Closely related is the issue of a new framework and system of rules for governing bargaining in the districts; through this, the widespread phenomenon of failed observance of labour contracts - even those specifically dealing with labour and small-firm relations - can be confronted. So significant is this lack of contract observance that the very ability of the unions to act as representatives is jeopardised.

In respect of remuneration, we can sketch out the following proposals: a maximum limit of weekly working time (to be fixed at a level of around 48 hours); a legal threshold for the beginning of overtime work (to be fixed at about 40 hours); prohibition of a situation where employers might ask workers to compensate for a reduction in factory working hours by taking work away to be carried out elsewhere; hourly wages which are not lower than some portion (e.g. 75 per cent) of the nationally-agreed average rates; definite procedures for the payment of wages, and definite procedures for measuring actual working time. We suggest that these proposals become a set of unbreakable, minimum individual labour rights, not open to further bargaining, and possibly ratified by law.

There would remain an area between such an unbreakable minimum level and clauses of nationally negotiated contracts where it is difficult to enforce agreements: this margin should be dealt with using the instrument of firm bargaining. Firms which provide rates and conditions below the national level might not be allowed exemption from contributions to the national social security fund. We could envisage a progressive range of exemptions from contribution for those firms which admit to being in such situations, and which agree with the unions on a gradual and progressive realignment in respect of the national contract, with a further increased benefit whenever the realignment is realised immediately and fully.

Our consideration of the structure and characteristics of labour markets in the districts leads us to conceive of a radical change in the system of labour rights that would hinge on a worker who is no longer just identified with a particular task and a particular working place, but is a an active participant *in a process* made up of phases of work, training and exchanges between different production activities. The idea of labour as a circuit, and not just a position, brings to light dynamic values, and makes necessary a greater homogenisation of the circumstances of work performance, precisely because the paths of work are not closed, disconnected and opposite dead ends of the labour market. For this reason it is necessary to take account of the interlinking and blending of working experiences typical of the districts, and to remove the distinctions which the *Statuto dei lavoratori*[5] and subsequent legislation defined in the past: distinctions between workers in small and large firms concerning dismissal, rights of assembly, the existence and powers of shop stewards, temporary employment subsidies and other measures to favour labour mobility.

In respect of the question of individual dismissal, there cannot be any rational and socially fair solution other than a thorough application of the principle of "right cause". Lacking this element, reinstatement in the position must be granted, leaving the judgement on the existence of valid reasons for substituting reinstatement by forms of fair compensation to a referee; the judgement should take into consideration the size of the firm - not the size of the unit of production - which carries out the dismissal.

As far as assemblies and union delegates are concerned, the emerging issue is that they must be seen as the means and the subjects for representing and protecting widespread interests (often of a collective sort). This requires a qualitative change in the powers possessed by these figures. The delegate, for instance, inasmuch as he is the accepted voice of the workers in the area, and at the same time a union representative, should be given the duty and power of entering the different units of production, of talking to the workers, of monitoring labour and safety conditions, and of making both judicial and administrative decisions directly or by means of the power to convene a workers' meeting.

The proposals sketched thus far move in the direction of the new industrial policy for labour mentioned above, for which the industrial districts could be a first test case.

5. *Statuto dei Lavoratori* refers to Law No. 300 passed in 1970, which defines the individual rights of workers and the collective rights of unions to be exercised within working places with a minimum of 15 employees.

IV. A model of development for the South

To conclude our discussion we would like to refer - albeit briefly - to the question of the South, since, on the basis of the analyses carried out on the few district-like phenomena found in this part of the country, we have come to the conclusion that the district model may represent an important reference point for reassessing the entire system of public intervention provided by the Italian Parliament in favour of the South.[6]

A new industrialisation of the South will be able to count on large industry only in part, while an ever more crucial role will have to be played by small- and medium-sized firms organised in the form of a district: that is, as areas of production specialisation.

The initiation and further development of such areas might be fostered by using the ample public resources which are already available, whilst the production complexes might take the form of a "network of suppliers" for firms in the North.

V. Final comment

The thesis on the districts which we have presented is ambitious: from the districts as strange and peripheral forms in the industrial life of the country, to districts able to provide new foundations for industrial policy, planning and intervention in the South, and for union contracts. In particular, we would like to give special emphasis to the expansion of industrial districts in the South, and to the relationship between legislation for safeguarding minimum contractual levels and flexible bargaining conditions in the districts. There is much scepticism on both counts in the unions, where different views and interests supporting public intervention prevail. As the districts have never benefited from public expenditure, the unions do not have easy "handholds". Quite apart from ideological considerations this might be the reason why these issues have been neglected for so long. Against whom could a battle for or against the districts have been fought, and how?

We have begun to realise that the way to address these issues is not, as might be expected, by focussing on social conditions, but rather by concentrating on more fundamental questions of production. A broader, more general union interest might follow if the embryonic non-hierarchical production organisation, along with primitive forms of democratic control of the way in which labour is organised, develop further in the districts. Reflections and conclusions about rights of labour intervention and self-regulation may then be drawn for the entire network of capitalistic firms.

---

6. The last law passed in March 1986, No. 64, put aside 120 thousand billion Italian Lire for a period of 10 years.

9 Small-scale enterprise in the ideology of the Italian Left

Sebastiano Brusco and Mario Pezzini

I. Introduction

Since the end of the 1960s, industrial economists, sociologists and local economists have begun to take an interest in systems of small companies concentrated in specific areas that have been termed industrial districts. The idea has emerged that in post-war Italy a particular mode of organising the productive process has slowly developed and spread, distinct from that of single vertically-integrated companies, be they large or small. Industrial districts, it is increasingly felt, represent a new unit of analysis and intervention for industrial policy-making.

The productive units of industrial districts are predominantly small firms, the development of which - and therefore of the industrial districts which they constitute - is strongly influenced by policies promoted by dominant political parties, both at a national and at a local level. These policies are, in turn, partly outcomes of the role small firms are perceived as playing by political ideologies.

In Italy industrial districts are often located in regions where one political party - either the Communists (PCI) or the Christian Democrats - is much stronger than all others. Thus, almost all local authorities in the industrial districts of Emilia-Romagna, Tuscany and Umbria are dominated by the Communist Party, whilst the equivalent areas in Veneto, Friuli and the Marches are controlled by the Christian Democrats. As Trigilia has shown [Trigilia, 1986], these political forces have provided firm support for small business both by legitimising it and by introducing specific policies. Yet this commitment is based on considerations and objectives that vary from party to party and from one area to the next. This chapter sets out to uncover the system of values and judgements that has informed the policy of providing assistance to small enterprise and to consider the way in which this ideology has influenced the policy measures taken at national and local levels.

Attention will be focussed less on the particular measures adopted than on the theoretical background and the ideology from which those measures derive. Above all, an attempt will be made to pinpoint the specific historical outlook and the strategic options that have prompted support for small-scale enterprise. In other words, the object of analysis is the political and cultural climate in which the decisions to back small business have been reached. How widespread, for example, has been the conviction that small companies can be efficient? What role ought small companies to play in the Italian economic system?

The responses to such questions might help to account for the origin and the logic of currently prevailing trends in industrial policy. If the conviction is held that industrial districts are bound to be replaced by more efficient modes of production, any measures taken to help small firms will assume the form of bolstering mechanisms prior to their inevitable extinction. In such circumstances, the most ambitious objective would be to slow down the process of restructuring and to make it as painless as possible. By contrast, if industrial districts are viewed as viable productive systems, set to maintain or even to increase their importance, any measures taken to assist them could be seen as support for a specific form of development.

Given the immensity of this field of enquiry, our analysis will concentrate on the Left, and above all on the Communist Party, and will examine the most important positions that it has articulated over the years.

The analysis will be organised under five headings:

(1) the original positions;

(2) post-1945 and the position of Togliatti;

(3) the 1970s - the decentralisation of production, and the debate with the trade-union Left;

(4) the policies of the Left towards small enterprises at national level.

(5) the policies of the Left in favour of small enterprises at local level and in the industrial districts.

II. The original positions

From the outset, the productive efficiency and the economic and political roles of large and small-scale business have been frequent topics in the debates on early industrial capitalism. Marx argued at length about the inevitability of the change-over from small manufacturing to factory production being concentrated in large plants. He also held that, given the economies of scale involved in energy generation, productive units, in order to be efficient, would have to grow ever larger.

In the discussion on the future of self-employment, held in Erfurt in 1891, the German Social Democrats prophesied bankruptcy and ruin for artisans and peasants, and maintained that to help artisans and peasants *as producers* [our emphasis], by shoring up their outdated forms of enterprises, ran counter to economic development and was not practicable.

Looking closer at this issue, it is perhaps worth referring to Kautsky's *Die Agrarfrage*[1] [Kautsky, 1959]. Whilst in general, especially in

1. References and quotations are from the Italian translation of *Die Agrarfrage* - *La questione agraria* [Kautsky, 1959].

Italy, Kautsky's position is not deemed decisive, the aim here is to use it mainly as a yardstick, i.e., as terms of reference for comparisons with the positions which emerged subsequently in the debate in Italy.

It should be stated at once that Kautsky was utterly convinced of the technical superiority of large-scale agricultural and industrial enterprise. *Die Agrarfrage* - moderating, to some extent, the view expressed at Erfurt - concludes that "we must not expect either the end of the large firm nor that of the small one", but that "nothing is more absurd than the idea that the small company can withstand competition from the big one". If small business retains its importance, this is basically due to:

- the time it takes for large-scale business to penetrate the different sectors of industry [p. 161];
- the "political reasons" for which "state power supports social strata that have lost their economic strength" [p. 161];
- "fashionable society's preference for handwork as against machine work in the case of products intended for their own personal use" [p. 164].

The positions of Kautsky and of Marx were shared by many exponents of the Left and they exerted a significant influence on the entire subsequent debate. For example, Lenin, an admirer of Kautsky's *Agrarfrage*, commenting on the section on "The technical superiority of large companies" referred, albeit cautiously, to a "*law* [our emphasis] of superiority of large-scale production" [Lenin, 1962, p. 319]. In respect of industry, the point is made even more categorically and mention is made of "the indisputable fact of the elimination of small-scale by large-scale production" [Lenin, 1962, p. 318].

But what role, in Kautsky's view, do small companies play in the economic system? For a first approach to this question, it is worth looking at Kautsky's attempt to classify companies from a socialist perspective, i.e., in terms of a society from which all the irrationalities of the capitalist market would be expunged. From this point of view, there are "necessary" and there are "parasitic" small firms [Kautsky, 1959, pp. 493-500]. The "necessary" firms include artisans working in sectors not yet "conquered by the machine", "in which big business does not yet predominate", but where it is clearly destined to do so. Then there are those artisans who meet the need for more expensive products that are better tailored to individual requirements. Given the increased affluence of the masses - which would come about under socialism - these artisans would survive and might even "flourish". "Parasitic" companies, i.e., those "that have long been technically obsolete and economically superfluous", might gradually disappear - if large-scale business were ready to take on a sufficient number of wage earners under tolerable conditions.

Kautsky was quite certain as to the relative importance of the two types of firm: with the ever growing spread of machines, more and more small companies would fall into the "parasitic" category. These would make up the overwhelming majority: even in a situation of widespread affluence (i.e., under socialism), the "necessary" small companies would constitute "merely an exception to the general type of production", based on large-scale business. Small parasitic firms, furthermore, would live on.

Kautsky wrote that, "the more acute class struggle becomes, and the more menacing Social-Democracy grows, the more inclined are governments to allow small firms that have become economically superfluous to lead a more or less parasitic existence. In this way, the process of their disappearance might perhaps be slowed down..." [Kautsky, 1959, Part I, Chapter VII, p. 162].

The answer to our question is therefore that the small firm is not viewed only, and not even principally, as a survival from the previous stage in the development of the productive forces. On the contrary, under capitalism it assumes important functions that go far beyond its own efficiency, and which account for the *mystery* of its lasting presence [Kautsky, Part I, Chapter VII, p. 162].

It should be added that at the end of Kautsky's analysis there are a number of references to Chapter 23 of *Das Kapital* [Marx, 1974], in which Marx introduces the concept of "relative overpopulation". The process of accumulation creates a working population that is surplus to the requirements of capital. That section of the population that is not fully employed in the productive process thus becomes part of the "industrial reserve army". This army, partially enlisted in phases of rapid expansion and partially demobbed in periods of crisis, constitutes, with its alternate swelling and shrinking, an element of flexibility that proves useful in the regulation of wages and the handling of conflict. The point, however, is that this overpopulation assumes many forms: the ranks of this army include not only those who are actually jobless, but also those workers who are formally "employed" in irregular forms of work, e.g. home workers, and, among others, a set of independent or "freelance" workers employed in agriculture and industry.

So, according to Kautsky, what type of approach and what elements of active policy should be introduced towards small business on the basis of this analysis? The answer, at least in part, can be inferred from what has already been stated. The process of capitalist accumulation obstructs the full development of the productive forces and makes use of "parasitic firms" as an indirect instrument for smoothing over its own contradictions. Owners of small business cling to their firms "because a purely proletarian existence strikes them as even more uncertain and miserable than their own, but sometimes also because they cannot find any means of subsistence within the wage-earning proletariat" [Kautsky, 1959, Part II, Chapter V, p. 493]. If, therefore, Social-Democracy pursues social development and if, in accordance with this aim, it does not defend the interests of entrepreneurs, there is no reason, either, why it should defend the interests of companies whose owners are in fact proletarians disguised as entrepreneurs.

In Kautsky's opinion, however, there is one aspect of the mentality of "independent workers" that needs to be taken into account. Such workers simultaneously possess a "proprietorial soul" and a "proleterian soul", and, however subject they may be to "proletarianisation", they remain susceptible to the illusory "hope" of one day becoming completely independent. It is in the interest of the conservative parties, but not in that of the Social-Democrats, to cultivate this illusion. As a result, social-democracy has, on the one hand, to address the problem of how to "neutralise" the conservative impulses of small entrepreneurs in such a way that they are not open to the manipulation of the bourgeoisie; and, on the other, to promote alternative and non-entrepreneurial models of identification. This entails the promotion of measures that have more to do with the goals of social policy (education, health, justice, transport) and with the defence of civil rights, than with enterprise growth and development. Further, it entails the development of forms of organisation constructed around the notion that proletarians in entrepreneurial disguise should be organised not as entrepreneurs but rather in close association with those who are proletarians in both name and fact.

III. Post-1945 and the position of Togliatti

The new thinking of the Italian Left in the years following the Second World War is of great relevance to this whole topic. The Italian Communist Party was engaged in drawing up an innovatory strategy that contrasted with traditional "roads" to socialism. This strategy accorded a crucial role to the policy of fostering alliances between the working class and the "productive middle classes", i.e., peasants, small shopkeepers, artisans and small industrial entrepreneurs. The range of potential allies of the working class was gradually extended to take in this set of social groupings foreign to the revolutionary alliances of Marxist tradition. Whereas Kautsky, in *Die Agrarfrage*, wrote that "Social-Democracy does not represent the interests of entrepreneurs" and that "small entrepreneurs" had if anything to be "neutralised", Togliatti, in 1946, at Reggio Emilia, in his famous speech entitled "The Middle Classes and Red Emilia" [Togliatti, 1974], declared that "there is no clash between the interests that we defend and those of intermediate social groups".

The reasons for the offer of alliance and collaboration made to small business were very complex and demand thorough analysis. Such analysis would need to focus on the specific cultural roots of the Italian Left, taking into consideration the influence not only of the Third International, but also of the tradition founded by Benedetto Croce, and that of marginalist liberal economic thinking. Put extremely succinctly, the Left appears to have derived its strategy of alliances from two sources: a) the conviction that - once the war of liberation was over - there was a pressing need to draw the productive petty bourgeoisie out of the conservative camp, and b) the determination to remove those obstacles that had hindered Italian industrial development. The basis of this thinking is already discernible in Togliatti's *Lezioni sul fascismo* [Togliatti, 1970], but in the years following the Second World War it was fully ratified and became official PCI strategy.

Let us look first at the more immediately political reasons. In the early post-war years, the parties of the Left feared a new wave of reaction.

The reasoning ran as follows. The material bases of Fascism lay in the strategies of the major economic groups which, in Italy, exercised great power and influence over the political system. But Fascism also enjoyed an extraordinary degree of consensus among the broad masses. As Togliatti formulated it, Fascism was a "mass-based reactionary movement". It was therefore considered that an important task for the Left was to construct a broad democratic and anti-fascist front, while averting the danger of any future convergence between the economy's commanding heights and the petty bourgeoisie.

To the leaders of the PCI, and especially to Togliatti, this task appeared very complex. Fascism left in its wake a social structure in tatters. By means of corporatism and a variety of far-reaching cultural policies, it had succeeded in prising apart social groups that had shared common interests and the problem was only partly alleviated by the Resistance movement which was led not only by skilled workers employed in the large factories, but also by artisans and share-croppers.

Consequently, Togliatti believed that the workers' movement needed to face up to its own tradition and to eliminate the errors that it had committed during the struggles that it had supported between the end of the First World War and the rise of Fascism. Togliatti was convinced that the Left's exclusive commitment to and defence of the interests of workers and labourers had pushed the middle classes into the arms of the Fascist movement.

As for the economic reasons, the position that prevailed within the PCI in the post-war years may be summarised - again, very succinctly - as follows: Italian development suffers from "original taints" and is held up by the control that monopolies exert over the economy. In particular, large monopolies:

- limit output - and avoid increasing their own productive capacity - in order to maximise their profits: this leads to high unemployment, low wages, and economic stagnation;
- prevent competition with large foreign companies through their rigid control of foreign trade, and provide support for autarchy;
- limit, as far as they can, the setting-up in business of new competitors, not only through market mechanisms, but also by means of all those administrative and political measures that they are in a position to demand and obtain: among other things, this strategy acts as a decisive brake on the growth of smaller companies.

Seen from this standpoint, monopolies were a pathological component of Italy's retarded capitalist development, rather than its fruit. The task of the Left was above all to overcome this "blocked" development or, to put it differently, to ensure the full development of the productive forces with a view to attaining that stage at which a transition to socialism becomes possible. The so-called "new course in economic policy", supported by the Left in Italy at the end of the 1940s, was articulated within a fundamentally free-market perspective. Admittedly, there was no evidence of any conviction that the market could regulate itself and optimise resources. Yet there was an apparent certainty that this optimisation could indeed be guaranteed once competitive conditions were restored. And it was precisely this that the State had to set out to achieve through the public ownership of companies, credit controls, and the ensuring of even-handed behaviour by the institutions.

This combination of political and economic grounds set the conditions for a political trade-off: while small entrepreneurs were called upon to take part, alongside the working class, in the struggle to defend and expand democracy, they were given the assurance that restrictive autarchic policies as well as artificial obstacles to the growth of their companies would be removed. Furthermore, based on the convergence of material interests, this alliance was to prove much more solid than a straightforward political pact. For, as they grew, small companies tended to restore competitive conditions and thereby to counter monopolistic stagnation with increased incomes and an expansion in employment.

Evidence that this alliance was not merely tactical but in fact represented a fundamental choice of strategy was provided in the programme statement issued at the 8th Congress of the PCI in 1956: "given the structure of the Italian economy, the artisan sector must be protected and developed, and co-operation with small and medium-scale production must be fostered" [PCI, 1957]. And again: "... the possibility of a *permanent alliance* between the working class and layers of the middle class in both town and country is provided by a convergence of economic and social interests that is rooted in the historical development, and in the present structure, of capitalism. The deadweight of the monopolies on the country's economy is so suffocating that it is in the interest of non-monopoly companies within industry and commerce to support the struggle of the working class against the monopolies" [PCI, 1957].

This alliance was so important that in 1959 Togliatti was prepared to countenance the development of different industrial relations for large and small-scale business. Later this was referred to as a policy of granting "discounts" to small business.

In essence, the positions of the Italian Left in the post-war period, at least up until the years of the "economic miracle" may be summarised as follows:

- large-scale business is the most efficient form of production, but it may lead, as in the case of Italy, to the creation of monopolies and resulting distortions;
- small businesses are small because they have not yet grown; some small companies will successfully grow and come to compete with large firms: in a competitive market, the presence and growth of small firms will counteract monopolistic trends;
- artisans and small businesses are strategic allies of the working class and should be given active assistance to expand and be defended from the monopolies.

In so far as large-scale business is deemed technologically superior and more efficient, this view is obviously similar to that taken by Kautsky and by most of the Leftist tradition. Yet it differs sharply both in the role it assigned small companies, and in the attitudes that the Left was to adopt toward them. Small companies were not seen as an indirect instrument in a process of accumulation wholly controlled by big business, but rather as its potential competitors. And, finally, rather than having to be "neutralised" small companies were to be helped.

IV. The 1970s - The decentralisation of production, and the debate with the trade-union Left

At the end of the 1960s, and more so during the 1970s, a fresh outlook on the problem began to gain ground in certain sectors of the Communist Party. This was strongly influenced by the increasing decentralisation of production, i.e., the commissioning by large companies of outside (usually small) firms to take over stages in the manufacturing process previously carried out internally.

The ideas underlying this line of analysis run as follows. Faced with the rigidities imposed by the unions, and the escalation of conflict on their shop-floors, the big Italian companies fall back on a kind of "threadbare" capitalist response: instead of seeking to regain their competitive edge by means of investment and technical innovation, they decide to decentralise, putting work out to businesses which are small enough to elude union control. The low technological level of these small firms is more than offset by their low wage levels, their poor (unhealthy and hazardous) working conditions, their evasion of tax and social contributions, their extreme labour intensity, and their ability to hire and fire, introduce overtime or cut working hours at will.

The technological backwardness of small firms, it is further argued, is destined to become increasingly pronounced. Those that have "grown up in the shadow of large-scale business" generally work for a single major customer: in practice they are separate units of a single company. In a buyer's monopoly, such as this, the buyer can fix prices. The large company therefore suffocates the small one, by squeezing profits and thereby undermining its ability to make the investments necessary to update its technology.

As Claudio Sabattini wrote in 1972 [Sabattini, 1972]: with the process of decentralisation, "an industrial sector is created - comprising small and medium-sized companies - much of which is characterised by utter subordination to the plans of the large company, and by stagnation of investment. This sector is economically extremely fragile and is continually exposed to decisions taken by the large companies, who determine the small firm's level of production, the use made of its equipment, and hence indirectly even the number of its employees. The result is a sector that expands and contracts in response to the economic cycle of big capital, with all the obvious consequences that this entails for workers' conditions and for levels of employment".

It is not hard to discern in this suggested interpretation many elements of the line prevailing in those years in the trade-union Left. Most strikingly, just as in the theoretical frame of reference applied to the struggles of Italy's "Hot Autumn", the large company is deemed central, both as a site of power and capital management, and, as we shall soon see, as the privileged battle-ground between capital and labour, the only place where the workers' movement is able to score some successes.

In this context, the role of the small firm is totally subordinate. Its job is to enforce exploitation for the benefit of the big company, which is prevented from so doing itself by the higher degree of control exerted by workers and trade-unionists.

In contrast with Kautsky's analysis, small firms are not seen as an indirect instrument of large business, allocated the task of looking after segments of relative overpopulation, but as a direct instrument enabling big business to regain flexibility and to reduce costs without the burdens of major investment, simply by means of a sharp reduction in wages and a worsening of workers' conditions. In contrast with Togliatti's analysis, small firms are not seen as potential competitors of big business, supposedly paralysed by the monopolies' control over the economy. Small firms only produce intermediate products of large companies and, far from being their competitors, could almost be said to be their collaborators or tools.

From this standpoint, the issue of alliances looks quite different. If small firms are blind tools of large ones, and if - when confronted with big business - they are unable to defend their own profits, it is hard to see how there can be any co-operation between them and the workers' movement. Workers and small entrepreneurs certainly share some interests: both would like to see a reduction in the power of the large companies or groups and a reasonable expansion of the productive system. Such changes might pave the way to an improvement in workers' conditions and make available to small businesses forms of development that would free them from dependency. But any trade-union policy that grants concessions to small companies has to be rejected: it might after all merely serve to reduce the costs of the large companies and hold back development, triggering further decentralisation and a drop in investment in large and small companies alike.

In short, if small firms are a direct instrument of exploitation, a Kautskyan policy designed to ignore or neutralise them is simply not thinkable - nor is a policy of 'discounts'. Instead, working conditions in large and small firms should be brought into line, so that decentralisation becomes a pointless manoeuvre. Furthermore, in large companies, it is essential that union control over investments be tightened and that the practice of decentralisation be actively combated. It would also be a good idea to seek investments in small companies to ensure faster growth. Finally, bargaining at firm level should become more frequent for small firms, and the workers in small businesses should be involved (as had not happened before) in the process of formulating the bargaining platform at the national level.

If the new position was commonly expressed in the early 1970s within the CGIL (*Confederazione Generale Italiano del Lavoro*) and the CISL (*Confederazione Italiana Sindacati Lavoratori*), and also within some sections of the PCI, the leadership of the PCI did not essentially alter its attitude towards small business. Even if the economic and social context had changed since the post-war years, it was still felt that a policy of alliances with the so-called "middle classes" was essential to isolate and defeat conservative and reactionary groups and to carry through a "programme of moral and economic recovery".

The concluding remarks at the most important conference that the PCI had so far devoted to small and medium-sized business - held in Milan in 1974 [Amendola, 1974] - were entrusted to Amendola. His speech resounded with the classic themes of the party line and emphasised the essential continuity with the positions that the party had expressed at its 8th Congress in 1956. He declared: "The Communist Party does not aim to conclude a precarious tactical agreement, but rather to lay the foundations for an alliance between the working class and the productive middle classes destined to set the Italian economy on a new course, within the framework of a democratic programme and a policy of reforms. ...A labour alliance is also essential to beat back Fascist attempts at revival. In 1919-22 the middle classes were pushed to the right, in part due to errors made by the workers' movement, and they formed part of the mass base of Fascism. Today the alliance between the working class and the middle classes is vital to the defence and renewal of democracy."

This line and this overall strategic design served as the basis for the rebuttal of arguments fielded by those who pointed to the significance of "dependent decentralisation", and who urged that the policy of alliances be followed with greater caution. In view of the increasing weight of small companies in the Italian industrial structure it was argued that, apart from certain exceptions in the South, the small company was no longer 'marginal' and that, in the majority of cases, it was in a position to make use of new technology, able to orient itself toward new products and to adapt existing ones to new tastes, able to penetrate international markets and to pay salaries comparable to those paid by large companies. For this type of company, "an active policy of support and of technical, commercial and financial assistance" was envisaged. The aims of this policy would be: "to enhance those business skills already present in most small- and medium-sized firms; to provide services that small- and medium-sized firms are not often in a position to organise for themselves; to free small and medium-sized firms from the burden of rent" [Peggio, 1974].

The focus of these arguments was almost always on *individual* small firms that - even if this was not stated explicity - produced for the final market. The fact that such companies were not isolated, and were bound up in a dense fabric of relations and a division of labour, was not given much attention: the analysis overlooked organisational and structural relations between firms. This neglect had two consequences: on the one hand, it made it easier to gloss over the real problems posed by increasing decentralisation - which in many cases, especially in the early 1970s, really did lead to relations of dependency; and on the other hand, there was the failure to observe that many of the innovative and efficient small companies were located within new forms of industrial organisation, which were beginning to emerge just then, and which indeed were subsequently labelled "industrial districts".

Essentially, the PCI still held that the representative small company was one that, despite its efficiency and innovative flair, remained small because of obstacles preventing it from growing (credit, technical assistance, relations with public authorities). These obstacles were thought to be a result of the control of large economic groups over the economy, their influence on economic policy, and inefficiencies in public administration. It was still believed that there existed a kind of competition for development between large firms on the one hand and small firms on the other. This view led to the notion that what the Italian economy needed was firmer management and guidance to ensure a smoother and better balanced development.

As regards union policy, the PCI acknowledged that conflict between the working class and small- and medium-sized entrepreneurs could give rise to contradictions undermining a strategy of alliances. The refusal to grant wage "discounts" to small firms was reaffirmed ("equal pay for equal work"), but unions were encouraged to adopt a policy of "careful attention", involving tailored, or "differentiated", contracts, and of a step-by-step approach to struggles. What this ought to mean in practice was never clarified. But the fact remains that no proposals were formulated for the removal of inconsistencies in regulations affecting workers employed in small firms and those employed in large firms; nor was there any mention of possible ad hoc proposals on industrial democracy to take account of the specific conditions and needs of those employed by small business.

V. The policies of the Left toward small-scale enterprises at national level

Having commented on the declarations of principle and policy, it will now be worth examining the provisions in favour of small enterprises that the PCI has promoted and implemented. In this section we will only deal with policies followed at national level. Those developed and financed at local level will be considered in the next section.

The aim is not so much to assess the effectiveness of the policies pursued, as to lay bare the model of industrial structure around which the measures introduced were constructed.

Firstly, the parties of the Left have argued in favour of legislation to provide backing for small firms and for their consortia. Although the Christian Democratic Party has never put up strong opposition to such demands, the Left has been almost alone in its insistence on the need for the state to grant small firms favourable terms of credit and no-security loans, and in lobbying for the introduction into company finance legislation of provisions for the allocation of specific funds to small companies. Given Italian rituals of partnership-based democracy, the increase in funds earmarked for small firms and their associations has always represented an essential stage in the process of securing the passage of these laws.

Furthermore, the effort to create the conditions for a stable alliance with small entrepreneurs has generated a different framework of industrial relations. The Left has given its backing to a trade-union policy that distinguishes between large and small firms. The bargaining tables for small firms have always been separate, and the forms of struggle used less incisive. National work contracts affecting smaller companies have, almost without exception, been more favourable to employers than is the case with specific contracts with the larger firms. By the same token, with the agreement of the Left, labour legislation has also differentiated between large and small companies. In this connection, the two most important and exemplary cases are Law No. 604 (1966) and the Workers' Statute of 1970. In accordance with Law No. 604, in cases of unfair dismissal the employer has a choice between reinstating the worker and paying a penalty. But these sanctions are only envisaged for firms with more than 33 employees. The 1970 Workers' Statute provides for the reinstatement of an unfairly dismissed worker, but only in production units with more than 15 employees.[2]

As a further element in this strategy towards small enterprises and the middle classes, it may be noted that, unlike in other European countries, the Italian Left has found itself in agreement with the Christian Democrats regarding the need for legislation to control the growth of large-scale distribution; and has promoted a policy aimed at hindering the growth of large companies by severely restricting the granting of licences. This is the sole reason why in present-day Italy small and very small retail shops are still so thick on the ground, and the gap between wholesale and retail prices is so wide.

How should this attitude towards small firms, and towards protecting them, be interpreted? On what model of industrial and productive structures is it based? From what kind of analysis does it derive?

Some authors (suffice it here to quote Paggi and D'Angelillo [1986]) argue that this behaviour bears witness to a profound shift in the ideology of the PCI. According to them, the Italian Communist Party, in pursuing its alliance with the middle classes, has modified its relationship with the working class and the subordinate workers who have made up its real constituency. In so doing, it has lost sight of the essential questions of industrial strategy for Italy and has devoted less and less attention to the need to modernise the financial system, to keep the large economic groups under control, and to orient and govern technological innovation.

This reading of the data has many points in common with that of the union Left in the first half of the 1970s. In our opinion it is mistaken. For, all the interventions described above have taken as their basic point of

---

2. It should be noted, however, that since 1988 the PCI and the CGIL have been arguing that there should be less discrimination in favour of small firms and that some guarantee should be introduced against dismissal even for workers in firms with less than 15 employees.

reference a single small enterprise, potentially efficient but incapable of actually being so by virtue of its size; requiring to grow and needing to be assisted to do so. Thus several interventions - especially those offering loans to firms, and those that restrict licences for retailing to the large firms - make a point of insisting that the smaller firms should actually become bigger by associating together in consortia, which are to be granted countless privileges. Moreover, the small enterprise so considered is always a firm producing for the finished goods market. Indeed, no specific provisions whatever are made for firms engaged in intermediate stages of production. One can plainly see the contradiction inherent in this policy which proclaims the maximum faith in the small enterprise: provided that it grows - either by itself or by associating with other firms - and ceases to be small. Moreover, there is still the same fast conviction that the success of Italian products in the international markets depends entirely on what happens in the large companies, that struggle in large factories is of central importance, and that large firms are the only ones which heavily influence the practice of government. This line of thinking is amply witnessed not only by the official documents of the Communist Party, but also by the various conferences dedicated to analysing the party line towards small enterprises; and, above all, by the want of attention towards the ever-growing role assumed by small firms in the Italian system of production during the 1970s and 1980s.

VI. The policies of the Left in favour of small enterprises at local level and in the industrial districts

Local policies of the Left in favour of small enterprises show sharp differences from one another. Certain regions, such as Sicily and Sardinia, are endowed by law with an autonomy in industrial policy that is much more extensive than that enjoyed by other areas. These regions, which show a much lower growth rate than that of Northern Italy, have experienced only two kinds of intervention: those for establishing infrastructures and industrial areas, and the more conventional, more familiar kinds providing for financial incentives of every sort for all industrial enterprises, and especially for the smaller firms. These latter funds - no-security loans, low-interest credits for investments, easy-term credits for working capital - are no different from those provided at national level, except for the fact that they are often available to large as well as small enterprises and involve larger amounts.

In contrast, the regions of Tuscany, Emilia, Umbria, and others equipped with numerous industrial districts, have very much less power of decision in industrial policy - indeed, almost none. These regions, moreover, have been confined by severe budget restrictions to taking initiatives that could be implemented with only slender funds. Consequently, the industrial policies pursued by the regional, provincial and municipal authorities and the Chambers of Commerce have been less conventional and more innovatory.

For a long time industrial policies in these areas took the form of a kind of town planning. As in Southern Italy, though on a much more extensive scale, small firms were allotted plots of land suitable for the development of industrial plants. This enabled them to sidestep both the excessive costs resulting from property speculation, and the long and tiresome search for an appropriate site. These very simple measures were followed, however, by various more complex initiatives. Among these mention must be made of local authority-initiated work training schemes (an area in which local authorities have considerable expertise), the establishment of, and continuing support for, technical high schools, and, of course, the positive effect - albeit indirect - of interventions in matters relating to social services (nursery schools, aid for the elderly, public transport, etc.).

More recently, and in particular at the end of the 1970s, and above all in Emilia-Romagna - which since the end of the Second World War has been governed without interruption by the Left - a variety of new and original measures have emerged. The most interesting of these have been the centres offering companies "real services".

These centres came into being to provide services that small companies, owing to their size, were unable to handle on their own, and which the market had failed to supply spontaneously. For example, small firms do not always possess the ability to obtain up-to-the-minute information on new products and technologies, or the skills needed to assess the latest international market trends, or a familiarity with regulations applying to the importation of goods into different countries. Private consultants are unlikely to set up in business to supply such specialised needs. Often there are too few firms to induce a consultant to acquire the requisite specialisation, the start-up investment is too great, and returns are likely to be too slow in materialising. Moreover, one of the tasks of these centres is to show the relevance of information or procedures that companies themselves do not know, or see as outside their range, or consider unimportant for their marketing strategy.

Among the local initiatives, mention must also be made of the artisan associations. The most active of these is undoubtedly the CNA (Confederazione Nazionale dell'Artigianato) which, in many provinces, started in the period immediately after the Second World War as a sectoral federation of the CGIL thereafter to become autonomous in the early 1950s. Both the CNA and, to a lesser extent, the other artisan associations began by offering services relating to matters such as book-keeping and the preparation of pay packets, then broadened their field to include areas such as the calculation and payment of indirect taxes, income tax declarations, and insurance contributions.

As a result of the popularity of the services provided to its members, the CNA has attained levels of expertise that often outdo those of private consultants, and yet prices have remained lower. Recently, these organisations have branched out still further: they now promote professional training courses, establish associations for the purchase of raw materials, help companies to take part in trade fairs and exhibitions, co-ordinate the demand for credit with the banks so as to secure low-interest loans and set up associations to provide credit guarantees.

Some figures may help to give an idea of the importance that these organisations have assumed in certain areas. In the province of Modena, where approximately 24,000 small businesses are based, the CNA has about 13,000 member firms, some 40 local offices, and 540 employees on its payroll. In Emilia-Romagna as a whole, where there are approximately 140,000 small businesses - 50% of which are members of the CNA - the CNA keeps the books of 40,000 businesses, and each month prepares roughly 70,000 pay packets. With the passage of time the "left wing" connotations of CNA have gradually faded, so that today it operates over the whole artisan range, offering itself as a centre of association for all artisans.

As can easily be seen, all the above mentioned interventions relating to the central areas of Italy - those by local authorities and those by trade associations - are of another kind altogether from the interventions in Sardinia and Sicily, and those carried out by national authorities. Instead of loans, the small enterprises are offered services. Instead of reducing the expense of keeping accounts and preparing pay packets by providing financial assistance, the organisations themselves have set up an office to perform these tasks at a lower cost. Instead of giving a contribution to a firm that commissions market research, or requires a consultant for information on, say, French or German technical standards, a centre is funded to gather this information and disseminate it throughout the production system. The associations may follow this line in order to swell their membership, the local authorities do so in order to equip the entire district with skills that would otherwise not be available. All of which suggests, among other things, that the organisations, too, are gradually moving from the provision of, so to speak, common or garden services - book- keeping, for instance - towards riskier areas of activity, for which they need to acquire expertise that is rare on the local market.

In order to return to the specific topic of this chapter - without confining ourselves merely to recounting established facts - we must now enquire into the relationship between day-to-day operation and principles, between achieved policy initiatives and the ideology that inspired them. The fact that so often the initiatives have been tailored to the needs of the industrial districts may lead one to think that the analytical hypotheses of Togliatti have been revised and modified. Actually this is not so. Only in Emilia, between the late 1970s and early 1980s, did the local administration take steps in this direction and attempt to establish an original theoretical framework. But the attempt was unsuccessful and has not altered the opinion current among party cadres, so that neither in Emilia nor elsewhere has there ever been any explicit and detailed rethinking of the analysis of industrial structure put forward by the Eighth Congress of the PCI.

The industrial policies described above sprang from the need to "do something", from attention paid to the ongoing processes, from the care taken to discover people's requirements and the commitment to tackling these problems; but not from any change in perspective or interpretation. By way of confirmation, suffice it to consider how much stress has been laid on the need for small enterprises to associate in production consortia, even when it was obvious that the only consortia that could succeed were those engaged in purchasing or in the production of services. But what is most significant is the record of the real service centres. The first of these was started almost by chance as a spin-off from a successful experience of work training. The others were then set up and grew under the stimulus of good intentions and the common sense and pragmatism of people who were eager to repeat a successful experience. But there has never been any theoretical reflection on the specificity of the firms in the industrial district, or the needs of the district, or its role in the national economy where small isolated businesses, industrial districts and large companies exist side by side. It is as though there were a sort of schizophrenia between efficient operation based on what actually goes on in the area and involving whole communities, and the basic analytical standpoints. Perhaps this diagnosis is too harsh and, in Emilia at any rate, there may have been some theoretical reflection. But it is quite certain that the innovative thrust and specific value of these interventions - targeted at the products of the district and carefully singled out to overcome the bottlenecks impeding development within the district - have still not managed to gain access to the store of policy demands of either the PCI or PSI (Partito Socialista Italiano).

VII. Conclusions

The foregoing pages have shown that the reference model employed by the Left to define the role and the requirements of small firms has remained practically unchanged from the post-war period to the present. The view put forward by Togliatti, and confirmed by the Eighth Congress of the PCI in 1956, has remained unaffected by the debate over decentralisation, by the changes in Italy's productive structure, by the successes of Italian-made products, and by the discussions of economists and sociologists of the "Third Italy" and industrial districts.

Nevertheless at the local level, as on the periphery of the Communist Party, where the needs of the communities in question can be more easily perceived, several important initiatives have been implemented that represent innovations with respect to the past. The result is that the small enterprises in the districts - however belatedly and in spite of insufficient means - have found backing and assistance for their growth from the institutions.

However, whether at the periphery or at the centre of the Party, theory has yet to take the opportunity to focus adequately on the new producers. And although some steps have been taken in this direction in a few regions, the problem has never attracted the attention of the Party as a whole, let alone stimulated a fresh look at the dominant paradigm.

The penalty paid for this shortcoming has been high. The blame must be laid entirely on the hypothesis of the Togliattian model according to which the small firms are all equal and all have strong growth potentials as long as certain conditions are guaranteed.

Thus, for example, not enough thought has been devoted to the nature of many of the retail shops which have enjoyed such staunch support. These small businesses - which Kautsky would have called "parasites" - were, and are, merely a refuge for relative overpopulation. Perhaps the "proprietorial soul" of these entrepreneurs has been "cultivated" too assiduously, thus delaying for too long the development in Italy of an efficient retail distribution system. One rather particular but nonetheless significant instance of this policy is the excessive readiness to heed protests from shopkeepers over the closure of city centres to traffic.

The Left has perhaps been hasty in taking for granted the capacity for growth of small companies in the South. More precise data are needed, relating to the technological level, the outlet markets, and the professional and managerial skills of these firms. But the data that are available show that very few local companies have grown big enough to operate on the national market. And this is in spite of an extremely favourable system of incentives, as regards investment loans, working credit, and whatever form of funding the entrepreneur may seek. It is of course possible to blame the snail's pace of local bureaucracy: but other data suggest that bureaucratic inefficiency is not as rife as is sometimes claimed. The effects of organised crime are certainly devastating; but firms in Puglia and Sardinia, regions where organised crime poses a less serious threat, also suffer from arrested growth. So the problem must lie elsewhere.

The fact is that these small firms - unlike the ones Togliatti spoke of - are small traditional businesses, suited to operating on a local market: in other words, the small businesses which Marx predicted would collapse before the "heavy artillery" of low-priced mass production.

Lastly, the hypothesis that the small enterprises are uniform and, as Togliatti said, ready to grow and achieve efficiency, has obscured the fact that Italy has been developing an original mode of production: namely, the industrial district where small firms can often be efficient even without growing. Consequently, the steps to support small firms currently envisaged in proposals for legislation by the Left are not innovatory; they take no account of the successful experiences in various regions and, twenty years after the first debates on this subject, they do not even bother to develop specific measures to tackle the needs of the firms in the various districts.

Most importantly, the old ideology has obscured innovations in analysis put forward by students of the industrial districts. Of particular significance, in this respect is the increasingly common position which holds that a productive system must be defined not only on the basis of its technical characteristics, but also in relation to its cultural background and social relationships. This, in its turn, leads to the conclusion that there is a whole range of different ways of meeting the demands made by technology, and that there is no single *technically efficient answer.* Sometimes the large multinational comes off better, thanks to its political clout, its control over prices for mass produced articles, or its ability to make rapid changes and innovations. At other times, industrial districts may be at an advantage, due to their ability to stimulate local imagination and intelligence. On yet other occasions, a company from Eastern Europe or from a newly-industrialised country may conquer the market, on the strength of its low labour costs. Or, lastly, a large Japanese firm may make effective use of its ability to penetrate markets by using a long-term investment strategy.

We would therefore argue that different mixes of technology, social relations, levels of agreement, value systems, research, and state assistance can compete on the market. Each productive system has a different pattern of strengths and weaknesses and can therefore, in turn, score successes and suffer setbacks.

Viewed from this perspective, there is no longer any sense in raising those old sacred questions of Marxist discussion: "Are large or small companies more efficient?", "Are small companies able to compete with large ones?", and "Why is it that small firms survive?" For it is obvious that a different measure must be tailored to each different case, in accordance with the desired objectives.

References

Amendola, Giorgio. 1974. "Conclusioni", in *La piccola e media industria nella crisi dell'economia italiana*, Atti del convegno tenuto a Milano il 4-5-6 novembre 1974, Rome, Editori Riuniti.

Kautsky, K. 1959. *La questione agraria*, (Italian translation of *Die Agrarfrage*), Milan, Feltrinelli.

Lenin, V.I. 1962. "La piccola produzione nell'agricoltura", in *La teoria della questione agraria*, Milan, Feltrinelli.

Marx, K. 1974. *Il capitale*, Turin, Libro Primo, UTET.

Paggi, Leonardo; D'Angelillo, Massimo. 1986. *I comunisti italiani e il riformismo*, Turin, Einaudi.

Peggio, Eugenio. 1974. *La piccola e media industria nella crisi dell'economia italiana*, Rome, Tipografia ITER.

Sabattini, Claudio. 1972. "Relazione introduttiva", in FIM-CISL, FIOM-CGIL, uilm-uil Emilia-Romagna: *Atti convegno piccole e medie aziende metalmeccaniche industriali e artigiane*, Bologna.

Togliatti, P. 1970. *Lezioni sul fascismo*, Rome, Editori Riuniti.

---. 1974. "Ceto medio e Emilia Rossa", in *Politica nazionale ed Emilia Rossa*, Rome, Editori Riuniti.

Trigilia, C. 1986. *Grandi partiti e piccole imprese: comunisti e democristiani nelle regioni a economia diffusa*, Bologna, Il Mulino.

10 Work and politics in the Third Italy's industrial districts

Carlo Trigilia

I. Introduction: An institutional perspective

Small firm development has been a crucial aspect of the Italian economy in recent years. The purpose of this chapter is to draw attention to labour relations in the small-firm industrial districts of the Third Italy's regions. It will be argued that the quality of work in these settings has been significantly shaped by an institutional context characterised by a peculiar equilibrium between "traditional" and "modern" components. But one cannot understand the formation and operation of such a context without considering its political features: i. e. the role of local political subcultures.

It is now well known that the regions in which small firms and industrial districts have grown fastest, and predominate in the industrial structure, are mainly located in the centre and north-east of the country. It is true that the phenomenon is also to be found in the north-west and in the south, but in the case of the former there is also a particularly strong concentration of large firms and metropolitan areas, whilst in that of the latter there still are major problems associated with underdevelopment. It is the regions of the so-called Third Italy (Central and North-east Italy, fig. 1), therefore, that are characterised by the marked predominance of small firms. Indicators such as the rate of growth of value-added, investments, productivity and employment show the dynamism of industry in these areas, especially in the 1970s and the early 1980s. The traditional sectors of industry - textiles, clothing, shoes and furniture - predominate, but there is also a significant presence of modern sectors, particularly the machine-tool industry. Small firms tend to be found clustered together in "industrial districts". They form integrated territorial systems with varying degrees of sectoral specialisation.[1] These districts usually coincide with small urban areas and consist of one or more communes.

Numerous economic studies of these small-firm economies have been carried out, indicating clearly that there is a relationship between this form of development and the social context in which it occurs. However, less attention has been devoted to the role of the local political context. Yet the regions in the Third Italy which are most typical of small-firm development (as well as similar areas in Piedmont and Lombardy) are usually characterised by the existence of specific subcultures. In these areas,

---

1. The definition of industrial district which is used here is looser than that proposed by Becattini with regard to the concept of "Marshallian industrial district" (see Becattini's contribution to this volume).

one often finds the predominance of a particular political tradition whose origins usually go back to the beginning of the century, and a complex of institutions (parties, interest groups, cultural and welfare structures) which derive from the same politico-ideological matrix. Thus, the central regions, which were originally socialist in orientation, are now communist strongholds, while there is a deeply-rooted Catholic sub-culture in the regions of the north-east.

Interpretations of the origins and characteristics of small-firm development in Italy have been progressively refined over time. In the early stages, the emphasis was on the idea that the growth of small firms was brought about principally by the attempts of larger firms to circumvent restrictions imposed by the unions, by devolving parts of the productive process to smaller firms. Their aim was to reduce labour costs and to re-establish the flexibility of the workforce.

This initial conception was later complicated by various developments. Economic research showed that in some areas the relationships between firms could not wholly be explained by the phenomenon of productive decentralisation introduced for the purpose of cutting labour costs. These relationships often entailed increased specialisation and division of labour among small firms and were rooted in economies of scale, external to the single units of production, but internal to the industrial district in which they were located. The same studies stressed that changes in technology and the growth of demand for non-standardised goods enhanced the chances of autonomy and innovation for small firms.[2]

At the same time, another line of research, this one sociologically oriented, contributed to the clarification of certain essential aspects. It was pointed out that small firms are concentrated, mainly, in the central and north-eastern regions [Bagnasco, 1977]. In these areas a trend of autonomous development emerged. This was not primarily brought about by the decentralisation of existing production, although it was combined with the latter in various ways according to the sectoral specialisation of industrial districts. The role of the institutional context (in particular, traditional institutions and identities) is considered, by this approach, to be an important variable in explaining why the new economic and technological opportunities for small-firm development were especially likely to be seized upon in the central and north-eastern regions. In particular, some studies have used this perspective to examine the characteristics of the extended family and its relationship with the small-firm economy [Ardigò, Donati, 1976; Paci, 1980].

The research on which I draw here can be located within this institutional approach. The project consisted of an analysis of the central and north-eastern regions, as well as of case studies of two typical districts with differing political subcultures, Bassano in Veneto and Valdelsa in

2. See for example: Becattini [1978, 1987], Varaldo [1979], Garofoli [1981], Rullani [1982], Brusco [1982, 1986], Brusco and Sabel [1981], Sabel and Piore [1984], Sabel [1987].

Tuscany.[3] However, the results indicate that diffuse industrialisation was supported by a more complex institutional architecture which consisted not only of social components like the extended family and the local community, but also of specific political components - such as industrial relations and the activities of local governments - related to the role of the Communist and Catholic subcultures at the local level.

Section II will summarise some results of the comparative study of the districts of Bassano and Valdelsa, with particular reference to labour relations. Drawing on this study and on more general findings on the central and north-eastern regions, three basic questions will be discussed in section III: (a) What is the quality of work in the small-firm industrial districts? (b) What has been the role of political subcultures in the formation of the peculiar institutional context in which labour relations are embedded? (c) How have labour relations specifically been affected by the activities of unions and local governments? It is worth pointing out that the answers that will be proposed refer to an ideal-type model with specific space and time boundaries. The questions refer to industrial districts in the Third Italy's regions, in the period of their formation and consolidation (usually from the 1960s to the early 1980s).

II. A story of two districts

A summary of research on two small firm districts is presented in this section. The intention was to select areas that were socio-economically similar but which yet had very different political characteristics. The aim was, on the one hand, to identify key socio-economic characteristics of two typical industrial districts and, on the other, to assess the role of the subcultural "red" and "white" political contexts in small firm development. We obviously did not expect to achieve the impossible target of having all the forms of small firm development in the central and north-eastern regions well represented statistically. The aim was rather one of studying cases which were as close as possible to the types of district which were most widespread in such regions.[4] The areas of Valdelsa in Tuscany and Bassano in Veneto were eventually chosen. The former lies across the border of the provinces of Florence and Siena. The latter is in the northern part of the province of Vicenza.

---

3. For a comprehensive picture of the research project, see: Bagnasco and Pini [1981], Trigilia [1981], Bagnasco and Trigilia [1984, 1985], Trigilia [1986a, 1986b], Bagnasco [1988].

4. This enquiry was carried out between 1982 and 1985. The methodology employed was the typical one for case studies: conversations with "inside" observers, analysis of existing data and research, interviews with political, economic, and union leaders. The main tool was a standardised questionnaire for interviewing three representative samples in each area: workers (400 cases), entrepreneurs (100 cases), middle class people (200 cases). The overall results of the research are presented in Bagnasco and Trigilia [1984; 1985].

1. Socio-economic structure

The areas chosen are typical small firm districts, whose development began in the late 1950s. They had an overall population of less than 100,000 in 1981. Their largest centres, Poggibonsi and Bassano, accounted for 26,000 and 38,000 people, respectively. A diffuse type of settlement is a long-standing feature of these areas that can be traced back to the period of the Italian city-states. The rural population became scattered in the countryside as a consequence of the prevailing production relations: sharecropping in Valdelsa, very small peasant property and sharecropping in the area of Bassano.

Figure 1: Central and North-Eastern Regions and the Industrial Districts of Bassano and Valdelsa

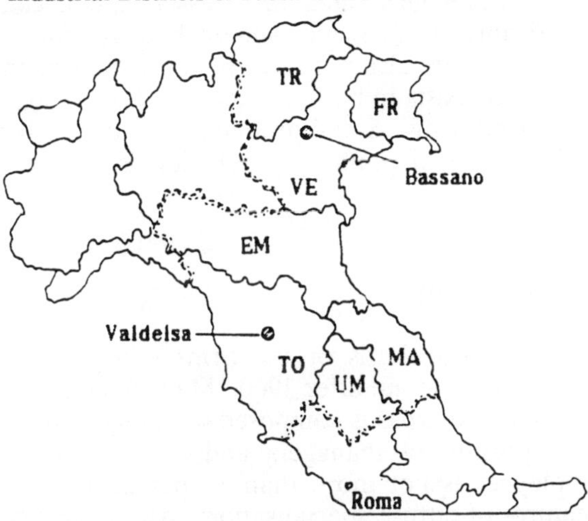

--------- = central and north-eastern regions (Third Italy)

TR = Trentino Alto Adige
FR = Friuli
VE = Veneto
TO = Toscana
MA = Marche
UM = Umbria

In both cases, the economy was mainly agricultural until after the Second World War; but there are local traditions of commerce and handicraft, and some early industrialisation was brought about by external initiatives.[5] Around Bassano, ceramics and woodwork are local traditions.

5. Economic and social change in Valdelsa during the second half of the nineteenth century has been reconstructed by Mori [1957]. As far as Bassano is concerned, a good number of contributions which appeared in Storia di Bassano - and especially that of Signori [1980] - are worth looking at.

A flourishing wool industry died out at the end of the eighteenth century. The art of printing also went into a crisis during the nineteenth century, after a period of strong growth; but some traces of it remain. In the case of Valdelsa, the industries of paper and glass, and the activities of weaving and spinning, which were practised by sharecropping families, were of early significance; woodwork arrived later.

After the Second World War growth was extremely fast in both cases. In 1951 agriculture was still an important sector, accounting for 40 per cent of employees in the area of Bassano, and for 60 per cent in Valdelsa. Between 1951 and 1981, manufacturing industry grew by about 250 per cent in Valdelsa and 160 per cent in the already more advanced Bassano area.

In both cases the prevailing sectors in the 1980s are the "traditional" ones: in Valdelsa, furniture, glass and, to a lesser extent, clothing and shoemaking are significant; in Bassano, shoemaking is more important whilst furniture and ceramics are also of note. But a mechanical engineering branch of some importance exists in both districts and is growing, organised in small- and medium-sized firms. Small production units clearly prevail in both areas (the average size of units of production is 9.3 employees in Valdelsa and 9.5 in Bassano).

2. Source of entrepreneurship

Between half and two-thirds of the firms - both industrial and artisanal - of our sample were set up after 1960. Management in more than 60 per cent of firms in the two areas is composed of family members and/or relatives, and the proportion of managers and white-collar workers in relation to total employees is not more than 15 per cent in either case. These are typical features of diffuse specialisation. Also typical is that only 24 per cent of industrial entrepreneurs (that is, in firms with more than 10 employees) and artisans (that is, in firms with less than 10 employees) interviewed in the Bassano area and only 22 per cent in the Valdesa area said that they have a father of the same professional status. The vast majority are therefore first generation entrepreneurs, who receive assistance from family members and relatives. About 50 per cent of them, both in Bassano and Valdelsa, have had past experience as waged workers.

Our research allows for an evaluation to be made of the relative contribution of the town and the countryside to the formation of entrepreneurs [Bagnasco, 1988]. In this respect, a direct relationship between a past experience of sharecropping or peasant farming, and small firm entrepreneurship has often been assumed. But this hypothesis seems to require some qualification. Most industrial entrepreneurs have urban roots: more than two-thirds of their fathers - both in Bassano and in Valdelsa - are, or were, in urban trades. The peasant mould is, relatively speaking, more widespread in the case of artisans; about half the artisans in Valdelsa and 40 per cent in Bassano have, or had, a father employed in agriculture as a sharecropper or peasant farmer. The overall greater contribution to the formation of entrepreneurship - especially of the most strategic industrial sort - has come, therefore, from the traditions of manufacture and commerce existing in the small central and north-eastern towns. Even in the case of the formation of artisanship, where the countryside has made a greater contribution, people with fathers in agriculture would usually have intermediate experience as waged workers in small firms before setting up their own businesses.

3. Political cultures

Whilst the two districts have very similar socio-economic structures, politically they are very different; this emerges clearly in the vote for the Christian Democratic Party and for the Communist Party in the two areas. Both Valdelsa and the area of Bassano are zones of ancient subcultural settlement. The Socialist movement in Valdelsa and the Catholic movement in Bassano developed and settled in the two areas at the end of the last century.

In Bassano, Catholic identity has roots which go far back into the past; but it is especially between the end of the nineteenth and the first decades of the twentieth century that a network of secular institutions linked with the Church developed alongside the strictly religious ones.[6] In 1909 a Catholic MP was elected for the first time, and this result was to be confirmed in the next elections in 1913. The extension of suffrage and the beginning of full participation of the Catholics in political life brought about a clear superiority in the polls. The *Partito Popolare* (the Catholic party) won the elections held after the war, in 1919 and 1921, by acquiring 55 per cent of the votes. After the Fascist period, the historical traditions reasserted themselves in the elections of 1946; the DC (the Christian Democratic Party), which took the place of the *Partito Popolare*, gained more than 50 per cent of the vote in Bassano.

The subculture in the Valdesa area also goes far back in time. The social changes which occurred in the last decades of the nineteenth century, with a worsening situation for sharecropping agriculture and a growth of urban centres, laid the conditions for a penetration of Socialist ideas.[7] These were supported, in particular, by the formation of the first nuclei of a working class, and by the existence of social strata of urban, artisan, commercial, and industrial lower middle classes, which were under the influence of democratic and liberal opinion. In 1897, the Socialists achieved a majority of votes in the local elections of the Colle Val d'Elsa, which became the first Socialist municipality in Tuscany. The political experience of a "Municipal Socialism" in the first decades of the twentieth century left a deep mark on local self-identity which Fascism did not manage to erase

6. For a treatment of these developments, see Berti [1980] in the already quoted Storia di Bassano.

7. On the development of the Socialist movement, see Mori [1957] and Caciagli [1961].

and which the *Resistenza* brought back to light. It was indeed through the activity of the *Resistenza* against Nazism and Fascism that the Communist party acquired a dominant role; this was to be further developed after the war during struggles of the sharecroppers. In such a way the PCI (Communist Party) ended up as the heir to most of the preceding Socialist political experience.

4. Family and community institutional context

At the beginning of the 1950s, the majority of the population in our areas was made up of agricultural labourers, mainly of a self-employed type: small peasants and sharecroppers. By the 1980s, however, small firm industrial workers had come to make up the largest social group. The working class appears to be young, of local origin, and to a large extent of the first generation (Table 1).

Despite the new preponderance of industrial workers, the districts display a number of features that contribute to a particularly low degree of proletarianisation. Within the small units of production the way labour is organised inhibits strong class differentiation. Both small entrepreneurs and the members of their families participate directly in the running of the firms (we have already observed that the number of white-collar workers and managers is very small). This often requires direct and personal contacts with the workers.

Of further significance are the high expectations of social mobility across socio-economic statuses. Whilst only 20 per cent of workers believed, at the time the research was carried out, that they had concrete possibilities of setting up their own businesses within the next few years (particularly in the tertiary sector), 70 per cent of them held this as an aspiration. We should not, therefore, underestimate the importance that mobility has in maintaining the existence of a social and cultural *continuum* between workers, artisans, and small entrepreneurs, and in avoiding the erection of rigid class barriers.

This tendency is then strengthened by the fact that uprooting from the community is very limited (see Table 2). Contact with an agricultural background is maintained. This is especially the case in Bassano, probably partly because of the greater historical importance of small peasant property there. Hence, whilst only 22 per cent of workers in Valdelsa were found to live in isolated houses or cottages, the level went up to 66 per cent for those in Bassano. The latter were also found to more frequently have kitchen gardens[8] and to raise poultry.

The gradual move from agriculture to industry inside the same area has consequences for family structures and relations. The average size of the family (4.1 in Bassano and 3.4 in Valdelsa), and the average number of

---

8. Research carried out in some communes in Marche [Paci (ed.), 1980] revealed that 45 per cent of working class families owned kitchen gardens, and 20 per cent raised poultry.

Table 1: Personal and employment characteristics of workers in Valdelsa and Bassano, 1984 (percentages)

		Valdelsa	**Bassano**
(a)	**Gender**		
	- male	70	70
	- female	30	30
(b)	**Age**		
	- up to 29	37	53
	- 30 - 39	25	25
	- 40 - 49	21	16
	- 50 and over	17	6
(c)	**Place of birth**		
	- the same commune as that of residence	39	52
	- other communes in the same province	36	37
	- other communes in the same regions	13	5
	- other regions or abroad	12	6
(d)	**Distribution of firms by size**		
	- up to 10 employees	24	17
	- 11 - 50	53	40
	- 51 - 200	21	35
	- over 200	2	8
(e)	**Distribution by sector**		
	- machine tool	28	40
	- furniture	35	11
	- clothing		16
	- shoes	20	9
	- glass and ceramics*	17	24
	Number of cases	**372**	**381**

Note: * These are employees in the glass sector in Valdelsa, and in ceramics in Bassano.

See: Trigilia [1986a].

Table 2: Workers' environment and living conditions in Valdelsa and Bassano, 1984

		Valdelsa	Bassano
		Absolute values	
(a)	**Family**		
	- average family size	3.4	4.1
	- average number of family members who are able to work	2.2	2.4
		Percentage levels	
	- families with a cohabiting member who is employed in agriculture	9	9
(b)	**Housing**		
	- workers owning their home	59	69
	- workers who live in a single or a two-family house, or in a cottage	22	66
(c)	**Additional family agricultural production**		
	- workers who have a kitchen garden cultivated directly by the family	42	74
	- workers whose families raise poultry	24	44
(d)	**Family relations**		
	- workers exchanging mutual help with non-cohabiting siblings in the vicinity	46	48
	- workers who define relationships with non-cohabiting relatives as very or fairly "frequent and friendly with everyone"	72	70
(e)	**Relations with friends**		
	- workers having "many friends with whom they exchange help and advice "	28	39
	- workers having friends among the self-employed:		
	- artisans	26	43
	- shopkeepers	28	29
	- entrepreneurs	15	12
	- peasants	19	28
	Number of cases	**372**	**381**

See: Trigilia [1986a].

working household members, continues to be large. Most of those working are employed in non-agricultural sectors. To this it must be added that about half the workers in the two districts said that they have close (non-cohabiting) siblings with whom they exchange different sorts of help. There were also found to be a good number of workers who declared that they have many friends with whom they exchange help and advice.

This is the overall context which must be borne in mind when we consider the substantial level of savings of the families; more than two-thirds of them had been able to save part of their income in the year preceding the poll. In the light of the data, it can therefore be said that the family and community institutional context - which was shaped by the previous agrarian structure - has not been radically uprooted by small firm development. This context gives workers access to substantial resources which make possible the maintenance of a degree of independence from the conditions of the labour market. It also favours the ability of the individual - with the help of his family - to adapt to the need for the mobility and flexibility which are proper to small production units.

The large percentage of workers who stated that they have frequent and friendly relationships with non-cohabiting relatives, and the existence of networks of acquaintances where different social groups are involved, suggest that family and community continue to have a relevant role in the shaping of individual behaviour. This factor, together with the close personal relationships within the firms and the high rates of social mobility, prevents the formation of deep class cleavages.

5. Automomous working conditions

The process of production in small units leaves the individual worker a greater scope for self-management in comparison with the more rigid organisation which is typical of large firms.

In order to assess this claim, an analysis of the work tasks carried out in the two districts was attempted. The first two categories listed in Table 3a group tasks which require low skill levels, whether they be in more traditional (craft production) or more standardised production contexts.

The other three categories group tasks requiring higher skills. In this case the more traditional skills involve some "on-the-job" know-how, or the ability to perform different tasks and to intervene in different phases of the production process. The more modern ones involve the control of complex machinery (such as numerically controlled machines).

The data show a prevailing presence of fairly skilled tasks in both districts - more so in Bassano than in Valdelsa - but the traditional, craft, versions are more widespread (on-the-job know-how and ability to perform different tasks). These may not usually require a high level of technical skill, but may, nevertheless, involve some relative autonomy of the worker in the process of production (this is another factor which limits the proletarianisation of workers).

Table 3a: Workers' skill evaluation of their tasks in Valdelsa and Bassano, 1984 (percentages)

	Valdelsa	**Bassano**
- you only need to repeat a series of manual, possibly heavy, but simple operations	40	28
- it simply consists in manning one or more machines which operate almost on their own	8	6
- it is necessary to know the job, a bit like the old artisans	15	37
- you need readiness of mind and the ability to intervene in a number of different tasks, with respect to ever-changing problems	31	24
- you need to know how fairly complex machinery operates	5	5
	99*	100*
Number of cases	**372**	**381**

Note: * rounded figures

See: Trigilia [1986a].

Table 3b: Workers' evaluation of their work in Valdelsa and Bassano, 1984 (percentages)

	Valdelsa	**Bassano**
Judgements of one's own work *(percentage answering "very" or "fairly")*		
"You think your work is":		
- interesting	75	80
- tiring	62	43
- dangerous or harmful	53	41
- secure (with regards to dismissal)	73	68
- well paid	49	66
- done under good regulating conditions	84	90
Number of cases	**372**	**381**

See: Trigilia [1986a].

Some confirmation of the craft-type organisation may be derived from the judgements the workers made about various aspects of their work (Table 3b):

Eighty per cent of Bassano workers and 75 per cent of the Valdelsa workers found their work interesting. Job security was evaluated as high by 70 per cent of all those interviewed; and contractual conditions were considered good. The work was considered well - or fairly well - paid by 66 per cent of workers in Bassano and by 49 per cent in Valdelsa. On the negative side, 42 per cent of workers in Bassano found the work tiring and dangerous or harmful, while an even worse judgement (53 per cent) was given by those in Valdelsa.

Taken as a whole, these data give us a picture of a largely positive attitude towards the jobs carried out which, in the light of the most widespread tasks, seems to be related more to aspects of self-management than simply to matters of skills. It is likely that these judgements are affected by the informal relationships and the general "climate" existing in small factories. In connection with this, one has to consider that 80 per cent of those interviewed in Valdelsa and 65 per cent in Bassano declared that "relationships between people in our work place are usually co-operative: we quite often help one another".

6. An enterprise culture

The majority of workers appear to appreciate the "spirit of enterprise" (Table 4) and the role of the small entrepreneurs who are seen as active agents in the district model of development. A typical component of Social-Communist and Catholic cultures is, therefore, widespread in the areas under scrutiny. We found no evidence supporting an interpretation of this response as "traditional deferential" [Lockwood, 1966], that is, as a consensus based on a shared system of values, whereby entrepreneurs are given an exclusive role of guidance in exchange for protection, following a typically paternalistic model. Most workers interviewed were found not to subscribe to this model; they did not agree with the statement: "local entrepreneurs try to favour workers; they help them out of difficulties, and are also prepared to make sacrifices before resorting to dismissals".

Consensus on entrepreneurs as organisers of production activities is not followed by an unconditional acceptance of the market as a regulating mechanism. Only 40 per cent of workers in Bassano and 30 per cent in Valdelsa were prepared to have incomes and employment levels dependent on the business cycle. Consistent with this was the common awareness of the negative side of working in the small firms.

All this suggests the existence of a sort of "contractual" consensus to the district model of development; that is, an agreement based on a concrete evaluation of the advantages and disadvantages which the model is able to generate[9] This is a generalised tendency. In neither contexts did a strong critical attitude towards production relations emerge. All the same, Tuscan workers seemed to be more reluctant to accept the market as a regulator of employment and income levels, and to pay greater attention to the negative side of their work relations. This difference does not seem to be explained by living and working conditions, which appear to be largely similar in the two districts. One explanatory factor is the continuing existence in the Veneto area of stronger ties with agriculture, together with a lower concentration of settlements in urban centres; but this alone cannot explain the observed differences in attitudes. These are much more likely to reflect the different effects of the Socio-Communist and Catholic cultures in the two areas. One can presume that the more critical attitude shown by Tuscan workers is connected with greater expectations of political regulation, while traditional "background" resources continue to be relatively more relevant in the "white" area.

Apart from differences, the analysed data have revealed that in any case the diffuse industrialisation has generated only limited proletarianisation. A considerable economic transformation has occurred without any violent social upheaval, and without causing marked social divisions likely to jeopardise the basis for a reproduction of political subcultures. This outcome has been fostered by processes of co-ordination and mediation between interests which the subcultures themselves allowed for, and which we are now going to examine.

7. Industrial relations

A. Trade union organisation

While the role of the social and cultural context is largely recognised, the characteristics of industrial relations in areas with a diffused economy are less well known. An image of "weakness" of trade union organisations usually prevails, but this is not confirmed by the research data.

The rate of union membership among workers in the two areas was ascertained as being 80 per cent in Valdelsa and 48 per cent in Bassano. As might be expected, values rise with the size of the firm. Almost all the Tuscan workers in firms with more than 50 employees are trade union members, whilst membership in firms of that size is also very widespread in the Bassano area. In the size bracket which is crucial for the economy of both districts - firms with 10 to 50 employees - the rate reaches 90 per cent in Valdelsa and 43 per cent in Bassano. In smaller, artisan-like firms in the Bassano area, only a minority of workers (17 per cent) belongs to a union, while 40 per cent do so in the Valdelsa area. Of the unions, CGIL (the Communist and Socialist union) is a near monopolist in the "red" area and

9. The notion of a negotiated adaptation of the working class to capitalistic social relationships has been employed by Parkin [1971].

Table 4: Judgement of workers in Valdelsa and Bassano on the small firm model of development, 1984 (percentages)

		Valdelsa	Bassano
(a)	**Workers in agreement with the following statements:**		
	- many difficulties may be overcome by the spirit of enterprise in the society we live in	65	71
	- small entrepreneurs are not like big businessmen: they must pay attention to competition, should not waste resources, and should improve production	85	82
	- local entrepreneurs try to favour workers: they help them out of difficulties, and are even prepared to make sacrifices before resorting to dismissals	38	34
	- it is to everyone's interest that industry produces, but there are good years and bad years: it can't be helped if in some periods workers have to work and earn less	20	40
(b)	**Distribution of answers to the question: Workers are said to have been generally satisfied in these last few years with their work in small firms. Why do you think this is?**		
	- because it is the most natural form of industry and everyone has found his advantage in it	39	59
	- because many people do not consider the other side of the coin: heavy and sometimes dangerous work, little free time, etc.	61	46
Number of cases		**372**	**381**

See: Trigilia [1986a].

CISL (of a Catholic bent) has the majority in the "white" area, but it is not as dominant.

Negotiations in 80 per cent of industrial firms in the sample in Valdelsa, and 60 per cent in Bassano are controlled by the unions - mostly via the factory council, but also with the participation of union representatives in some firms. The scope of union negotiations can be assessed from information taken from the sample of workers. Such negotiations involve about 70 per cent of the Tuscan workers and a bit more than 50 per cent of the Veneto ones; they involve the industrial sector almost exclusively, that is, all firms with more than 10 employees (non-artisan firms); and are particularly important in larger firms. In the 11 to 50 employees size bracket, union negotiations involve 84 per cent of workers in Valdelsa, and 49 per cent in Bassano; in the 50 employees or over size bracket, the figures are 97 per cent and 83 per cent, respectively.

B. *Negotiated issues*

In respect of the issues which are subject to negotiation, it can be seen that wages are of central relevance (Table 5). This is even more apparent in Bassano, where other issues are less frequent. In the Tuscan area the average level of wages was estimated to be 19 per cent higher in the furniture sector and 15 per cent higher in machine tools and glass than the standard levels fixed by the national general contracts. In respect of the Veneto district, the average level of firm wages, for the same task levels, was 10 per cent above the national standard for furniture, and 6 per cent for clothing and shoes.[10]

Table 5: Issues in firm contractual agreements in Valdelsa and Bassano, 1984 (percentage frequency of each item in the total number of agreements)

	Valdelsa	**Bassano**
Wages	100	94
Working time, holidays, overtime work	84	40
Job classification	74	26
Canteens and other services	11	32
Right of information on firm's activities and investments	80	56
Subcontracting	18	2
Employment, mobility, professional training	66	28
Work environment	80	48
Union rights	41	32
Number of agreements	**117**	**81**

See: Trigilia [1986a].

10. These are not isolated cases either. Cases of locally agreed upon consistent wage increases have been observed in Prato [Trigilia, 1989] and in Modena [Perulli, 1989] as well.

Another issue present in firm agreements is that of schedules and overtime. In our research it appeared in 84 per cent of cases in Valdelsa, and in 40 per cent in Bassano. The main difference between the two districts consisted of a greater number of clauses concerning overtime work, shifts, and compensating periods of rest in Valdelsa. However, this difference did not seem to affect the actual patterns of hours worked, nor the more general modes of labour force utilisation. Ninety-four per cent of respondants in Valdelsa, and 86 per cent in Bassano declared that they normally worked eight hours. On the other hand, a quarter of the respondants worked for nine or more hours "during busy periods", stretching from one to three months. Twenty-five per cent of Tuscan workers and 36 per cent of Veneto workers also declared that they worked on Saturdays or during holidays, but many of these did so only occasionally. It can be added to this that 30 per cent of workers in both areas "stayed at home for some time during the last few years, due to production declines".

All in all, the data do not reveal the existence of strong working time differences between the two districts. The most striking feature is, rather, that times and modes of labour force utilisation were objects of more active contractual negotiations in the Tuscan area; and that this was followed by more markedly beneficial results in terms of wages and job hierarchies.

C. Flexibility

Labour flexibility appears to be high in both areas, but it has not reached the levels which are often believed to occur. This flexibility seems to have been more a result of negotiations, with the Tuscans receiving better compensation. This interpretation receives indirect confirmation from indicators of labour mobility. About the same number of respondants (56 per cent in Valdelsa and 57 per cent in Bassano) had had one to three jobs in other firms before their present position, and 10 per cent more than three. Only a minority of those who changed jobs mentioned dismissal explicitly as the reason for change. Rather they stressed reasons such as voluntary choice and a search for better paid and safer occupations. The data revealed that labour force mobility has certainly been an important factor in local economic development. Differences between smaller, artisan-like firms and industrial ones do not appear to be particularly marked. Flexibility seems rather to be a distinguishing feature of the local system of production in its entirety, although it is certainly better compensated in industrial firms.

III. Work and politics

The small-firm economy can take many different forms. Research work carried out in Italy on this topic has shown the importance of a particular form which is based on the industrial district and which is characterised by a specific institutional context. Labour relations in these settings are shaped by cultural, social and political factors which were forged in the long term. However, clarifying the quality of work and unravelling its intricate relationship with politics can help locate the Third Italy's experience in a comparative perspective.

1. The quality of work

The story of our districts - as well as that of other areas that have been examined - suggests that the Italian districts cannot usually be considered as high-tech districts in which small units largely utilise the new computer-based technologies such as numerically-controlled machines and other forms of sophisticated flexible equipment. Rather we find small firms that are specialised in the production of non-standard goods, but that usually rely on more traditional multi-purpose technologies and craft-like skills. This does not mean that the new electronic technologies are absent from the districts or that they are not growing. So far, however, their diffusion remains limited, with important exceptions such as that of machine-tool districts, especially in Emilia-Romagna.[11] In other industries - for example in textiles, clothing, footwear - it has been more often a question of a blending of old and new technologies.[12] In any case, from an economic point of view, the characteristics of technological equipment require careful evaluation. In many cases, multi-purpose machines - even though they are not based on new technologies - can remain particularly suitable for short runs [Brusco, 1986]. However, what mainly interests us here is the impact of the prevailing equipment on the quality of work.

It is usually recognised that an assessment of the quality of work clearly requires a multidimensional evaluation. It certainly involves psycho-physiological aspects as well as other features such as work environment, level of skills, autonomy in the productive process, and chances of social mobility. But one should not neglect that work experience is also significantly shaped by the cultural, social and political environment external to the factory. From this perspective, other dimensions should be considered: the influence over living conditions - both cultural and material - of factors such as the family and local community, industrial relations and the activities of local government. Evaluation of the quality of work is therefore particularly complex and caution is required in any generalisation. However, a sketchy framework could be proposed in the following terms.

First, "working hard" seems to be the rule in our districts. However, it is related more to working time than to a rigid labour organisation. In addition, working hard becomes less important in the more advanced small firms, in which the available equipment limits the need for a "quantitative" flexibility. The latter is more dependent on a flexible organisation of labour and higher levels of skill. In respect of safety and health, in general workers

11. For a recent account of the case of Modena, see Perulli [1989].

12. On the case of Prato, see Colombo and Mazzonis [1984), Trigilia [1989].

are not exposed to extreme risks. Both aspects, however, could entail serious problems and are objects of growing concern for the workers.

Workers' skills are obviously influenced by the above-mentioned features of the technological equipment. In this respect, one has to take into account that significant sectoral differences exist. But, on average, only a minority of workers possess high levels of technical skills, such as those involved in the ability to control complex machinery (e.g. numerically controlled machines). In addition, there are very few managers and white-collar workers. At the same time, the small firms of our districts rely on a pool of unskilled labour which should not be overlooked. However, the standard pattern seems to involve a widespread presence of fairly skilled workers of the traditional kind (craft-like skills and ability to perform different tasks).

If one considers the autonomy of workers, the picture becomes even more different from that prevailing in mass production. As a matter of fact, the most distinctive feature of the quality of work in our districts is the higher degree of autonomy that the workers in small firms enjoy in comparison with their colleagues in the large mass production firms. It is the limited subdivision of the productive process into rigid tasks, more than the level of technical skill, that mainly characterises the work experience in the districts. In addition, one has to consider the higher rates of occupational and social mobility that the small-firm workers enjoy. Even though the real chances of mobility - especially in terms of a shift to an independent entrepreneurial position - seem to decrease over time, this aspect significantly affects the expectations and attitudes of workers.

Within the industrial district, market mechanisms and social institutions such as the family, the kinship network and the local community are closely interwoven. These social institutions provide cultural and material resources for the development of entrepreneurship and flexible productive structures. They motivate people to start new activities and help them to sustain the costs of setting up and operating small firms. At the same time, they also mitigate the effects on industrial workers of greater small-firm discontinuity of employment and working time, and enable the costs of reproduction of labour to be lowered and incomes to be supplemented at the family level. Furthermore the persistence of community values which cut across social classes plays an integrative role that should not be underestimated in evaluating the "success" of small firm areas. Workers enjoy a low degree of proletarianisation, not only with reference to the organisation of labour and the chances for mobility, but also in relation to a working experience that does not entail a sharp uprooting from their original communities.

These social aspects of the small firm economy are well known. The studies carried out in Valdelsa and Bassano also confirm that they are of great importance. Nevertheless, the insistence on the role of traditional institutions and identities runs the risk of being misleading, especially when it is applied to those areas where industrialisation is more consolidated and where there is a well-established political subculture. In these situations, the role played by a specific form of interest mediation, shaped through the influence of political subcultures on union representation and the activity of local government, must also be taken into consideration.

While the skills of small-firm workers are often overemphasised, the level of wages is usually underestimated. The experience of the Third Italy suggests that small-firm development is not necessarily bound to low wages and to the evasion of labour regulations. Over time there has been an increase in real wages.[13] In many districts, the average wages are currently above the standards which are fixed by the national agreements between unions and business associations. This is due to the influence on wages of agreements that are negotiated at a local level. Industrial relations, therefore, play a role that should not be overlooked, one which is significantly affected by the institutional context, in particular by the local political subcultures. In this respect, one has also to consider the activity of local governments. The provision of services in the field of transport, housing, schools, day-care centres and health care have often anticipated or enriched national policies. Social services, therefore, contribute significantly to improving the living conditions of the workers. In effect, our districts benefit more than other areas from a kind of "local social wage". Together with the material effects of these policies, the symbolic and cultural influence of local welfare is also to be considered: citizenship is enlarged by removing important areas of living standards, such as those relating to schooling, or to health, from the direct domain of the market. Again, one cannot understand these outcomes without considering the political context of our regions.

The role of politics can be analysed at two levels. Firstly, it is important in shaping the peculiar equilibrium between the "traditional" and "modern" components that characterise our districts and affect labour relations, and which help to explain the origins and particular locations of small-firm development in the Third Italy's regions. Secondly, politics strongly influence the operation of districts through industrial relations and the activities of local governments.

2. Politics and the origins of the institutional context

The Italian literature clearly indicates that there is a relationship between small-firm growth and the social context in which it occurs. Among the factors which have attracted attention, one finds: the agrarian class structure with a strong presence of non-waged work (sharecropping, peasant, and tenant farming); the persistence of extended families and local communities; and a tight network of small artisan and commercial centres. As a result of the combination of these factors a peculiar equilibrium between traditional and modern components has emerged over time. One could also say that our regions have been able to avoid mass production, with all its social, cultural and political effects.

---

13. Besides the cases that were considered in the previous section, see the more general data that are reported in Trigilia [1986a, Ch. 3, p. 172].

However, we cannot understand the formation and the persistence of the social equilibrium of these regions - and therefore the origins and the location of industrial districts - without taking into account the political context. What has been the role of political subcultures in this process? The development of the Socialist and Catholic movements at the end of the nineteenth century was certainly influenced by the social structure which favoured the transformation of these movements into territorial political structures. Both of them cut across class boundaries and assumed wider community dimensions. Both of them shared a particular feature: they tried, although in different ways, to *defend the local society*[14] from the penetration of the market and of the national state; they tried to contain social disintegration and proletarianisation by experimenting with localised forms of organisation. As a matter of fact, the exclusion of the Socialists and Catholics from central political power led them to strengthen their positions at a local level, where conditions were more favourable.

In the "red" areas, a tight network of unions, friendly societies and co-operatives developed in close collaboration with the Communes. The central regions were characterised by a lively "Municipal Socialism". In the "white" areas of the North-east, unions were less present, but there was a network of rural savings and other banks, agricultural organisations, co-operatives, friendly societies, and charities, all of which were linked to the Church. It is not possible here to go into the details of the differences between the two subcultures - which, it should be said, are not to be underestimated - but at least three similar consequences of their influence on the model of economic growth should be considered.

First of all, both subcultures made an important contribution, through their organisations, to the formation and to the persistence of a social and cultural background based on a peculiar mix of traditional and modern components. They strengthened a localist kind of political economy and therefore preserved local communities and helped contain the erosion of productive relations based on non-waged work, both in the small towns (artisans) and in the country (sharecroppers and farmers). Secondly, and more specifically, they contributed to the high degree of legitimacy of entrepreneurship and to a work ethic which were very important later for small-firm growth. Thirdly, they brought about an emancipation of the political system from civil society. Contrary to what happened in the South, where the Socialist and Catholic movements were very weak, politics became more autonomous from individual or family interests and more bound to the defence of collective interests, even though with a strong localist connotation. Again, this factor was a crucial legacy which helped the political economy of the small-firm areas.

---

14. I use this concept in the sense proposed by Polanyi [1944].

3. Industrial relations and local government activities

In Italy the debate on industrial relations has centred mainly on the experience of large firms and on the central political system. This brought about a long-lasting distortion: productive structures different from the large industrial firms were usually considered as if they were not covered by industrial relations. However, research conducted in small-firm areas, in the early 1980s, provided evidence which questioned an interpretation of labour relations conceived in terms of "dualism".[15] In order to understand this neglect of industrial relations in small and medium-sized firms, one has probably to consider that in the Italian debate industrial relations are often synonymous with conflictual industrial relations. Since the prevailing model of industrial relations in small firms is not conflictual, it is usually thought that in these settings there are no industrial relations at all.

What is the prevailing model of industrial relations in the small-firm areas, especially in the central and north-eastern regions? First, the rate of unionisation grew significantly in the 1970s, and it was always higher than in the large firms of the North-west (the average rate of unionisation for the two major unions - CGIL and CISL - reached almost 50 per cent of industrial workers in the central regions and almost 40 per cent in the north-eastern regions, while in the regions of mass production, the rate of unionisation was less than 30 per cent). In the 1980s, there was a decline, though it was not as strong as that in the large-firm areas. The research conducted in industrial districts has shown that unionisation was fostered by the particular features of the local political systems. Political traditions provided identity and organisational resources which facilitated unionisation, in spite of the very fragmented productive structure. The stronger political subcultures were, the more unionisation increased. While in the "red" areas CGIL (the Communist and Socialist union) prevails, in the "white", Catholic, areas CISL is stronger.

Of course, one could remark - as many observers did in Italy - that this kind of unionisation is bound to have a subcultural character, with limited effects on industrial relations. But there is evidence to show that although this was true in the initial stages of small-firm growth - in the 1960s and early 1970s - in the following period unions exploited their organisational resources and acquired increasing autonomy from political parties. Again, there are differences between "red" and "white" areas (for example, unionisation is higher in the "red" areas), but in both cases a specific model of industrial relations, different from that prevailing in large firms, was triggered off. This is a co-operative and localist model. Unions have not placed constraints on the flexible use of labour - both within and among the local firms - in exchange for increases in local wages, the maintenance of full employment at the local level, and the provision of welfare benefits by local governments. The territorial level of unions is

15. This category was proposed by Goldthorpe [1984] to point to the expansion of labour relations in which the representation of workers' interests by trade unions were excluded or strongly discouraged.

usually more important than the firm level for bargaining local agreements, although in some districts agreements at a firm level are also significant (usually in non-artisan firms with more than 20 employees); in such cases, for example, aspects related to flexibility and work organisation can be directly negotiated by members of the works councils and the employers [Perulli, 1989]. In general, the model is based on what we could call a "compensated flexibility". Unions contribute indirectly to the social acceptance of high labour flexibility by raising its wage value, but without negotiating its actual implementation, which is more frequently left to direct agreements between workers and their employers.

Two main factors fostered the institutionalisation of this model. The first is related to the social and cultural features of the working class which we have already considered; in particular, the low proletarianisation of this social group which derives from the prevailing organisation of work in the small firms, from deep-rooted family and community ties, and from the high opportunities for social mobility. These factors have not favoured the kind of militant unionism and conflictual relations that prevail in large firms and industrial cities.

The second aspect is related to the activities of the local governments. In the small-firm areas local governments have usually been able to provide a certain quantity of collective goods which have reduced costs for both employers and workers, and which have thereby encouraged local compromise. These goods include social services for workers (transport, public housing, schools, day-care centres) and, for local firms, the provision of industrial estates, infrastructures, professional training, and support to consortia for marketing or export facilities. Communes also have become increasingly involved in attempts to find solutions to crises in those firms which are particularly important to the economy of the area. This has often involved putting pressure on regional and national governments to grant redundancy payments to the workers and even interceding with local banks on questions of credit. It has also involved mediating between local unions and entrepreneurs. The Communes, however, have limited powers in the economic field. Their social policies have had a much greater impact. Again, there are differences which cannot be considered in detail here. Suffice it to say that the "red" administrations have tended, on the whole, to be more interventionist, while the "white" ones have been less interventionist in land-use and urban policies and have delegated most social services to the network of Catholic associations; the former have tried to increase the regulative role of politics, while the latter have been more oriented towards sustaining traditional institutions.

Why have local governments in these regions been able to play the role described above? Two aspects should be considered. Firstly, contrary to what has happened in other areas, political subcultures have provided a generalised support which has freed local leaders from the concerns of particular and fragmented demands. Success has been more dependent on the ability to provide collective goods for the local community. Clientism has been contained. Secondly, the diffuse character of industrialisation, especially in its initial stages, has limited the problems that local governments have had to face. That the traditional family and the community background have not changed dramatically, that there has been no great inflow of immigrants, and that employment and consumption have been sustained, has not only facilitated the task of local administrators, but has also allowed traditional institutions to be used as regulative resources.

On the whole, the influence of the political context on industrial relations and local governments' activity has helped to establish a social compromise based, on the one hand, on the high flexibility of the economy and, on the other, on the control of costs and the redistribution of the benefits accruing from economic growth. Politics have been able to play this role by combining traditional and modern regulative resources. However, the institutional context that has emerged in this process is not to be considered as a set of external conditions facilitating the working of the market. Our areas cannot be described in terms of a *laissez-faire* society. Borrowing from Dore [1986], we could rather define the role of social and political institutions in terms of "flexible rigidities". Economic relationships have been shaped by social and political mechanisms which limit the role and scope of the market. But in this way they have fostered flexibility and the ability of the local economy to innovate.

A final remark. It is appropriate to emphasise the *local* dimension of the small-firm political economy in the Third Italy. The economic, social and political resources that have affected the operation of industrial districts have been mostly endogenous. This aspect is important because it could offer a key to the problems of modernisation that are likely to affect the small-firm areas in the future. Of course, this point deserves a more specific treatment, but I wish to conclude by mentioning that new problems are now menacing the localist kind of political economy that we have described. There is, therefore, a need for new research in this field.

An aspect which should probably attract attention is the emergence of new types of external economies and diseconomies which cannot be easily dealt with at a local level. For example, on the one hand, problems of innovation are emerging that require resources that are not always available at the local level: technological research and information, marketing and export services, more sophisticated financial services, managerial and labour training, etc. On the other hand, new external diseconomies have clearly appeared: pollution, waste disposal, traffic congestion and transport, energy supply, etc. Again, it is difficult to tackle these problems only at a local level and with endogenous resources. In other words, it seems that the development of industrial districts is facing a problem of scale. Constraints of scale make the local economy more dependent on a wider mode of regulation of a *regional* kind. This is not to say, however, that industrial districts are bound to become less important as institutional forms of economic organisation. What is hypothesised is that they could probably consolidate their role if the original isolation was broken and new, more complex, forms of interaction and co-operation were built. However, it is worth considering that, in this regard, the strong localist aspect of the industrial districts' political economy could change status: from a past source of strength to a menacing future constraint.

References

Ardigò, A.; Donati, P. 1976. *Famiglia e industrializzazione*, Milan, Angeli.

Bagnasco, A. 1977. *Tre Italie: La problematica territoriale dello sviluppo italiano*, Bologna, Il Mulino.

---. 1988. *La costruzione sociale del mercato*, Bologna, Il Mulino.

Bagnasco, A.; Pini, R. 1981. "Economia e struttura sociale", in *Quaderni della Fondazione Feltrinelli*, No. 14.

Bagnasco, A.; Trigilia, C. (eds.). 1984. *Società e politica nelle aree di piccola impresa: Il caso di Bassano*, Venice, Arsenale.

---. 1985: *Società e politica nelle aree di piccola impresa: Il caso della Valdelsa*, Milan, Angeli.

Becattini, G. 1978. "The development of light industry in Tuscany: An interpretation", in *Economic Notes*, Nos. 2-3.

Becattini, G. (ed.). 1987. *Mercato e forze locali: Il distretto industriale*, Bologna, Il Mulino.

Berti, G. 1980. "Otto e novecento", in *Storia di Bassano*, Vicenza.

Brusco, S. 1982. "The Emilian model: Productive decentralisation and social integration", in *Cambridge Journal of Economics*, No. 6.

---. 1986. "Small firms and industrial districts: The experience of Italy", in Keeble, D.; Wever, E. (eds.): *New firms and regional development in Europe*, London, Croom Helm.

Brusco, S.; Sabel, C. 1981, "Artisan production and economic growth", in Wilkinson, F. (ed.): *The dynamics of labour market segmentation*, London, Academic Press.

Caciagli, M. 1961. "Nascita del partito socialista in Valdelsa", in *Miscellanea storica della Valdelsa*, Nos. 1-2.

Colombo, U.; Mazzonis, D. 1984. "Integration of old and new technologies in the Italian (Prato) textile industry", in Bhalla, A. et al. (eds.): *Blending of new and traditional technologies*, Dublin, Tycooly I.P.L.

Dore, R. 1986. *Flexible rigidities. Industrial policy and structural adjustment in the Japanese economy, 1970-80*, London, Athlone Press.

Garofoli, G. 1981. "Lo sviluppo delle aree periferiche nell'economia italiana degli anni '70", in *L'industria*, No. 3.

Goldthorpe, J. 1984. "The end of convergence: Corporatism and dualist tendencies in modern western societies", in Goldthorpe, J. (ed.): *Order and conflict in contemporary capitalism*, Oxford, Oxford University Press.

Lockwood, D. 1966. "Sources of variations in working-class images of society", in *Sociological Review*, No. 3.

Mori, G. 1957. *La Valdelsa dal 1848 al 1900. Sviluppo economico, movimenti sociali e lotta politica*, Milan, Feltrinelli.

Paci, M. (ed.) 1980. *Famiglia e mercato del lavoro in un'economia periferica*. Milan, Angeli.

Parkin, F. 1971. *Class inequality and political order*, London, MacGibbon & Kee.

Perulli, P. 1989. "Il distretto industriale di Modena", in Regini, M.; Sabel, C. (eds.): *Strategie di riaggiustamento industriale*, Bologna, Il Mulino.

Piore, M.J.; Sabel, C. 1984. *The second industrial divide*. New York, Basic Books.

Polanyi, K. 1944. *The great transformation*, New York, Rinehart & Winston.

Rullani, E. 1982. "L'economia delle differenze: Il capitalismo industriale delle periferie", in Goglio, S. (ed.): *Italia: Centri e periferie*, Milan, Angeli.

Sabel, C. 1987. *The reemergence of regional economies: Changes in the scale of production*, Paper prepared for the SSRC Western European Committee.

Signori, F. 1980. "L'economia di Bassano dalle origini a oggi", in *Storia di Bassano*, Vicenza.

Trigilia, C. 1981. "Le subculture politiche territoriali", in *Quaderni della Fondazione Feltrinelli*, No. 16.

---. 1986a. *Grandi partiti e piccole imprese. Comunisti e democristiani nelle regioni a economia diffusa*, Bologna, Il Mulino.

---. 1986b. "Small-firm development and political subcultures in Italy", in *European Sociological Review*, No. 3.

---. 1989. "Il distretto industriale di Prato", in Regini, M. and Sabel, C. (eds.) *Strategie di riaggiustamento industriale*, Bologna, Il Mulino.

Varaldo, R. (ed.) 1979. *Ristrutturazioni industriali e rapporti tra imprese*, Milan, Angeli.

11 Industrial districts and regional development: Limits and possibilities

Ash Amin and Kevin Robins

I. Introduction

The purpose of this chapter is to address the significance and the potential of industrial districts for regional economic development in the present period, and this in the light of grandiose claims now being made about industrial districts. The task is at once empirical and theoretical. At one level, it is a matter of assessing available evidence about the similarities and differences between these new spaces of production. To what extent do idealising claims about, and for, regions like the Third Italy actually stand up to scrutiny? To what extent do all the new industrial spaces derive from the same process? It is a question of disentangling the realities from rapidly proliferating myths of a future golden age. At another level, there are important conceptual and theoretical issues to be raised about the extravagant scenarios being projected around industrial districts and flexibly specialised regional economies. Any consideration of this phenomenon must be located within a broader political economic perspective on the nature of contemporary capitalist development and transformation. The new myth-makers, with their optimistic and celebratory visions of decentralised production, high-tech cottage industries and flexible futures, base their claims on what we consider to be an extremely simplistic and contentious understanding of historical change. A more adequate account and one that acknowledges the complex and contradictory nature of the restructuring process - and particularly of its spatial dimensions - must, we shall argue, raise considerable problems about the industrial district paradigm.

The crucial issue is whether industrial districts do indeed constitute a blueprint for the regeneration of local and regional economies. Our discussion can only proceed by way of confronting this contentious hypothesis. For Jonathan Zeitlin [forthcoming] it is clear that "the economic development of the Third Italy has important implications for local industrial strategies in other advanced countries such as Britain" and that it holds out "the possibility of creating a high skill, high wage and high value-added economy". So clear is the relevance of such developments to Charles Sabel [1989, p. 52] that the burden of proof in fact lies with the critics rather than the protagonists of industrial districts: "To ask why flexible economies should not diffuse under competitive pressure is as reasonable as to ask why they should". Industrial districts and flexible specialisation are confidently invoked as the "third way" to economic and social development and as a universally applicable model. They are at the heart of a fundamental and benign historical transformation, an "epochal redefinition of markets, technologies, and industrial hierarchies" [Sabel, 1982, p. 231], a "second industrial divide" [Piore and Sabel, 1984].

The arguments in this paper are directed against what we see as an influential and imposing orthodoxy that is coming to cohere around this perspective. In developing our critique, however, we do not intend to lose the baby along with the bathwater. We are not suggesting that it is a matter of business as usual, nor are we saying that debates around flexible specialisation and industrial districts are simply without substance. On the contrary, the perspectives we are criticising do indeed identify dimensions and dynamics of structural change in the present period. The issue is, what weight to give them. How significant are these new phenomena, and how are we to interpret them? Whilst important changes are most certainly happening, there are real problems in suggesting that they represent a distinct break with the past and the dawning of a wholly new era of accumulation. Furthermore, we would argue that the significance of the new industrial agglomerations is overstated by the orthodoxy as a result of its tendency to collapse very diverse processes and areas into one category, and then to treat this as a symbol of the new area of accumulation. There are also problems with that kind of intellectual synecdoche, as it were, which takes one element or dimension of contemporary developments as equivalent to the whole. The dynamics of the restructuring process are, in fact, quite contradictory and divergent. Thus, in spatial terms, whilst there are indeed tendencies towards industrial districts and other types of localised agglomerations, there are also powerful countervailing and competing tendencies towards transnational networks and a "global space of flows" [Castells, 1987]. How these various developments might work themselves out is not at all clear. The issues are far more difficult and unpredictable than the initiates of this new orthodoxy would have us believe.

In the following section, we deal more fully with this important question of the broader political economic and historiographical framework within which thinking about industrial districts and flexible economies has been elaborated. We also deal more substantively with the composition and influence of what we have termed the new orthodoxy, a new radical consensus. In the second section, we assess how far, using the example of Italy, a narrower definition of industrial districts stands up to scrutiny. We then offer a critique of the more ambitious and generalising conceptions of this phenomenon as developed by the new orthodoxy, before going on to suggest something less idealised and less fervent to capture the new realities. The final section of the paper begins to move beyond the new orthodoxy by sketching the outlines of a more complex account of the nature of contemporary restructuring.

II. A new orthodoxy

The importance of industrial districts for local and regional development has been forcefully argued by Michael Piore and Charles Sabel [see, particularly, Piore and Sabel, 1983; 1984; Sabel, 1989] and by Allen Scott and Michael Storper [Scott, 1988; Storper and Scott, 1989]. Both pairs of researchers have grounded their valuation of industrial districts in a developed and sophisticated analysis of broader macroeconomic and macrosocial transformations in the current period. The work of Piore and Sabel, which has had a profound impact on research and policy communities alike [Hirst and Zeitlin, 1988; 1989; Kern and Schumann, 1987; Sengenberger and Loveman, 1988], is predicated on the idea of a radical shift from a model of industrial development founded on mass production to a possible, and even probable, coming era or regime of flexible specialisation based on flexible technologies, skilled workers and new forms of industrial community. The second industrial divide is characterised by a transition from one technological paradigm to another.

If the writings of Scott and Storper draw on this conceptual scheme, their analysis is also informed by the somewhat different perspectives of the French Regulation School of political economists. Their economic geography mobilises the Regulationist concepts of "regime of accumulation" and "mode of regulation" to argue that the present "historical rupture" represents the crisis of Fordism as both model of accumulation and regulation. If there are real problems with what adds up to an implicit conflation of the perspectives of Piore and Sabel ("flexible specialisation") and those of the Regulation School ("regime of accumulation"), further difficulties arise with Scott and Storper's particular reading of Regulation theory. Scott and Storper inscribe their work within an interpretation, that in the end tends to reduce it to being simply a variant of neo-Schumpeterian long wave theory elaborated by Carlota Perez and Christopher Freeman [Perez, 1983; 1985; Freeman and Perez, 1988]. The Regulationist categories of regime of accumulation and mode of regulation are in the end superimposed on the neo-Schumpeterian concepts of "techno-economic sphere" and "socio-institutional framework".[1] Thus, according to Storper and Scott [1989, p. 22], "capitalist production apparatuses may assume many alternative technological and institutional configurations ... Each particular

---

1. Whilst there is indeed a structural-functionalist current within the Regulation school, there is also another "wing" which has been more sensitive to class struggle and class agency. The work of Benjamin Coriat [1978] and of more "marginal" figures like Jean-Paul de Gaudemar [see de Gaudemar, 1980] reflects a more complex variant of Regulationism strongly influenced and shaped by the ideas of Italian *operaismo* as developed by such writers as Bologna, Negri, Tronti and Panzieri. We should also note that writers within the Regulation perspective who are apparently closer to neo-Schumpeterianism, are in fact extremely guarded about theoretical convergence. Thus Robert Boyer warns against the economic and technological determinism of long wave theory [Boyer, 1986, pp. 69, 83-4]. More recently, Boyer has suggested that "the concepts of technological system and technological paradigm" display the same features as the 'régulation' approach for institutional forms and that "*a priori*, one could imagine a marriage of these two lines of analysis", but he still emphasises the dangers of collapsing into a deterministic and reductionist model [Boyer, 1988, p. 89].

configuration consists in a historically determinate technological-institutional model of production ... Each such model is also roughly equivalent [sic] to what theorists of the French Regulationist School call a regime of accumulation and a model of social regulation". Whilst certain researchers have been quite explicit about building bridges between Regulation perspectives and long wave models [Roobeek, 1987; Cooke, 1987; Boyer, 1988], the over-riding tendency is for such a relation to be implicitly and wishfully presumed (a tendency that is only reinforced by the tentative invocation of regulationist terms in the recent work of Freeman and Perez [1988]).

What we have then is a complex theoretical syncretism, an unholy and congealed alliance of the ideas of Piore and Sabel, the economic geography of Scott and Storper, Regulation theory (in its most reductionist form) and neo-Schumpeterian long wave theory. Whilst there are clear differences in the components of this invisible college, what tends to get emphasised are the apparent convergences and commonalities. If there are those who are more explicit about their attempts to combine these various strands into a coherent theoretical synthesis [e.g. Mahon, 1987], for the most part it is a matter of conceptual elisions, jumps and slippages. Thus, although the notion of "technological paradigms" is much invoked, there is no acknowledgement that it means quite different things in Piore and Sabel than it does in long wave theory. Similarly, concepts of crisis and historical rupture are used very loosely and vaguely, as are notions of historical phases or stages. There is, for example, a substantiated assumption that regimes of accumulation correspond to kondratiev cycles. There is also a great deal of confusion about the object of analysis: at times it is the labour process or industrial organisation, whilst at other times it is the macroeconomy or even society as a whole.

The real and serious confusions and inconsistencies within this theoretical nexus, however, have not prevented it from establishing itself as an influential school of thought. It has become a new radical consensus for the 1980s. In the context of crisis and restructuring it has become drawn into the project of selling the future [see Webster and Robins, 1986, ch. 2], of projecting a new vision for social and economic progress. What is being promised is the end of centralisation, concentration, massification, standardisation, and so on: a kind of anti-Fordist utopia characterised by flexibility, diversity and, in spatial terms, localism. As Karel Williams and his colleagues [1987, p. 438] argue in their critique of Piore and Sabel, this kind of radical, and often romantic, futurology "strikes comforting and responsive chords". Ideas of flexible specialisation and of a new regionalism or localism have obvious appeal. And this is further enhanced by a historical perspective that suggests some absolute epochal transformation from mass society to flexible communities, and by an underlying technological and institutional determinism [Foster, 1988] that makes these changes seem not just desirable but also necessary and inevitable. It all adds up to a powerful and persuasive set of arguments, one that subtly "fuses description, prediction and prescription towards a self-fulfilling prophecy" [Pollert, 1988, p. 43].

We want now to look a little more closely at two variants of what we have called the new consensus - the flexible specialisation perspective of

Sabel and Piore, and the Regulation-type approach of Scott and Storper - in order to explore the significance they attribute to industrial districts.[2] How do they explain the development of this kind of territorial complex? Why do they attribute so much importance to this industrial paradigm for local and regional regeneration? And how do industrial districts fit into their understanding of change and restructuring and their schemes of historical development?

1. Flexible specialisation and industrial districts

Piore and Sabel argue that flexible specialisation is a consequence of a crisis of mass production: mass markets have become saturated and consumers are now demanding specialised and differentiated goods to which the mass production system cannot respond. "It is not clear", according to Piore, "why the environment has shifted in this way ... But prominent on the list are consumer tastes and the new flexibility of technology itself, factors which are viewed by the business community as unlikely to go away, hence compelling a permanent institutional adjustment". In the new unstable and uncertain environment where "markets can no longer be effectively managed and controlled", it is important for organisations to "be able to respond quickly and 'flexibly' as market conditions change" [Piore, 1986, p. 162]. Flexibly specialised firms are "flexible by comparison to mass producers, and hence more competitive in volatile environments" [Sabel, 1989, p. 53].[3] Having asserted the centrality of flexible specialisation as a new social paradigm, the argument then goes on to suggest that this has particular spatial implications. The relation between the economy and its territory is changing: "The more volatile markets became, the more firms experimented with flexible forms of organisation which permitted rapid shifts in output. As they did, they encouraged the reconsolidation of the region as an integrated unit of production" [ibid., p. 18].

The reasons for this new territorial logic are difficult to adduce. Piore and Sabel seem to assume that it is necessary to a regime of flexible specialisation, but their account is more descriptive than analytical.

---

2. The new orthodoxy includes other variants. Our critique, therefore, is not restricted only to the work of Scott, Storper, Piore and Sabel. For instance, similar ideas, though less theorised, are proposed by a group of French regional specialists attached to GREMI, a Paris-based network of researchers studying innovative milieus [see, for example, Aydalot, 1986, 1988; Loinger and Peyrache, 1988; Perrin, 1986, 1988]. Their assertion is that Fordism, dictated by the "functional" logic of the large firm, is giving way to a new "territorial" logic of development. The latter is based upon a technological innovativeness that is best realised through social and industrial networks, for which the best guarantor is the local milieu. Only the latter is capable of providing the necessary material, social and institutional conditions for innovative and networked production [see Crevoisier, 1988, for an exposition of this approach].

3. This argument about the centrality of markets as the defining principle of restructuring is problematical in both empirical and theoretical terms [see Williams et al., 1987, pp. 424-429; Pollert, 1988, p. 44]. In the work of Piore and Sabel, it seems to depend upon a very shaky behaviourist rationale.

Flexibility, they argue, depends on specialisation, which demands a new articulation of the division of labour both within and between firms. In an account of the textile machine industry in Baden-Württemberg, Sabel and his collaborators describe this phenomenon:

> The more specialised each firm became, the more it depended on the success of products complementing its own. Firms became more interested in exchanging information with related producers. They also began to further the well-being of the industry as a whole by supporting broad institutions - vocational schools, research institutes, and marketing agencies. The industry was not simply the sum of autonomous production units, but rather a set of institutions that made the survival of individual companies possible [Sabel et al., 1987, p. 31].

In the case of Italian industrial districts, this need for spatial agglomeration is again emphasised. The capacity to innovate, it is suggested, depends on "the firm's internal organisation, its close relations with workers, its clients and its collaboration with other firms in the sector", all of which leads to a relationship between firms which "resembles the collegial relation between good doctors, good lawyers, or good university teachers", and to an awareness on the part of the firm that "its success and very survival is linked to the collective efforts of the community to which it belongs and whose property it must defend" [Brusco and Sabel, 1981, pp. 106, 108]. It is the over-riding need of inter-firm collaboration, trust and social solidarity, reminiscent of the emphasis ascribed by Dore [1983] to "goodwill" in Japan, which gives rise to the tendency towards spatial agglomeration in the present period. There is no other necessary or sufficient condition for the resurgence of regional economies in Sabel's view.

Sabel emphasises the importance of industrial and social networks, pointing to "the learning advantages of network systems as industrial organisation" [Sabel, 1989, pp. 30-31]. Such networks, he argues, are crucial not only to small firms but to an increasing number of large corporations that are "imitating and allying with the industrial districts" [ibid., p. 31]. In the context of market fragmentation, "even the largest firms no longer know exactly what to produce or how" [ibid., p. 35]; the adaptive capacities of hierarchical mass-production corporations are exhausted. This has given rise to a significant reorientation of corporate organisation with the deverticalisation and decentralisation of operating units, the blurring of hierarchies, and the growth of external subcontracting relations being the most evident. Large firms, like small businesses, are becoming organised through network structures and shaped by the productive communities and "clan cultures" that form around these new structures.

Having described this combined logic of economic, social and spatial development, Sabel goes one step further to advertise the transformative potential of the new industrial districts and to emphasise the potential for endogenous development by flexible regional economies. From here it is possible to go on to argue that the proliferation of industrial districts could produce a new form of inter-regional collaboration. Flexible regions will evolve to share knowledge and resources and create an expansive net of solidarity: "If the pooling of knowledge succeeds, it can easily become the political metaphor and matrix for the pooling of other resources as well.

The more knowledge available to each industrial district, the less the probability of being tripped up by costly ignorance; the greater number of prosperous industrial districts, the more likely that each can draw on the resources of the others in its moments of distress" [Sabel, 1989, p. 58]. And on this basis, Sabel suggests, it is possible to see the structural and regulatory basis for a new form of national, and perhaps even international, economy.

There are two broad areas (in addition to others developed later in this paper) in which we would contest these claims about the special destiny of industrial districts. In the first place, the structural transformation, namely the break-up of mass markets, upon which the entire theory of flexible specialisation and local economies is constructed, is a dubious one. Williams and his colleagues [1987] have criticised Piore and Sabel for their lack of attention to the widespread diffusion of batch and craft production during Fordism itself. They, like Smith [1988], also demonstrate the persisting importance of scale, capacity-raising investment and mass demand in the so-called mature markets today, due to the continued expansion of replacement demand, the absorption of ever-increasing market shares by the major competitors and the ability of market leaders to cope with differentiated demand by continuing to draw upon a very large number of common standardised and mass-produced parts. Could it be that all we have today is greater product differentiation rather than the break-up of mass markets? If so, fragmentation and local agglomeration may not be an inexorable trend.

The second area of difficulty concerns the nature of the explanations offered by Piore and Sabel of restructuring across the second industrial divide. Whilst they develop elements of a structural account of transformation, there are in fact strong contrary tendencies in their thinking that push the analysis towards a behaviourist logic. The rationale for the growth of flexible specialisation and the emergence of industrial districts is built around the "strategic considerations" of social actors and "their tactics in particular instances" [Sabel, 1989, p. 53]; around such variables as trust, solidarity, community allegiance and local pride. To some extent, this psychological, or psychologistic, framework reflects a desire on the part of Piore and Sabel to avoid technological or economic determinism and to maintain a sense of openness and possibility. It remains inadequate, however. The language of individual choice is inserted into a discourse on collective actors and political agency [Solo, 1985]. The atomistic and individualistic framework of behaviourist theory cannot be combined or reconciled with a broader perspective on structural and political transformation. The approach of Piore and Sabel remains an unsatisfatory blend of determinism and voluntarism.

2. Vertical disintegration and new production complexes

The recent work of Allen Scott and Michael Storper represents a second important variant of the new consensus we have been discussing. It is in many ways a more theoretically sophisticated perspective and is based, unlike the work of Piore and Sabel, on a structural theory of transformation. Beginning from the analyses of the Regulation School, Scott and Storper describe the present period as one in which the crisis of Fordism as a regime of capitalist accumulation is now leading to the emergence of a brave new regime of flexible accumulation. In the late 1970s, they argue, the Fordist model of industrialisation was in disarray: new "emerging structures of flexible production helped to intensify the crisis of Fordism by exerting strong competitive pressures on mass production industries", whilst, at the same time, "the advent of flexible production organisation was potentiated by the problems of Fordist industry" [Storper and Scott, 1989, p. 26]. As with Piore and Sabel, we have again a simple binary opposition between mass production and flexibility underpinning the logic of economic transformation. Out of the ashes of Fordist mass production is rising the phoenix (the new "hegemonic model") of "flexible production methods" and "ensembles of flexible production sectors".

This industrial transformation also manifests itself in spatial terms through a "new geography of flexible accumulation". Basing their argument on a Marxist variant of transactions cost analysis, as developed in Scott's earlier work [e.g. Scott, 1986], Storper and Scott identify "the tendency for internal economies to give way before a progressive externalisation of the structure of production under conditions of rising flexibility, [which] leads at once to a revival of proclivities to locational convergence and reagglomeration" [Scott, 1988, p. 175]. The fundamental observation is that "vertical disintegration encourages agglomeration, and agglomeration encourages vertical disintegration" [Scott, 1986, p. 224]. Production flexibility is necessarily associated with the clustering of firms into localised geographical spaces: "the turn towards flexibility has been marked by a decisive reagglomeration of production and the emergence of the phenomenon of the industrial district" [Storper and Scott, 1989, p. 27]. Scott and Storper emphasise the emergence of Marshallian industrial districts, of "spatially agglomerated production complexes together with their dependent labour markets and intercalated human communities" [Scott, 1988, p. 176], as the essential feature of the new geography of production. But, in contrast to Sabel's self-contained regional economies, the agglomerations of Scott and Storper are situated in a wider spatial division of labour.

In many ways, Scott and Storper offer a very neat and coherent account of the proliferation of industrial districts: intensifying flexibility results in the vertical disintegration of organisational structures, and this in turn leads to locational convergence and spatial agglomeration. On this basis, we can differentiate the late Fordist regime of accumulation, characterised by branch plants and the decentralisation of production to peripheral regions, from its successor regime, with its strong agglomerative tendencies in flexible production sectors and its "reaffirmation of the significance of place as the foundation for efficient and effective production apparatuses" [Storper and Scott, 1989, p. 37]. In the transition from Fordism to flexibility, a functional logic of organisational structure gives way to a new territorial logic. This, clearly, is a more coherent and systematic rationale for the centrality and importance of industrial districts than that offered by Piore and Sabel, based as it is on the necessary logic of the restructuring process, rather than on the relative contingency of behavioural dynamics.

Neat and coherent. But, really, too neat and coherent. Scott and Storper are caught up, like Piore and Sabel, in the idealisation of flexible specialisation and industrial districts and the demonisation of Fordism and mass production. This is based on a kind of binary thinking that opposes flexibility against rigidity: these terms are at the heart of a splitting process, common to many forms of futurological speculation, that polarises a "rigid" past against a "flexible" future [Robins and Webster, 1988]. Reality is more equivocal, more ambiguous, more obscure.

Such a conceptual opposition is a rather limiting organising principle for a theory of socio-economic development and change. Scott and Storper do, nonetheless, mobilise it as the key to understanding the nature of the restructuring process between Fordism and so-called post-Fordism. But in so doing, they fall prey to that tautological thinking that Werner Bonefeld sees as characterising the new consensus more generally: "first of all a model or norm is abstracted from disparate historical tendencies, and then it is in the light of this model that the significance of these same tendencies is assessed" [Bonefeld, 1987, p. 124]. The "heresy of reality" is stripped and compressed into the diminished and constricting grip of a schematic model. In the case of Storper and Scott, this leads them into a totalising vision that sees flexible specialisation and locational agglomeration, and only this, wherever they look. Countervailing and divergent processes can then only be understood as anachronistic and residual elements of the "ageing regime" of Fordism. There is also a desire to identify "a common underlying system of structural dynamics" [Scott, 1988, p. 181] in all forms of localised agglomeration. Despite their recognition of differences at some moments, Storper and Scott collapse together such heterogeneous developments as Italian industrial districts, high-tech growth centres and metropolitan business agglomerations, into one master paradigm. The consequence, as the gap opens between model and reality, is an abrupt contrast between the old and the new orders: "the old industrial spaces of the Fordist regime and the new spaces of flexible accumulation, in their purest and sharpest expression, contrast starkly with one another" [ibid., p. 171].

Scott and Storper claim not only to identify an "evolutionary tendency" towards flexible specialisation as a form of industrial organisation, but also towards flexible accumulation as a historically new social epoch. Their account of transformations in the prevailing economic and technological paradigm is supplemented by an emphasis on the "complementary social phenomena", the "multiplicity of sociopolitical relations" that make up the "mode of social regulation" [Scott, 1988, p. 172]. Scott and Storper tend to see the transition to post-Fordism as a consequence of the objective laws of capitalist development and the process of historical change as "explained mainly by the laws of reproduction immanent in the structure of a mode of production" [Gartman, 1983, p. 660]. Within this model of structural change, there is no space for social struggle and agency in the making of historical change. Social relations are relegated to the secondary sphere of the mode of regulation where they are seen as more or less functional to the prevailing regime of accumulation.[4] The regulatory forms "help the regime of accumulation to adjust" to crisis conditions; they "come into being alongside the regime of accumulation as a means of stabilising its operation through time" [Scott, 1988, p. 172]. In the account of Scott and Storper, the emergence of flexible economies and of localised industrial districts is "matched" by "corresponding" regulatory institutions and ways of life. They are complemented by a new "place-bound business culture"; by "communal processes of the habituation of workers into the local culture of production"; by a "Marshallian 'industrial atmosphere'" [Storper and Scott, 1989, pp. 31, 33]. At the same time, "the distinctive neighbourhoods and communities that emerge within any agglomeration become integral to the legitimation and stabilisation of socio-economic divisions in the local area" [ibid., p. 34]. They see the emergence of a "new post-Fordist politics of place", that is, "the formation and appropriation of systems of place-bound norms integral to the functioning of any locale as a centre of economic and social life" [ibid. p. 34].

For Scott and Storper, this stabilisation and coherence of accumulation is the normal state of affairs, whilst crises are exceptional periods of transition during which social institutions and behaviour are realigned and refunctionalised in line with a new technological and economic paradigm. Such periods of coherence and cohesion represent the distinct *stages* or *phases* of capitalist historical development. In the present period of instability which marks the crisis of Fordism, we are awaiting the new functional synthesis of the post-Fordist era. Massification will inevitably and ineluctably cede to flexibility as the organising principle of a new historical epoch. It is in this context that Scott and Storper confidently observe the proliferation of flexible production complexes and assume them to be "the cores of the new growth centres of the world system" [Scott, 1988, p. 178]. An abstract and idealised template is imposed on disparate and contradictory historical tendencies. Certain tendencies in the present period are absolutised as the hegemonic model, and then projected forward as the paradigm for a future regime of accumulation, for a new historical phase of capitalism; and then it is in the light of this reified, ideal-type model of post-Fordism, that the events of the present period are assessed and explained. The historical trajectory to a post-Fordist society is a determined and inexorable process, one that is rooted in the logic of capital itself. Our own view (see section IV) is that the process is far less determinate than is suggested by this new orthodoxy. As more careful and nuanced research within the Regulation perspective makes clear, the resolution of the present crisis could take many different forms. The crisis of Fordism, for example, could take a very long time to be resolved, or it might even "provoke catastrophic regressions" [Aglietta, 1982, p. xii]. The world is more complex, contradictory and ambiguous than the new orthodoxy allows for, and the

---

4. The dangers of a functionalist conception of the mode of social regulation are emphasised by Boyer [1986, pp. 26-7, 30-1, 43] and by Lipietz [1987], and can be attributed to the origins of Regulationism in systems theory. Whilst the most careful examples of Regulationist analysis avoid functionalism, it remains a constant temptation, and it mars the analyses of less scrupulous exponents of this perspective.

possibilities that can emerge are more problematical than it suggests. The re-emergence of regional economies is not simply and unequivocally written into the scheme of things beyond Fordism.

We are moving too quickly, however. First we need to describe what the new orthodoxy has to say about the re-emerging regional economies and to see what is wrong with its conceptualisation. We also need to see how well the concept of "Marshallian industrial district" stands up to empirical scrutiny in relation to the country, Italy, which more than any other country is supposed to be the hallmark of the new regime.

III. The new industrial spaces

It is only recently that the rise of all newly industrialising areas in the advanced economies has been interpreted in terms of an emerging hegemonic regime of capitalist accumulation. Hitherto, work on this resurrection of locally contained and self-sustaining growth has tended to confine itself to the focused study of particular places and phenomena. Theoretical endeavour at its best has been concerned with teasing out some of the abstract processes behind one or several very similar realities. Thus, for instance, Giacomo Becattini [1987], Marco Bellandi [1982] and, to a lesser extent, Sebastiano Brusco [1986] have attempted to understand the growth of the highly competitive small firm agglomerations in the central and north-eastern regions of Italy (the "Third Italy") in terms of the deliberations of Alfred Marshall, at the turn of the century, on the "concentration of specialised industries in particular localities" [Marshall, 1961, pp. 267-277].

Marshall emphasised the role of external economies of scale deriving from the division of tasks in an industry among many producers. He also referred to the benefits deriving from the spatial agglomeration of an economic network; benefits such as the easy exchange of ideas, information and goods, the accumulation of skills and innovative capability, and the development of a cultural homogeneity allowing co-operation, trust and consensus among and between employers and workers. For these Italian authors, Marshall's rationale comes very close to explaining the contemporary dynamics of areas in the Third Italy in which each closely-knit network of small firms, reliant upon a design and innovation-intensive craft tradition, specialises in the production of a particular good, for sale to quality-discerning and price-flexible consumers. So close are the affinities seen to be, that the term "Marshallian industrial district" has been coined to capture the essence of these localities in Italy. How well does it stand up to empirical scrutiny?

1. Industrial districts in the Third Italy

There is now an extensive body of empirical literature which describes the characteristics and origins of the small-firm based production complexes which have emerged in the regions of the Third Italy (Emilia-Romagna, Tuscany, the Marche, Abruzzi, and Veneto) during the last 20 years.[5] There seems to be a broad consensus that the renewal of small firm activity, notably in the engineering industries, was due to the extensive use of the putting-out system by medium-sized and large corporations after the period of intense labour conflict in the early 1970s. However, the consolidated growth of small firms, especially in the traditional consumer goods industries, has been traced to their ability to act as an integrated network of producers relying upon a number of factors for their success. Inter alia, these are: economies of scale and scope arising from the division of labour between specialist producers; an entrepreneurial ingenuity arising from the combination of *petit bourgeois* traditions and the skill and technical advantages of artisan production; the sedimentation of appropriate skills and innovative capability in the milieu as a result of clustering; active support from local authorities and other local institutions in the provision of infrastructure, training, finance and other collective services; the development of marketing agents to facilitate exports; a reputation (e.g. "made in Prato") that attracts buyers; and the consolidation of trust and consensus-based local subcultures which permit social collaboration and the exchange of ideas.

These are the conditions which have generated innovative small firm networks producing internationally competitive machinery and machine tools in Bologna and Modena, knitwear in Carpi, textiles in Prato, ceramics in Sassuolo, and furniture or shoes in the Marche. The documentary evidence reveals quite clearly that the conditions vary between areas, but it also reveals striking locational and organisational similarities, hence justifying their description, within Italy, as areas of "diffuse industrialisation", "specialised areas", or "industrial districts". There is a consensus that they are the differentiated manifestations of one phenomenon: the widespread industrialisation, since the 1960s, of semi-rural areas and small towns with very similar social and economic structures (self-contained communities of artisans, peasant farmers and merchants, near or in towns with strong

5. Bagnasco's [1977] pioneering general work on the Third Italy has been accompanied by very detailed studies, with Trigilia, of localities in Tuscany and the Veneto [Bagnasco and Trigilia, 1984, 1985]. Other early "discoveries" of small firm complexes include Becattini's [1975, 1978] work with IRPET on Toscana as well as that of Lorenzoni [1979] on Prato, the work of Brusco [1982] and Sabel [1982] on Emilia-Romagna, and the work of Frey [1974], Fuà [1983] and Paci [1980] on the role of family and informal labour in the Third Italy. In the 1980s, there has been an explosion of case studies, a tiny proportion of which are on the following: small rural firms in Lombardy [Garofoli, 1983]; ceramics [Russo, 1985], knitwear [Solinas, 1982] and engineering [Murray, 1987; Lazerson, 1988] in Emilia-Romagna; textiles in Prato [Berardi and Romagnoli, 1984; Macelli and Romagnoli, 1979]; small firm growth in the Marche [Mazzoni, 1981; Niccoli, 1984] and the Veneto [Anastasia and Rullani, 1981; Belussi, 1987, 1988].

municipal traditions). It is the systemic, agglomerative, and communal aspects of these areas [Trigilia, 1986], together with their distinctiveness from vertically integrated large firms or self-supporting independent small firms, which has earned them the label of being Marshallian. As a description of the Third Italy, this epithet has tended to be used in a less messianic way than in the writings of the new orthodoxy.

How far, then, do the realities conform to a homogeneous model of the Third Italy? Our review, below, of the evidence tends to lend support, with some qualifications, to a very broadly defined Marshallian interpretation rather than to the arguments of the flexible specialisation model. In a recent paper, Fabio Sforzi [1989], has attempted to identify the local travel to work areas in Italy which could qualify as Marshallian industrial districts. Eligibility in Sforzi's analysis is dependent upon an area's ability to meet three very broad conditions: the clustering and renewal of small firms specialising in the different phases of a particular industry ("a system of interacting parts"); a social structure characterised by a high level of small entrepreneurs, artisans, skilled workers, working wives, and extended family or youth labour; and proximity between home and work in the labour market. The study identifies about 60 areas with industrial districts, spread predominantly between eastern Lombardia (11 areas), Emilia-Romagna (8), Veneto (14), Tuscany (8), and the Marche (15). Interestingly, the vast majority of the districts are near small agricultural towns and, in contrast to Sabel's high-tech engineering areas in Emilia, over 50 of them produce fashionwear (textiles, clothing, shoes and other leather goods) or wooden furniture.

At a very general level, then, there are many clusters of small, family and craft-based firms in the rural areas of the Third Italy. To this extent they are similar as well as "Marshallian". However, a closer reading of detailed case studies reveals that there are significant differences between them in terms of their origins and their consolidation as industrial districts. A recent study by Roberto Camagni and Roberta Capello [1988] draws extensively on the published case studies to show, for instance, that in Tuscany the flexibility generated by the high division of labour among small firms and the region's highly integrated, self-supporting and co-operative social structure have been two key success factors. In contrast, areas in the Veneto appear to have benefited from low labour costs, the availability of specialised skills, as well as part-time labour from agriculture, and the pervasive influence of Christian Democracy and strong Catholic traditions, which have played a crucial role in shaping common social and business goals. The decentralisation of tasks among small firms appears not to be a distinguishing characteristic of Veneto areas [Belussi, 1988]. In the Marche, the areas of small firm development have been able to exploit similar labour circumstances as those in the Veneto, but they have also had to rely more on active local authority participation, rather than consolidated political subcultures or social traditions for the provision of common social and economic resources. In other words, significant differences exist between the industrial districts of the Third Italy - and the ones described above refer to only those areas which all produce similar traditional consumer goods.

The possibility that contemporary industrial districts may be a temporary or transitional phenomenon, and that they may be subsumed within new structures of concentration and centralisation is another question that the abstract and static model of the Third Italy has failed to address. A recent report [Signorini, 1988] based upon a Bank of Italy survey of technical change among firms of different sizes in Tuscany shows a relative slowdown in the uptake of technical innovations by small firms. This, for Signorini, presents a threat to the survival of the region's traditional small firm entrepreneurship, which could lead to the emergence of a small number of larger, "elite" firms. Similarly, Fergus Murray [1987] and Claudio Tolomelli [1988] refer to the growth in takeover activity within Emilia's engineering industries. For Tolomelli, the growing concentration of ownership is leading to the vertical integration of tasks and functions, as well as the insertion of the local economy into a wider spatial division of labour. These processes could not only alter the basis upon which the Emilian industrial districts have developed, but they could also threaten their survival:

> We see that the traditional organisation of the industrial districts will be overshadowed and replaced by an organisation based on groups of firms, with a variety of interconnections and tied to Italian and foreign corporations ... Groups of firms are not only taking over individual firms, but through them can enter the web of relations between firms within the districts and integrate them into their corporate network [Tolomelli, 1988, p. 8].

Finally, renewed competition from, or the flow of resources to, the traditional industrial heartland of the country could also threaten the economic buoyancy of these areas. It is said that extensive industrial restructuring, involving predominantly the greater uptake and utilisation of new technologies by large firms as well as their defeat of organised labour, has already begun to restore to the north-west regions their traditional industrial and economic hegemony. Camagni and Capello's study [1988] shows that since the mid-1970s, there has been a reversal of the previous ten-year trend of faster manufacturing productivity growth (GDP per capita) in the Third Italy regions. During the second half of the 1970s, productivity in Piemonte rose annually by 4.5 per cent and by 3.9 per cent in Lombardia, well above the rate in Veneto (2.5 per cent), Emilia-Romagna (2.8 per cent), Tuscany (2.9 per cent) and the Marche (3.5 per cent). Furthermore, the regional wage/productivity gap, which had worked to the locational advantage of the Third Italy during the 1960s and early 1970s because productivity rose faster than wages had, by 1981, begun to work in favour of the north-west regions since wages were rising more slowly than productivity. In view of the various internal and external pressures confronting the older and more successful industrial districts, what will happen to their organisational structure, and whether they will continue to remain Marshallian, remains an open question.

The majority of the remaining industrial districts, especially those in the traditionally less urbanised and less developed regions (Marche, Abruzzi) are new and quite different from the older established ones. Many of the areas of recent specialisation in the shoe, clothing and furniture industries appear to be little more than rural clusters of small, family firms producing the same finished or intermediate good (usually of medium-to-poor quality) for large subcontractors or for wholesalers selling in the open market. Often, these producers have few entrepreneurial or marketing skills. They have little immediate access to technology, specialised business services, finance and intermediate products. They are also often in fierce competition with each other as a result of close product similarities as well as severe pressures on prices, notably from subcontractors.

It is only in the loosest possible sense that these areas constitute an articulated industrial system. The producers possess a restricted degree of freedom in the market place and receive little support from the rest of the system. The firms tend to be isolated, highly dependent on a few buyers, and barely able to improve their market position. "Flexibility", here, tends to refer to an ability simply to survive and, on the basis of an artisanal capacity, to respond to new designs and new market signals. It also refers to self-exploitation and the use of family labour, the evasion of tax and social security contributions, and the use of cheap female and young workers, especially in the area of unskilled work. These conditions are also typical of the vast numbers of very small firms and artisans working in the traditional industries in many developing economies. They provide poor publicity for the ideal Marshallian model but they do have a very real and steadfast existence in Italy. Furthermore, as the experiences of the informal artisanal economy in developing countries have shown, there is no guarantee that the new small firm agglomerations will become internationally competitive industrial districts.

In this brief review, we have tried to show that even in the case of the Third Italy, where there are strong common characteristics between the areas of recent industrialisation, there are difficulties associated with the widespread empirical application of the term "Marshallian industrial district". However, there can be no doubt that as a description of a particular form of economic development based on local small firm synergies the term, better than any other, succeeds in capturing the experiences of the most successful areas in the Third Italy. Now, however, with the rise of the new orthodoxy, all kinds of different areas in different countries are being described as industrial districts in a bid to demonstrate that this form of growth is the globally enabling condition for a new post-Fordist economic regime. The empirical and theoretical circumspection of the best Italian writing on industrial districts has given way to a totalising approach. In the new orthodoxy, we are being asked to believe that the very laws of capitalist development are becoming, as it were, Marshallian (as opposed to Fordist). Consequently, not only are the new spaces all seen as forms of industrial district but, as such, they are also promoted as the "new growth centres of the world system" [Scott, 1988, p. 178].

2. The new orthodoxy and the new industrial spaces

The term which Storper and Scott [1989] use for the new industrial spaces of flexible accumulation is "flexible production complexes". Flexible production as a process is said to be particulary evident in the high technology sectors, in industries in which the craft tradition has been revitalised, in business and financial services, and areas of mass production in which Fordist methods have been abandoned. However, it is the growth of local agglomerations in the first two branches (high technology and craft), which receive the most attention, and which have sprung up in rural or agricultural areas untainted by Fordist traditions, and also in and around metropolitan areas such as Los Angeles or Boston which offer a "docile" immigrant or female workforce.

Storper and Scott cite the following areas as significant examples of the new high technology agglomerations: Silicon Valley, Orange County, Route 128 and Dallas-Fort Worth in the United States; the Cambridge-Reading-Bristol axis in Britain; and, in France, the Scientific City of the Southern Paris region, Grenoble, Toulouse and Sophia Antipolis. As for the craft sectors, artisanal or design-intensive industry is currently highly developed in the Third Italy, in Denmark, the Federal Republic of Germany, France, Spain and even parts of the USA (e.g. the clothing industry in New York and Los Angeles, motion pictures in Los Angeles). Though Scott is keen to stress that each area is caught up in a unique developmental trajectory, the differences assume a descriptive rather than analytical significance:

> A common underlying system of structural dynamics can be detected in virtually every case. These dynamics, as we now know, revolve for the most part around the social division of labour, the formation of external economies, the dissolution of labour rigidities, and the reagglomeration of production [Scott, 1988, p. 181].

The overall gist of Sabel's analysis is not too different from that of Scott and Storper, although his treatment of the "renaissance of regional economies" is less precise in meaning and broader in coverage, both in terms of process and place. For Sabel, the new regional economies are highly self-contained and composed of two broad realities: new Marshallian industrial districts composed of small firm networks; and new local production networks resulting from the reorganisation of large firms into separate product-based divisions, each with its own organisational autonomy. Both are portrayed as examples of the ever-increasing reconsolidation, as in the nineteenth century, of the region as an integrated unit of production.

By offering only a vague definition of the causes and key characteristics of spatial agglomeration, Sabel can refer to the re-emerged regional economies as both unique and the same. High technology complexes such as Silicon Valley and Route 128 come to stand alongside the craft-based industrial districts mentioned by Storper and Scott as well as new ones in Jutland in Denmark (textiles, furniture, machine tools), Småland in Sweden (metalworking), Baden-Württemberg in Germany (textiles, garments, machine tools, automobile components), Oyonnax in France (plastic injection moulding), Valles in Spain (textiles, wooden furniture and metalworking), and many industrial districts in small towns in Japan (e.g. Sakaki).

Sabel emphasises the following as the common aspects of the industrial districts: extensive and elaborate co-operation on a flexible basis between small specialist firms; the flexible use of microprocessor-based technologies in combination with craft skills; the expansion of privately or publicly provided collective business services; strong informal or institutionalised structures to ensure the provision of minimum pay scales and acceptable working conditions to regulate inter-firm co-operation and competition;[6] and the development of long-term collaborative relations with larger firms inside or outside the industrial district. It is interesting to note that the high technology areas such as Orange County and Silicon Valley, with their large firms that dominate the local electronics industry and whose division of labour is international rather than local, sit uncomfortably within this narrow, small firm and craft-based definition of industrial districts.

For Sabel, flexible specialisation is also about large firm restructuring, which he claims is leading to decentralisation strategies which are not only very similar to the organisational and spatial structure of the small industrial districts, but could also "blend with them".[7] Sabel argues that in the past 15 years, many of the largest multinationals, especially West German, Italian and Japanese, have begun to organise production on the lines of flexible specialisation in order to respond rapidly to market fragmentation and volatility on a least cost basis. This has involved - within textbook cases such as Bosch, Olivetti, Montedison and Xerox - a move towards autonomy and the integration of conception and execution within product divisions; the treatment of workers and subcontractors as worthy junior partners in production; and the devolution of responsibility for the development and production of sub-modules to sub-contractors.

We are being asked to believe that the organisational structure of the most progressive large corporations is now very similar to that of the industrial district in terms of the relaxation of centralised control, the devolution of responsibilities to local divisional units, and the replacement of coercion by collaboration with subcontractors and workers. Sabel acknowledges that not all corporations are pursuing this strategy. For instance, he notes [1989, pp. 37-38] that many US corporations (General Motors, Kodak) are adopting, in keeping with the classical model developed by Japanese corporations, the strategy of "flexible mass production", in order to cope with product fluctuations. However, these "neo-Fordists", who have decentralised production and not conception or control, and who are still wedded to dedicated machinery, still embrace the principles of mass production. They "appear unable to accommodate the currently necessary pace of product development" [ibid., p. 38]. This comment, together with Sabel's belief that even the large Japanese corporations are "adopting the organisational forms of the more decentralised large corporation" [ibid.,

---

6. The role of local regulatory mechanisms in ensuring the continued success of the industrial districts is also emphasised by Storper and Scott [1989]. The factors they single out to be important are "trust relations", "system-wide co-ordinating institutions", a consolidated "industrial atmosphere", and social consensus.

7. Though Scott, in his article with Storper [1989] does not attach any significance to this "discovery" of industrial districts by large firms, in another short piece written with Cooke [1988], he cites the example of Nissan in the north-east of England and General Motors' Saturn plant in the United States as nascent examples of such a process.

p. 38], leads us to infer that it can only be a matter of time before the textbook model becomes hegemonic.

Sabel avoids specifying the geography of the fully decentralised and benign corporation. However, there is a strong suggestion that each autonomously run division roots itself in its locality. Under flexible specialisation, the branch plant of the 1990s, like small firms, will nurture the growth of industrial districts:

> These activities of the giant corporations would more closely resemble and actually blend into the activity of the industrial districts. An engine plant which participates in the design of the engine and depends on highly specialised local suppliers to produce it is both part of a multinational car firm *and* an independent industrial district [ibid., p. 40].

That said, Sabel offers no explanation of why the new type of branch plant or division should establish its linkages in the area of location.

In the new consensus which has emerged through and alongside the work of Piore and Sabel, and of Scott and Storper, the term "industrial district", in sharp contrast to its more limited early use in relation to the Third Italy, has come to denote a wide variety of new regional growth experiences associated with the end of Fordism. In the rest of this section, we argue against such an all-embracing and epochal interpretation of the new industrial spaces, on the grounds that the processes of change behind these experiences are highly differentiated and also less epochal than made out by the new orthodoxy. The basis of our critique is not to make a bid for the uniqueness of any one industrial agglomeration: we do not wish to defend a purely descriptive empiricism but to reject an approach which squeezes quite different phenomena into a badly conceptualised analytical framework.[8]

3. Post-Fordist industrial districts?

The consensus broadly agrees on the key elements of the new industrial districts. But it is an agreement which is too vague to show how these elements are so fundamentally different from those of the growth areas which spearheaded Fordism. The industrial district is a locally co-ordinated

---

8. We do not wish to rebut attacks such as those by Harvey and Scott [1988] on arguments against generalisation and generalities in locality studies. We also agree with the rejection by Scott and Storper [1987] of approaches which offer endless lists of factors which explain, for example, the rise of high tech agglomerations. Our complaint is that the new "theory" treats as one the many and very different abstract processes shaping the new industrial spaces, and that some of these processes may not even belong to the model of structural change which is being proposed. Furthermore, we would argue with Massey [1984] and Hudson [1988] that there is no simple or linear relationship between the economic and the spatial. In any economic regime (e.g. mass production) there is a wide variety of ways in which production will be organised geographically, as places and strategies combine in novel and different ways. To condense all the new industrial spaces into one spatial form (the "industrial district") as well as one "structural" process (e.g. vertical disintegration) would be to appeal for a simple theory of spatial development. Our objection, then, is against vulgar theory.

and well articulated economic system, usually but not always specialising in one product, characterised by the division of tasks between firms, with the latter deriving all the benefits and economies of spatial agglomeration. Is this the distinctive characteristic of the post-Fordist locality, or have we perhaps come across this phenomenon before? Consider the following description by John Lovering of the local economy in Britain during the 1950s and 1960s when the consumer industries were taking off:

> But the new industries still tended to be regionally bounded, as for example in the Manchester electrical engineering industry, the Midlands car industry, the Bristol aircraft industry, the Sheffield steel industry, or the London radio industry. Expansion in one corner of the industry tended to generate ripple effects across the entire local economy ... As a result, the British economy was essentially a federation of distinctive regional economies ... Regional economic identities were defined, networks of directors interlocked, capital was supplied, and regional business interests were co-ordinated in the cities ... In the last couple of years a number of writers have captured this economic relationship under the term Fordism ... [Lovering, 1988, pp. 145-6].

The early years of the localised Fordist production complexes such as the car factories of Detroit or Turin also displayed a significantly high level of development of the social division of labour. There might have been more stages of the production process contained within the firm than today, but there was also an awful lot of the multi-part product that was bought in from local suppliers often, as with post-Fordism, on the basis of long-term, and even loose, collaboration among relatively autonomous partners. Furthermore, the principles of Fordism were also about purchasing the co-operation of workers and co-ordinating their work life with other aspects of their life. In ideological terms, this was presented then, as now, in terms of the worker as partner and co-operator; in reality, now, as then, this amounts to controlling, regulating and supervising the characters and the private lives of "new model workers".

We do not, in drawing these parallels, wish to claim that there are no differences between the so-called Fordist and post-Fordist production complexes. We wish simply to demonstrate that, with the exception of a period of crisis after the 1960s which provoked the break-up and internationalisation of the Fordist industrial heartlands, the broad definitions of the new orthodoxy also apply to an earlier period whose economic and geographical logic is supposed to be antithetical to that of post-Fordism. If there are indeed strong similarities between past and present, this would suggest that the rise of the new industrial spaces may not reflect the structural or organisational requirements of a new post-Fordist economic regime which demands the vertical disintegration and flexible specialisation of production. Mass production need not necessarily mean the supremacy of the technical over the social division of labour, and flexible or specialised production need not necessarily signify the pre-eminence of the social division of labour or its containment within local boundaries.

Capitalist development in this century has been characterised by the extensive and progressive deepening of both the technical and the social division of labour to produce an economic system, a *filière*, which is at the same time fragmented and integrated. The two divisions of labour co-exist, rather than displace each other. Furthermore, the historical example invoked above also suggests that there appears to be no structural reason (e.g. market size or composition, type of production technique or organisational framework) in any long phase which determines the balance between the two. Similarly, the spatial containment of the production *filière* need not be for reasons which are structural or historically bound. Richard Walker [1988], in a thought-provoking attempt to capture the many ways in which the *filière* can be organised or sub-divided, goes so far as to suggest that the territorial complex is an independent and trans-historical organisational form. It is not, for Walker, the necessary outcome of any particular form of industrial organisation (e.g. vertical disintegration). It may be more appropriate to conceptualise the new industrial districts as examples of an ever-present mode of geographical organisation (the "territorial complex") which can be activated, as it were, by a multitude of often unpredictable reasons, rather than as the specific product of post-Fordist deverticalisation. Its strengths, as Walker argues, relate to a variety of social, economic and organisational benefits that have always derived from spatial propinquity and agglomeration.

Of course, such a theorisation does not tell us much about the processes governing the development of the new industrial spaces today. All it tells us is that, as in the past, a variety of area-based circumstances combine with industrial ones to produce production complexes of one form or another (e.g. a "Fordist Detroit" or a "Marshallian Prato"). A general theory of post-Fordist industrial spaces as it has been proposed by the new orthodoxy is unacceptable. Such a theory tends to be either so vague and diluted that it can apply to any example of a local production complex or one which ignores continuities with the past. If an all-embracing or structural theory of spatial form is clearly highly problematical, how then should we think about the new industrial spaces? In our view, we should settle for something less grandiose and accept the possibility of there being several types of new production complexes which are very different from one another and whose development is not guided by one overarching structural transformation.

We would advocate a more cautious approach which does not collapse different realities into one or arrive at rash generalisations. The work of Bagnasco, Becattini, Brusco and Trigilia on the Third Italy is a good example of such an approach. It is only after rigorous theoretical inquiry and rich historical analysis that these authors have come to characterise some of the areas as new Marshallian industrial districts. Clearly, networks in other countries, of small specialist producers utilising a variety of local agglomeration economies as well as craft skills and transactional flexibilities to produce continually changing batches of goods for the high value added niches of mature markets, could also be recognised as examples of Marshallian industrial districts. Categorisations ought to be made at this level of detail. Perhaps the growth of such areas, too, ought to be put down to factors such as the development and extension of niche markets, rather than to monumental changes such as the end of mass consumption.

The other new industrial spaces, especially the agglomerations which have pioneered the development of new industries (Silicon Valley and

Grenoble) and those with extensive large firm subcontracting, ought to be treated separately and with less hyperbole. In a political economic sense these differences do matter. Variations in social and power relations among firms, institutions, employers and workers, play a critical role in shaping the social and economic characteristics of each type of production complex and its prospects. From the technicist organisational perspective of the new orthodoxy, for example, decentralisation and disintegration may seem highly significant. But if we are sensitive to the political and power structures of organisations, then these tendencies are likely to seem far less absolute. The new orthodoxy's analogy between the Marshallian industrial district and the local practices of the flexibly specialised multinational is a good example of a techno-institutionalist approach masquerading as political economy. Both developments are said to be characterised by a more or less loose association or network of autonomous buyers and sellers as a result of vertical disintegration. But are they really the same? The distinctive feature of the industrial district is the extensive division of labour among small firms which require each others' product, co-operation and proximity, but are also independent. The division of labour (including finance and marketing) is almost entirely locally contained and, through specialisation and interdependence, the production complex is, as it were, collectively controlled and regulated. In the subcontracting production complex, however, there is a more uneven distribution of power, and control ultimately lies in the hands of the major firms.

It is clear that the new divisional branch of the multinational corporation, with its own R & D facilities, its product and process complexity and its design capable suppliers, affords, in principle, many more economic opportunities to a locality than the traditional "headless" or task specific branch plant ever did. The autonomous division could act as a major innovation and growth pole for the locality. However, there is still no certainty that such a decentralised structure is becoming a standard formula for the multinational. If Sabel is wrong in assuming that mass markets have forever perished, then there is no reason to believe that the highly successful formula of partial decentralisation practised by many "flexible mass producers" in Japan and elsewhere is about to disappear. Here, complex subcontracting is combined with rigid and centralised control (Dohse, et al. [1985] call it "Toyotism"), to produce good quality products for volatile mass markets. This example of vertically disintegrated but centrally controlled production appears, at least for the present, to be more pervasively practised than Sabel's textbook example of the fully decentralised multinational. This model may well have a local production network, but as Loinger and Peyrache put it, "in this situation a sort of invisible wall isolates the large firm and its subcontractors from the rest of the local economy" [Loinger and Peyrache, 1988, p. 117].

The large firm locality is not an independent unit which sets the terms for its own development, but remains functionally integrated, albeit flexibly [Cooke, 1988; Camagni, 1988], into the wider division of labour of the multinational corporation. It is "autonomous" in its organisation, but "quasi vertically integrated" [Leborgne and Lipietz, 1988] in all other senses. As Poittier expresses it:

> We have no right to suppose that this new system is being locally reduplicated. It is more appropriate to conclude that it has found local support. Large firms seek to make the most of local traditions. This strategy involves taking a role in strengthening the local productive system, though the corporate policy is more of a means than an end in itself ... In the initial stages, the corporation promotes or merely watches the creation of innovative units, as relatively independent organisations embedded in the local environment. It then takes control of these units and terminates or diminishes their ties with the local area [Poittier, 1988, p. 117].

As with the classical branch-plant, the new production complex continues to be locked into the structure of the multinational corporation, and subject to its decisions. The concept of dependent regional development may have to be modified with the growth of the new large firm local networks, but we have a long time to go before we can abandon it. Nor should it be assumed that the change in definition could not be for the worse. Crowther and Garrahan's [1988, p. 52] description of Nissan's direct and indirect control "over organised labour, over its component suppliers, over land use control, over public authorities, indeed over the whole local economy" in the North-East of England is reminiscent of the one company town in which corporate philosophy sets the agenda for the social, economic and cultural development in the entire community. The locality may come to possess more elements of the production chain than did the single-task factory of the 1960s and 1970s. But this type of new production complex could be worse than the old branch plant since it could turn the entire locality into a branch plant.

Finally, the possibility that the new stand-alone operations may not stimulate much local economic development should also be kept firmly on the analytical agenda. Glasmeier's study [1988a] of new "technical branch plants" - independent profit centres with product related R & D attached to them - confirms this. Motorola's semi-conductor operation in Phoenix has generated few local linkages, like the highly specialised communications operation in Florida belonging to the Harris Corporation, despite the high "local development potential" of the plants, their products and their firms.

The "branch industrial complex", therefore, is governed by quite different laws from those affecting the Marshallian industrial district, and the two phenomena ought to be kept analytically separate. So, too, with agglomerations such as Silicon Valley and Grenoble, which have pioneered (as opposed to imitated) the development of new industries. Although, like most other dynamic agglomerations, these areas possess an articulated social division of labour, an innovative environment, social networks, and so on, they are also very different in terms of their constitution. Unlike the other agglomerations, their strength derives from a unique specialisation in new products with rapidly expanding demand in world markets.[9]

---

9. Our intention is not to claim that the distinctiveness of these areas derives from the nature of the product, but to insist that their status as pioneer areas binds them into one development logic. For this reason, we would not box all the high tech areas, for instance, into one category. "Branch complexes" such as those in Central Scotland, Silicon Valley and Route 128 near Boston, and policy induced Science Parks or Technopoles have very little in common

Silicon Valley, for instance, acquired a dominance in the world semiconductor industry through an initial specialisation which arose when the social division of labour in the industry was poorly developed elsewhere. This encouraged an agglomeration that consolidated as the area produced giant corporations which, in spite of their location of new factories overseas, continued to retain advanced manufacturing and R & D within California. Further agglomeration and diversification into other growing markets in electronics has occurred as a result of the area's capability of attracting capital and labour, new entrepreneurship from research laboratories, and the continual growth of highly specialised new firms due to spin-off from the larger corporations [see Gordon and Kimball, 1987].

Perhaps we should compare areas such as Silicon Valley with other areas which also have pioneered major product innovations (Detroit, with its motor vehicles in the 1930s) rather than with small firm Marshallian industrial districts, or branch-plant production complexes. As one commentator asks, how many examples of regional development are actually related to such major innovations? [Poittier, 1988, p. 111]. Do we really need an epochal theory of post-Fordist accumulation or flexible specialisation to account for the development of these product pioneering industrial agglomerations? Such growth has also occurred in the past. The bare bones of an explanation could draw on Vernon's [1966] hypothesis of clustering in the earlier stages of the product life cycle, Myrdal's [1957] theorisation of capital and labour being attracted to a growth pole due to the forces of "cumulative causation", and the continuation of local spin-off and innovation in "mature stages" due to vertical disintegration and specialisation [e.g. Del Monte, 1987]. But such an approach would not be fashionable enough for those who wish to see a future without antecedents.

We have tried, in this section, to argue against a simple and totalising theory of industrial districts. As we argue in the next section, the geography of production in the present period of change is to do with far more than simply a return to regional economies.

IV. The new order: Global space, local space

The new orthodoxy is a social science variant of what Boris Frankel [1987] describes as "post-industrial utopianism". What it has done has been to take one element of the present restructuring process, crystallised in the concept of flexibility, and to project it forwards as the one guiding principle of a new social era. Its conceptual framework is structured around a simplistic binary opposition (mass/flexible) which then becomes the basis for distinguishing "stages" of economic and historical development (and even progress) characterised as Fordist and post-Fordist.

---

with each other in terms of their key agents or processes [see, for example, Saxenian, 1987; Glasmeier, 1988b].

Our argument - and it seems strange to have to make it - is that socio-historical processes are more complex, more chaotic. There are indeed new trends emerging, but they are complex and contradictory, and they exceed what is designated by "flexible specialisation". The new is not marked by an absolute and fundamental break from the old: the old order of things does not, cannot, simply and conveniently disappear. More convincing, perhaps, than the idealising post-Fordist scenarios we have been discussing, is Joachim Hirsch's interpretation of a post-Fordism that extends and intensifies many elements of the *ancien régime*. Hirsch describes what is almost a kind of living-dead Fordism, a future of "hyperindustrialism" combined with "social dualism and segmentation", and watched over by an "authoritarian state" [Hirsch, 1985a, 1985b]. If one looks at the labour process or at industrial organisation, then it may be possible to emphasise the new - though even here there are in fact arguments that stress continuity [Pollert, 1988]. If, however, the focus broadens to the macroeconomy and to the international arena, then elements of continuity may be most apparent. From this perspective, for example, David Gordon does not see a change from Fordism to post-Fordism, but rather a period of prolonged and protracted crisis. Current changes, he argues, should be understood "*not* as a symptom of structural transformation but rather as a consequence of the *erosion* of the social structure of accumulation which conditioned international capitalist prosperity during the 1950s and 1960s. We are experiencing the decay of the older order and not yet the inauguration of a new one" [Gordon, 1988, p. 24]. Similarly, when he looks at the activities of transnational finance capital, transnational banks and multinational corporations, Wladimir Andreff [1984, p. 77] sees an international capitalist order "which does not have much of a new face".

The status of the new order in its relation to the past is clearly a matter of divided opinion. This is not an issue which we are able to elaborate or resolve here, but simply raise in order to broaden the debate on what are the constitutive features of contemporary macroeconomic change. And this is particularly the case with the changing geography of accumulation. Much has been made of a fundamental restructuring of space and territory in the supposed transition to post-Fordism, and industrial districts have been identified as symbols of the new order. They are the key elements of a new "spatial fix" that will, absolutely it would appear, replace the old fix of Fordism. In settling accounts with the geography of this allegedly anachronistic regime of accumulation, there has developed a new idealisation of the particular and the local. More adequate, in our view, than this notion of succeeding geographical "stages", is the "geological metaphor" developed by Doreen Massey [1984]. According to this heuristic conception, successive rounds of accumulation give rise to overlaying strata of industrial organisation and structure. "New and old forms of organising production profitably", as Ray Hudson [1988, p. 485] argues, "combine to produce changing spatial divisions of labour and have become intertwined in different ways in different times and places". There are indeed some conceptual difficulties with this kind of formulation [Warde, 1985], but its great advantage is in providing a more comprehensive and subtle framework for exploring geographical restructuring, one that does not overdramatise and fetishise the process of change.

What, then, of the nature of spatial and territorial transformation in the present period? Against the new orthodoxy, we would make the case that we are, in fact, seeing increasing tendencies towards internationalisation and the global integration of local and national economies. "World space", Henri Lefebvre reminds us, "is the field in which our epoch is created" [Lefebvre, 1979, pp. 288-289]. Regional and local economies have to be understood in the context of this global field. World corporations, we might add, have been the major force through which our epoch has been created. Discussion of entrepreneurial artisans and of disintegrating and localising corporations should not blind us to the growing power and influence of global industrial and finance capital. Multinational corporations are (need it really be said?) the real shakers and shapers of the world economy. And if we look at their activities in the current period, then the scenario of flexible production and independent localities must seem somewhat wishful. Andreff [1984] describes the emergence of a higher degree of centralisation and internationalisation of capital, a deepening of the capitalist mechanism of unequal development, and the domination of transnational finance capital, based on ever-closer links between multinational corporations and transnational banks. The multinational corporation remains the most powerful agent of the restructuring process, and there is little evidence that uneven development and transnational integration are being superseded.

What are the current strategies of multinational capital? How do they correspond to the projections of the new orthodoxy? In reality, global corporations are following a range of strategies, often antithetical to the localising and territorial logic, the shift towards flexibility and towards integration into the local economy, that Sabel claims to be the new logic of multinational capital. They may remain committed to "old", Fordist forms of organisation; they are also exploring a range of "new" possibilities. Beside the outright physical relocation of existing facilities, particularly during the recessionary 1970s, corporate management has developed a whole range of strategies, almost all on an international scale, to reassert its authority and control and, of course, to restore profitability. During the 1980s, there has been an unprecedented rise in the level of foreign direct investment, particularly through mergers, takeovers, joint ventures and various forms of strategic alliance between large corporations [Amin and Smith, 1986; Cooke, 1988; Martinelli and Schoenberger, 1989]. Keen to reduce costs and risks, maximise on scale economies, enter into new product areas, and maintain or extend market shares, these corporations have deployed strategies such as parallel production, multiple sourcing and multilateral co-production [Bluestone, 1987]; the international fragmentation and subcontracting of the production process, accompanied by greater control of the production network through the use of new information and communication technologies [Dunning, 1988]; and greater horizontal and vertical integration, through direct ownership or other means, especially in the areas of finance, Research and Development and marketing and distribution.

The new orthodoxy's singular and partial emphasis on fixity and the "politics of place" is clearly inadequate, denying as it does the growing internationalisation and international integration of the activities of major corporations. Capital is increasingly mobile, hypermobile even, tending towards an increasingly nomadic existence. Castells and Henderson describe a "space of flows":

> The development of the international economy, the dramatic growth of new information and communications technologies, the formation of powerful transnational organisations linked by subordinated, decentralised networks, are crucial factors in the process that provides the structural meaning for each territory in terms of the function that territory performs in the broader framework of interdependent operations. We certainly still have spatial forms, since societies and economies develop on a given territory and unevenly across the globe. Yet the logic and dynamics of territorial development are increasingly placeless from the point of view of the dominant organisations and social interests [Castells and Henderson, 1987, p. 7].

This perception contrasts dramatically with the flexible specialisation thesis.[10]

Rather than some fundamental shift from centralisation, concentration and integration towards a new historical era of decentralisation, dissemination and disintegration, what we are seeing in the present period are organisational developments that are in significant ways an extension of Fordist structures. What is at work is not corporate fragmentation but, in fact, more effective corporate *integration*. Philip Cooke [1988] refers to "flexible integration"; Roberto Camagni [1986, 1989] describes a process of ever-increasing functional and territorial integration, realised at different levels; Carlota Perez [1985] uses the term "systemation" to grasp the striving for management co-ordination and control; Danielle Leborgne and Alain Lipietz [1988] use the term "quasi vertical integration"; and Richard Gordon [1989] and Pierre Veltz [1989] describe the development of the networked economy as an alternative organisational and competitive form to the simple Williamsonian dualism between markets and hierarchies. Integration is a reflection of the search for a more effective and efficient corporate governance structure. We would agree with Flavia Martinelli and Erica Schoenberger's assertion that the "increasing fragmentation of the productive system must not be confused with a fragmentation of capital and control" [Martinelli and Schoenberger, 1989, p. 18]. Indeed, contemporary experimentations in the corporate economy tend to support the view that decentralised production, where it is occurring, is actually part of, rather than separate from, a wider deepening and extension of oligopolistic competition and control, now being realised through the development of a globally networked economy bestraddled and overseen by a relatively contained number of giant corporations.

As far as the geography of change is concerned, it is necessary to grasp the coexistence and combination of localising and globalising,

---

10. This "space of flows" applies not only to the flows of capital but also to those of labour. Whilst the "polyvalent" artisan, the skilled new model worker, may be settled in a particular place and may enjoy a sense of local allegiance and loyalty, the same may not be said for a growing underclass of peripheral workers. This new gypsy class, these *Gastarbeiter*, are destined to migrate, to wander, to flow across borders. For a theoretical perspective on this, see Cohen [1987] and Sassen-Koob [1987]; for a documentary reportage, see Wallraff [1988].

centripetal and centrifugal, forces. The current restructuring process is a matter of a whole repertoire of spatial strategies, dependent upon situated contexts and upon balances of power. Different companies may pursue quite distinct strategies; individual companies may themselves mobilise a number of different strategies. Context also clearly determines which form of intra- and inter-organisational linkages - integration, disintegration, quasi-integration, strategic alliances - is most appropriate. In some cases this might give rise to the formation of industrial districts, in others it will manifest itself in the increasingly global logic of development that Castells describes - a logic that could devastate or marginalise localities by abandoning them, or lock them as company towns into internationally integrated production complexes [see Hill, 1987, for a description, in the context of Japanese automobile production, of the blend between global factory and company town]. The point is that these different spatial dynamics are not contradictory or incompatible; we should not consider one as an emergent and another as a residual historical tendency. They are all contemporaneous, reflecting new articulations of global mobility and local fixity, new geographical options in the present corporate repertoire.

This less idealised outline of the nature and dynamics of socio-economic transformation throws a different light on the status and potential of industrial districts. In this context, the possibilities for the regeneration of local and regional economies are more problematical. Possibilities must and do, of course, exist in so far as the course of the restructuring process is not determinate. But there are also enormous problems and difficulties that must be recognised, and there must be strong doubt as to whether the industrial district can be the paradigm, the absolute model, for future development. The flexible specialisation thesis and the industrial district literature draw strongly on notions of local allegiance, co-operation and trust relations, and have as a sub-text the resurrection of "community". This, however, tends to take the local area in isolation and to obscure the growing significance of the local-global nexus [Alger, 1988]. In the late twentieth century, the local economy can only be seen as a node within a global economic network; and it can have no meaningful existence outside of this context. If we consider that this global arena is shaped and informed by formidable relations of power, then the scope for local autonomy and proactivity becomes considerably narrower. Perhaps the most striking effect of the new international economy on cities and regions, as Castells argues, "is the loss of their autonomy vis-à-vis the worldwide economic actors that control their activities in terms of a global logic largely ignored and uncontrolled by local and regional societies" [Castells, 1987, p. 58].

The question then arises as to whether the local economy can any longer be a significant category. One can see the obvious appeal of neo-Vidalian localism, but there is the real danger that the concept of locality fetishises and idealises the contradictory relations and processes that intersect over a specific territory [Jonas, 1988]. As John Lovering argues, some big cities may still contain a few Marshallian industrial districts, but for the most part, local areas now contain a variety of sectors all shaped by quite separate external influences. The "'local economy' is now a thing of fragments" [Lovering, 1988, p. 150], and the mechanisms of local interdependence are weak. If it is the case that local economies are sets of unrelated activities which are grouped together by a largely arbitrary territorial definition, then there is no basis for a "systematic localised filter-down". The new localism can then in one sense be seen as a kind of boosterism, creating a sense of pseudo-community in compensation for, and in defiance of, the collapse and disintegration of significant and meaningful localities. If local economies are, indeed, fragmenting, as Lovering suggests, then the idea of self-contained localities goes against the grain, rather than with it as the new consensus maintains.

Projections about the national implications of the emergent regional economies are still more problematical. Sabel, in particular, pushes his arguments towards suggestions for a macro-regulatory system of flexible specialisation, and towards the vision of a national confederation of flexible localities. Industrial districts, he argues, "are forced to acknowledge bonds extending beyond regional boundaries, and these ties can become the first strands in a net of broader solidarity" [Sabel, 1989, p. 58]. The nature of the restructuring process is, sadly, less benign and harmonious than Sabel would have us believe. David Harvey has pointed to growing competition and rivalry between cities, localities and regions: competition within the spatial division of labour; competition within the spatial division of consumption; competition for command functions; and competition for redistribution [Harvey, 1985, ch. 8]. As ever, under conditions of capitalist accumulation, economic development manifests itself through uneven development and spatial inequality. Bennett Harrison stresses "the technical, social and *political* importance of heightened inter-industry, inter-regional, and international competition in the current moment" [Harrison, 1987, p. 75]. In this process there will necessarily and inevitably be losers as well as winners. The question is how to deal with the costs of uneven development. How is macroeconomic and macrosocial regulation possible in this environment of intensified, and increasing, globalised rivalry?

Our argument in this and the preceding section has been, firstly, that the prospects for local economic revitalisation on a self-supporting and locally integrated basis are extremely limited, and secondly that, where such growth is occurring, it is a consequence of very diverse causes. A policy framework for localities must, in our view, be sensitive to these issues and not propose blanket solutions (e.g. Marshallian industrial districts) or others in which local policies come to substitute macroeconomic intervention at a national and international level. The resurgence of Marshallian industrial districts, and the development of new product-based agglomerations in some regions has shown, to be sure, that even under heavily internationalised and globally integrated circumstances, it is possible for a locally networked economy to arise. Where a base for such growth exists, local and national policies should seek to nurture and consolidate it.

There are limits, however, to this kind of growth. The competitive process is not benign but about winners and losers, and therefore in any industry there must be a limit to the number of agglomerations which can be tolerated. Furthermore, there is a distinct possibility of fracture within a local industrial system resulting from the concentration of ownership and insertion of the locality into the grip of multinationals. The loss of local control is very difficult to prevent. It should also be recognised that the so-called territorial logic of growth is not universally available as an option. Quite apart from the absurdity of the proposition that the building blocks and the complex inter-relationships of an industrial *system* can be policy induced, the fact remains that, despite assertions to the contrary, the key elements for success are very place-specific and non-transferable. For instance, in the case of the industrial district, it is not only trust and social solidarity which matter, but also a host of other conditions helping to contain the division of labour locally. Amongst these, as Trigilia [1986] so carefully illustrates, are conditions such as family-based and *petit bourgeois* traditions, community-wide social and economic rules, and municipal mercantilist traditions, which are historically sedimented in particular areas and virtually impossible to nurture *ex novo*. The same rule applies for the high-tech agglomerations: there has been an explosion of science parks and technopoles in Europe, Japan and the United States, all seeking to imitate Silicon Valley, but very few have come anywhere near revitalising the local economy.

Blanket solutions based upon the experiences of particular areas appear not to be a fruitful way forward for localities. Instead, it may be better for local institutions to support particular areas of expertise or local need, deploying and encouraging organisational strategies which build upon existing structures. That the success of such strategies will be piecemeal and limited should also be accepted. London, Singapore, San Francisco, Boston, Toyota City, Orange County and even areas in the Third Italy, are exceptions and not the rule for local economic development. It is precisely for this reason that support at a national and supranational level ought not to be rescinded but intensified and restructured in such a way that macroeconomic policies are able to plan the allocation of resources, control corporate behaviour, regulate the market, and orchestrate different local needs. Places are not microcosms, but vulnerable fragments of the wider economy. Consequently, national policies should be re-drawn to cope with local differences and local needs (even if it simply means the redistribution of income). Without this, we will be left with local interventionist strategies which work for a very small number of areas and confine others to the dustbin of history. Of course, we should not fetishise what macroeconomic policies can achieve. As Lipietz argues, the role of the nation state has become problematical, the global/local nexus, "in which the nation state has diminished responsibilities, seems at once macroeconomically unstable and socially regressive. Yet the possibilities offered by federal structures or multinational blocs seem themselves to be fragile and unstable" [Lipietz, 1985, p. 28]. Recognising this limitation, however, should not lead us to believe that everything can be left to local actors, especially if there is no real renaissance of self-contained regional economies occurring.

References

Aglietta, M. 1982. *Régulation et crises du capitalisme: L'expérience des Etats-Unis*, Paris, Calmann-Levy, second edition.

Alger, C. 1988. "Perceiving, analysing and coping with the local - global nexus", in *International Social Science Journal*, No. 117, pp. 321-340.

Amin, A.; Smith, I.J. 1986. "The internationalisation of production and its implications for the UK", in Amin, A.; Goddard, J.B. (eds.): *Technological change, industrial restructuring and regional development* London, Allen and Unwin.

Anastasia, B.; Rullani, E. 1981. *Nuova periferia industriale: Saggio sul modello Veneto*, Venice, Arsenale.

Andreff, W. 1984. "The international centralization of capital and the re-ordering of world capitalism", in *Capital and Class*, No. 22, pp. 58-80.

Aydalot, P. 1986. "L'aptitude des milieux locaux à promouvoir l'innovation", in Federwisch, J.; Zoller, H. (eds.): *Technologie nouvelles et ruptures régionales*, Paris, Economica.

Bagnasco, A. 1977. *Tre Italie. La problematica territoriale dello sviluppo economico italiano*, Bologna, Il Mulino.

Bagnasco, A.; Trigilia, C. (eds.), 1984: *Societa e politica nelle aree di piccola impresa: Il caso di Bassano*, Venice, Arsenale.

---. 1985. *Societa e politica nelle aree di piccola impresa: Il caso della Valdelsa*, Milan, Franco Angeli.

Becattini, G. (ed.) 1975. *Lo sviluppo economico della Toscana*, Florence, IRPET.

Becattini, G. 1978. "The development of light industry in Tuscany: An interpretation", in *Economic Notes*, No. 3, pp. 107-123.

---. 1987. "L'unita d'indagine", in Becattini, G. (ed.): *Mercato e forze locali: Il distretto industriale*, Bologna, Il Mulino.

Bellandi, M. 1982. "Il distretto industriale in Alfred Marshall", in *L'Industria*, Vol. 3, No. 3, pp. 335-375.

Belussi, F. 1987. *Benetton: Information technology in production and distribution. A case study of the innovative potential of traditional sectors*, SPRU Occasional Paper Series No. 25, Brighton, Science Policy Research Unit.

---. 1988. "Innovation diffusion in traditional sectors: An empirical investigation", Paper presented to the Regional Science Association's European Summer Institute, 17-23 July, Arco (Italy).

Berardi, D.; Romagnoli, M. 1984. *L'area Pratese tra crisi e mutamento*, Prato, Consorzio Centro Studi.

Bluestone, B. 1987. "Coping with labour and community: Capitalist strategies in the 1980s", in Muegge, H.; Stöhr, W.B. (eds.): *International economic restructuring and the regional economy*, Aldershot, Avebury.

Bonefeld, W. 1987. "Reformulation of state theory", in *Capital and class*, No. 33, pp. 96-127.

Boyer, R. 1986. *La théorie de la régulation: Une analyse critique*, Paris, Editions La Découverte.

---. 1988. "Technical change and the theory of 'regulation'", in Dosi, G. et al. (eds.): *Technical change and economic theory*, London, Pinter.

Brusco, S. 1982. "The Emilian model: Productive decentralisation and social integration", in *Cambridge Journal of Economics*, Vol. 6, No. 2, pp. 167-184.

---. 1986. "Small firms and industrial districts: The experience of Italy", in Keeble, D.; Wever, E. (eds.): *New firms and regional development in Europe*, London, Croom Helm.

Brusco, S.; Sabel, C.F. 1981. "Artisan production and economic growth", in Wilkinson, F. (ed.): *The dynamics of labour market segmentation*, London, Academic Press.

Camagni, R. 1986. "The flexible automation trajectory: The Italian case", Paper presented to the International Conference on Innovation Diffusion, Venice, 17-21 March.

---. 1988. "Functional integration and locational shifts in new technology industry", in Aydalot, P.; Keeble, D. (eds.): *High technology industry and innovative environments*, London, Routledge.

---. 1989. "Space, networks and technical change: An evolutionary approach", Paper presented at the GREMI International Workshop on Innovative Milieux and Transnational Firm Networks, EADA, Barcelona, 28-29 March.

Camagni, R.; Capello, R. 1988. "Italian success stories of local economic development: Theoretical conditions and practical experiences", Istituto di Economia Politica, Universita Luigi Bocconi, Milan, mimeo.

Castells, M. 1987. "Technological change, economic restructuring and the spatial division of labour", in Muegge, H.; Stohr, W.B. (eds.): *International economic restructuring and the regional economy*, Aldershot, Avebury.

Castells, M.; Henderson, J. 1987. "Techno-economic restructuring, socio-political processes and spatial transformation: A global perspective", in Henderson, J.; Castells, M. (eds.): *Global restructuring and territorial development*, London, Sage.

Cohen, R. 1987. "Policing the frontiers: The state and the migrant in the international division of labour", in Henderson, J.; Castells, M. (eds.): *Global restructuring and territorial development*, London, Sage.

Cooke, P. 1987. "Spatial development processes: Organised or disorganised?", in Thrift, N.; Williams, P. (eds.): *Class and space: The making of urban society*, London, Routledge and Kegan Paul.

---. 1988. "Flexible integration, scope economies, and strategic alliances: Social and spatial mediations", in *Society and Space*, Vol. 6, No. 3, pp. 281-300.

Coriat, B. 1978. *L'atelier et le chronomètre: Essai sur le Taylorisme, le Fordisme et la production de masse*, Paris, Christian Bourgeois.

Crevoisier, O. 1988. "Functional logic and territorial logic and how they inter-relate in the region", Unpublished conference paper, Institut de Recherches Economiques et Regionales, Université de Neuchâtel.

Crowther, S.; Garrahan, P. 1988. "Corporate power and the local economy", in *Industrial Relations Journal*, Vol. 19, pp. 51-59.

Del Monte, A. 1987. "Modelli di diffusione dell'imprenditorialita", Dipartimento di Scienze Economiche, Naples University, mimeo.

Dohse, K. et al. 1985. "From 'Fordism' to 'Toyotism'? The social organisation of the labour process in the Japanese automobile industry", in *Politics and Society*, Vol. 14, No. 2, pp. 115-146.

Dore, R. 1983. "Goodwill and the spirit of market capitalism", in *British Journal of Sociology*, Vol. 34, No. 4, pp. 459-482.

Dunning, J.H. 1988. "International business, the recession and economic restructuring", in Hood, N.; Vahlne, J.E. (eds.): *Strategies in global competition*, London, Croom Helm.

Fuà, G. 1983. "Rural industrialisation in later developed countries: The case of northeast and central Italy", in *Banca Nazionale del Lavoro*, No. 147, pp. 351-377.

Foster, J.B. 1988. "The fetish of Fordism", in *Monthly Review*, Vol. 39, No. 10, pp. 14-33.

Frankel, B. 1987. *The post-industrial utopians*, Cambridge, Polity Press.

Freeman, C.; Perez, C. 1988. "Structural crises of adjustment, business cycles and investment behaviour", in Dosi, G. et al. (eds.): *Technical change and economic theory*, London, Pinter.

Frey, L. 1974. "La piccola e media impresa di fronte al mercato del lavoro in Italia", in *Inchiesta*, No. 14.

Garofoli, G. 1983. *Industrializzazione diffusa in Lombardia*, Milan, Franco Angeli.

Gartman, D. 1983. "Structuralist marxism and the labour process: Where have the dialectics gone?", in *Theory and Society*, Vol. 12, No. 5, pp. 659-669.

de Gaudemar, J.-P. (ed.). 1980. *Usines et ouvriers: Figures du nouvel ordre productif*, Paris, François Maspero.

Glasmeier, A. 1988a. "Factors governing the development of high tech industry agglomerations: A tale of three cities", in *Regional Studies*, Vol. 22, No. 4, pp. 287-301.

---. 1988b. "The Japanese Technopolis programme: High-tech development strategy or industrial policy in disguise?", in *International Journal of Urban and Regional Research*, Vol. 12, No. 2, pp. 268-284.

Gordon, D.M. 1988. "The global economy: New edifice or crumbling foundations?", in *New Left Review*, No. 168, pp. 24-64.

Gordon, R. 1989. "Markets, hierarchies and alliances: A reassessment of industrial organisation and linkage theory", Paper presented at the GREMI International Workshop on Innovative Milieux and Transnational Firm Networks, EADA, Barcelona, 28-29 March.

Gordon, R.; Kimball, L. 1987. "The impact of industrial structure on high technology location", in Brotchie, J. et al. (eds.): *The spatial impact of technological change*, London, Croom Helm.

Harrison, B. 1987. "Cold bath or restructuring?", in *Science and Society*, Spring, pp. 72-81.

Harvey, D. 1985. *The urbanisation of capital*, Oxford, Basil Blackwell.

Harvey, D.; Scott, A.J. 1988. "The practice of human geography: Theory and empirical specificity in the transition from Fordism to flexible accumulation", in MacMillan, W.D. (ed.): *Remodelling geography*, Oxford, Basil Blackwell.

Hill, R.C. 1987. "Global factory or company town: The changing division of labour in the international automobile industry", in Henderson, J.; Castells, M. (eds.): *Global restructuring and territorial development*, London, Sage.

Hirsch, J. 1985a. "Auf dem Wege des Kapitalismus? Die aktuelle Neuformierung des Kapitalismus und ihre politschen Folgen", in *Das Argument*, No. 151, pp. 325-342.

---. 1985b. "Fordismus und Postfordismus: Die gegenwartige gesellschaftliche Krise und ihre Folgen", in *Politische Vierteljahresschrift*, Vol. 26, No. 2, pp. 160-182.

Hirst, P.; Zeitlin, J. 1988. "Crisis, what crisis?", in *New Statesman*, 18 March, pp. 10-12.

---. (eds.). 1989. *Reversing industrial decline? Industrial structure and policy in Britain and her competitors*, Oxford, Berg.

Hudson, R. 1988. "Uneven development in capitalist societies: Changing spatial divisions of labour, forms of spatial organisation of production and service provision, and their impacts on localities", in *Transactions of the Institute of British Geographers*, Vol. 13, No. 4, pp. 484-496.

Jonas, A. 1988. "A new regional geography of localities?", in *Area*, Vol. 20, No. 2, pp. 101-110.

Kern, H.; Schumann, M. 1987. "Limits of the division of labour: New production and employment concepts in West German industry", in *Economic and Industrial Democracy*, Vol. 8, No. 2, pp. 151-170.

Lazerson, M. 1988. "Organisational growth of small firms: An outcome of markets and hierarchies?", in *American Sociological Review*, No. 53, pp. 330-342.

Leborgne, D.; Lipietz, A. 1988. "New technologies, new modes of regulation: Some spatial implications", in *Society and Space*, Vol. 6, No. 3, pp. 263-280.

Lefebvre, H. 1979. "Space: Social product and use value", in Freiberg, J.W. (ed.): *Critical sociology: European perspectives*, New York, Irvington.

Lipietz, A. 1985. *Le national et le régional: Quelle autonomie face à la crise capitaliste mondiale?*, Paris, CEPREMAP, Couverture Orange, No. 8521.

---. 1987. "La régulation: Les mots et les choses", in *Revue Economique*, No. 5, pp. 1049-1060.

Loinger, G.; Peyrache, V. 1988. "Technological clusters and regional economic restructuring", in Aydalot, P.; Keeble, D. (eds.): *High technology industry and innovative environments*, London, Routledge.

Lorenzoni, G. 1979. *Una politica innovativa nelle piccole e medie imprese*, Milan, Etas.

Lovering, J. 1988. "The local economy and local economic strategies, in *Policy and Politics*, Vol. 16, No. 3, pp. 145-157.

Macelli, A.; Romagnoli, M. 1979. "Aspetti del decentramento produttivo nell'area tessile pratese", in *Inchiesta*, Jan-Feb, pp. 83-89.

Mahon, R. 1987. "From Fordism to?: New technology, labour markets and unions", in *Economic and Industrial Democracy*, Vol. 8, pp. 5-60.

Martinelli, F.; Schoenberger, E. 1989. "Oligopoly alive and well: Notes for a broader discussion on flexible accumulation", Paper presented at the International Colloquium on New Industrial Spaces: An International Survey, Université Panthéon-Sorbonne, Paris, 21-22 March.

Massey, D. 1984. *Spatial divisions of labour*, London, Macmillan.

Marshall, A. 1961. *Principles of economics*, London, Macmillan, ninth edition.

Mazzoni, R. 1981. "Alcuni aspetti del recente sviluppo economico delle Marche", in *Economia Marche*, No. 2, December, pp. 15-47.

Murray, F. 1987. "Flexible specialisation in the Third Italy", in *Capital and Class*, No. 33, pp. 84-95.

Myrdal, G. 1957. *Economic theory and the underdeveloped regions*, London, Duckworth.

Niccoli, A. 1984. "Alle origini dello sviluppo economico marchigiano", in *Economia Marche*, No. 1, June, pp. 3-17.

Paci, M. (ed.). 1980. *Famiglia e mercato del lavoro in una economia periferica*, Milan, Franco Angeli.

Perez, C. 1983. "Structural change and assimilation of new technologies in the economic and social system", in *Futures*, Vol. 15, No. 5, pp. 357-375.

---. 1985. "Microelectronics, long waves and world structural change: New perspectives for developing countries", in *World Development*, Vol. 13, No. 3, pp. 441-463.

Perrin, J.C. 1986. "Un bilan théorique et methodologique", in Federwisch, J.; Zoller, H. (eds.): *Technologie nouvelle et ruptures régionales*, Paris, Economica.

---. 1988. "New technologies, local synergies and regional policies in Europe", in Aydalot, P.; Keeble, D. (eds.): *High technology industry and innovative environments*, London, Routledge.

Piore, M.J. 1986. "Perspectives on labour market flexibility", in *Industrial Relations*, Vol. 25, No. 2, pp. 146-166.

Piore, M.; Sabel, C.F. 1983. "Italian small business development: Lessons for U.S. industrial policy", in Zysman, J.; Tyson, L. (eds.): *American industry in international competition: Government policies and corporate strategies*, Ithaca, Cornell University Press.

---. 1984. *The second industrial divide.* New York, Basic Books.

Poittier, C. 1988. "Local innovation and large firm strategies in Europe", in Aydalot, P.; Keeble, D. (eds.): *High technology industry and innovative environments*, London, Routledge.

Pollert, A. 1988. "Dismantling flexibility", in *Capital and Class*, No. 34, pp. 42-75.

Robins, K.; Webster, F. 1988. "Athens without slaves ... or slaves without Athens? The neurosis of technology", in *Science as Culture*, No. 3, pp. 7-53.

Roobeek, A. 1987. "The crisis of Fordism and the rise of a new technological paradigm", in *Futures*, Vol. 19, No. 2, pp. 129-154.

Russo, M. 1985. "Technical change and the industrial district: The role of inter-firm relations in the growth and transformation of ceramic tile production in Italy", in *Research Policy*, Vol. 14, pp. 329-343.

Sabel, C.F. 1982. *Work and politics*, Cambridge, Cambridge University Press.

---. 1989. "Flexible specialisation and the re-emergence of regional economies", in Hirst, P.; Zeitlin J. (eds.): *Reversing industrial decline? Industrial structure and policy in Britain and her competitors*, Oxford, Berg.

Sabel, C.F. et al. 1987. "How to keep mature industries innovative", in *Technology Review*, Vol. 90, No. 3, pp. 27-35.

Sassen-Koob, S. 1987. "Issues of core and periphery: Labour migration and global restructuring", in Henderson, J.; Castells, M. (eds.): *Global restructuring and territorial development*, London, Sage.

Saxenian, A. 1987. "The Cheshire Cat's grin: Innovation, regional development and the Cambridge case", Department of Political Science, MIT, Cambridge, Mass., mimeo.

Scott, A.J. 1986. "Industrial organisation and location: Division of labour, the firm, and spatial process", in *Economic Geography*, Vol. 62, No. 3, pp. 215-231.

---. 1988. "Flexible production systems and regional development: The rise of new industrial spaces in North America and Western Europe", in *International Journal of Urban and Regional Research*, Vol. 12, No. 2, pp. 171-186.

Scott, A.; Cooke, P. 1988. "The new geography and sociology of production", in *Society and Space*, Vol. 6, No. 3, pp. 241-244.

Scott, A.; Storper, M. 1987. "High technology industry and regional development: A theoretical critique and reconstruction", in *International Social Science Journal*, No. 112, pp. 215-232.

Sengenberger, W.; Loveman, G. 1988. *Smaller units of employment: A synthesis on industrial reorganisation in industrial countries*, Geneva, International Institute for Labour Studies, second revised edition.

Sforzi, F. 1989. "The geography of industrial districts in Italy", in Goodman, E. (ed.): *Small firms and industrial districts in Italy*, London, Routledge.

Signorini, L.F. 1988. "Innovation in Tuscan firms", Paper presented to the Regional Science Association's European Summer Institute, 17-23 July, Arco (Italy).

Smith, C. 1988. "Flexible specialisation, automation and mass production", Paper presented to the Conference on Questions of Restructuring Work and Employment, 12-13 July, University of Warwick, Coventry.

Solinas, G. 1982. "Labour market segmentation and workers' careers: The case of the Italian knitwear industry", in *Cambridge Journal of Economics*, Vol. 6, pp. 331-352.

Solo, R. 1985. "Across the industrial divide", in *Journal of Economic Issues*, Vol. 19, No. 3, pp. 829-836.

Storper, M.; Scott, A.J. 1989. "The geographical foundations and social regulation of flexible production complexes", in Wolch, J.; Dear, M. (eds.): *The power of geography: How territory shapes social life*, Boston, Unwin Hyman.

Tolomelli, C. 1988. "Policies to support innovation processes: Experiences and prospects in Emilia-Romagna", Paper presented to the Regional Science Association's European Summer Institute, 17-23 July, Arco (Italy).

Trigilia, C. 1986. "Small firm development and political subcultures in Italy", in *European Sociological Review*, Vol. 2, No. 3, pp. 161-175.

Veltz, P. 1989. "Nouveaux modèles d'organisation de la production et tendances de l'economie territoriale", Paper presented at the International Colloquium on New Industrial Spaces: An International Survey, Université Panthéon-Sorbonne, Paris, 21-22 March.

Vernon, R. 1966. "International investment and international trade in the product cycle", in *Quarterly Journal of Economics*, Vol. 80, pp. 190-207.

Walker, R. 1988. "The geographical organisation of production-systems", in *Society and Space*, Vol. 6, pp. 377-408.

Wallraff, G. 1988. *Lowest of the low*, London, Methuen.

Warde, A. 1985. "Spatial change, politics and the division of labour", in Gregory, D.; Urry, J. (eds.): *Social relations and spatial structures*, London, Macmillan.

Webster, F.; Robins, K. 1986. *Information technology: A Luddite analysis*, Norwood, New Jersey, Ablex.

Williams, K. et al. 1987. "The end of mass production?", in *Economy and Society*, Vol. 16, No. 3, pp. 405-439.

Zeitlin, J. (forthcoming). "The Third Italy: Inter-firm cooperation and technological innovation", in Murray, R. (ed.): *Technology strategies and local economic intervention*, Nottingham, Spokesman Books.

12 Three responses to Ash Amin and Kevin Robins

I. Charles F. Sabel replies

"Industrial Districts and Regional Development: Limits and Possibilities" is an awkward amalgam of a core argument about current economic reorganisation and criticisms of the flexible specialisation thesis and associated claims. If true, some of the criticisms might apply with equal force to the argument offered by Amin and Robins themselves; others might simply not be worth discussing if the larger core argument holds. I say "might" because, to judge the full import of the criticisms it is often necessary to interpret them in the light of the central argument; yet the latter is too fragmentary and too dependent on allusions to others' work to authorise the necessary interpretations. At the heart of these confusions, I will argue, is the contradictory desire to claim both that the current process of industrial reorganisations creates novel forms of organisation with unknown political implications, and that these new forms can be understood with the same categories used to explain traditional mass-production firms.

It would of course be possible to abstract from the core argument, address those criticisms which touch on the weaknesses of the flexible specialisation literature, and clarify the numerous points where disagreement seems to result from misunderstandings. But I believe that it will be at least as fruitful to enjoin Amin and Robins to clarify their position and their criticisms as a whole. Clarity about the large issues which divide us ought to be the starting point, not the result, of a debate about the interpretation of particular cases of industrial adjustment, and - more importantly - disputes over what kind of evidence bears on our arguments in the first place. Clarification of the deeper divisive issues, moreover, creates the rudiments of a common intellectual language. The following criticisms of "Industrial districts and regional possibilities" (Chapter 11) are thus intended to avoid a self-protective exchange of views by beginning a discussion.

Amin and Robins' core understanding of industrial reorganisation rests on assertions like these: "The break up of mass markets, upon which the entire theory of flexible specialisation and local economies is constructed, is a dubious one" [p. 190]. Proponents of this theory might have confused "greater product differentiation" with changes in the organisation of markets profound enough to provoke the transformations they expect or claim to have observed. For this and some combination of other reasons, in any case, multinational firms have been able to maintain, indeed strengthen, their control over local developments. "Multinational corporations are (need it really be said) the real shakers and shapers of the world economy" [p.209]. They are not responding to market changes by decentralising power, opening the way for increased local decision-making and hence even partial integration of individual production units into self-determining local economies. On the contrary there is a "higher degree of centralisation and internationalisation of capital" [p. 209]. "What is at work is not corporate fragmentation, but, in fact, more effective corporate *integration*" [p. 23, emphasis in original]. Capital is "increasingly mobile, hypermobile even, tending towards a nomadic existence" [p. 210]. The future will, perhaps, be so much like the past that it is best described as a kind of "living-dead Fordism": a world, to use Joachim Hirch's phrases, of "hyperindustrialism" combined with "social dualism and segmentation", and watched over by an "authoritarian state". [p. 208; references to Hirsch are from Hirsch 1985a, 1985b]. The best synopsis of current developments is provided by this passage from Castells and Henderson:

> The development of the international economy, the dramatic growth of new information and communications technologies, the formation of powerful transnational organisations linked by subordinated, decentralised networks, are crucial factors in the process that provides the structural meaning for each territory in terms of the function that territory performs in the broader framework of interdependent operations. We certainly still have spatial forms, since societies and economies develop on a given territory and unevenly across the globe. Yet the logic and dynamics of territorial development are increasingly placeless from the point of view of the dominant organisations and social interests [p. 210; Castells and Henderson, 1987, p. 7].

Given the persistence of mass markets and dominance of the multinational corporations, it is no surprise that Amin and Robins regard Marshallian industrial districts or regional economies with any degree of local autonomy as marginal phenomena. "In the late twentieth century, the economy can only be seen as a node within a global economic network; and it can have no meaningful existence outside of this context" [p. 211]. Hence "the scope for local autonomy and proactivity becomes considerably narrower", so questionable, indeed, that the "question then arises as to whether the local economy can any longer be a significant category". [p. 211]. There are "some" cases of locally networked economies. But there are "limits ... to this kind of growth" [p. 212]. These limits are set, naturally enough, by the international competitive process. In any case, it is impossible to build such economies by political means, for the "key elements for success are very place-specific and non-transferable" [p. 213].

I have been fastidious in the recitation of these arguments because I want to leave no doubt that Amin and Robins have very strong views about the current economic reorganisation. On another occasion it will certainly be necessary to address some version of this thesis of nomadic, large-firm hegemony. But such a discussion would be, I think, premature. Vehement as they are, Amin and Robins' claims are simply too imprecise to know whether they are consistent with or relevant to many of their own criticisms of flexible specialisation views, let alone whether they are empirically defensible.

Consider first the problem of agency: the question of which persons or groups acting under which constraints decide how restructuring is to proceed, and of how - if at all - this process can be directed. This is one of "two broad areas" - the other concerns the break up of mass markets - where Amin and Robins want to challenge "claims about the special destiny of industrial districts" [p. 191]. To judge by some oblique remarks, they want to "avoid technological or economic determinism and to maintain a sense of openness and possibility" [p. 191]. But it is notoriously difficult to capture the balance in any historical moment between the constraints imposed by the situation and the margin of manoeuvre where the actors can influence outcomes by exercising their discretion. According to Amin and Robins, Piore and I err on the side of voluntarism, imputing to the actors an illusory power to transform their situation. Despite our efforts at synthesis, our work "remains an unsatisfactory blend of determinism and voluntarism" [p. 191]. Scott and Storper err on the side of determinism. They see "the transition to post-Fordism as a consequence of the objective laws of capitalist development" [p. 193].

But why, supposing that I suddenly see the force of these criticisms, should I prefer the work of Amin and Robins to the works they attack? At first glance their notion of the "higher degree of centralisation and internationalisation of capital" sounds very much like it is founded on one of those "objective laws of capitalist development" whose existence they have just denied. At the very least writers such as Joachim Hirsch, whom they cite in support of their arguments, may well be thought to hold such views. In that case, Amin and Robins should obviously criticise Scott and Storper for having the *wrong* "structural-functionalist" model and say something more about the right one.

On the other hand, to judge by a fleeting reference to Aglietta [p. 194], Amin and Robins perhaps believe that the fundamental outcome of restructuring may have been or still is up for grabs. But given their view of the multinationals' hegemony, the actors cannot intervene locally. In that case Amin and Robins ought to specify at what times - past, present, or future - which actors could have, can, or could reshape the plans of the central corporate headquarters. It is impossible to judge whether a particular account of a situation is too "voluntarist" or too "determinist" unless it is juxtaposed to an alternative account which reveals the first to have ignored or overstated the constraints. If they are not somehow still attached to the necessitarian views they disavow, then Amin and Robins have confused an attack on the possibilities of local autonomy with an argument in support of the "openness and possibility" of the current situation. If they want the disavowal to be taken seriously, they must provide the argument.

Analogous considerations apply to their discussion of the literature of industrial districts. The criticism here is related to the problem of agency in that Amin and Robins accuse their opponents of assuming a necessary and all encompassing tendency for mass production to develop into some fundamentally more flexible and geographically decentralised form of production. "The world is more complex, contradictory and ambiguous, than the new orthodoxy allows for", they tell us [p. 194]. Nonetheless, Amin and Robins do not "wish to defend a purely descriptive empiricism". They merely "reject an approach which squeezes quite different phenomena into a badly conceptualised theoretical framework" [p. 202].

I, and all those accused of misleading simplification, agree that the problem of categorising and assessing the empirical significance of hybrids of Fordism and flexible specialisation - including, but not limited to, different types of industrial districts - is among the most difficult and challenging on our research agenda. The problem is crucial because the intermediate cases, to my mind, often result from the same kinds of strategic considerations which prompted corporations to question mass production in the first place. Just as firms use flexible forms of production to hedge against various types of market uncertainty, so they hedge their hedges by adopting hybrid organisations pursuing diverse strategies which allow them to adjust rapidly to changes in the form of uncertainty. To affirm that the outcome of restructuring is still open is to assert that firms are uncertain of the outcome as well, and hence that they will be unlikely to embrace *any* organisational form or strategy which cannot be redefined. In so far as hybrids by definition combine different structuring principles, they should proliferate in an openly uncertain situation.

But those are my reasons for wanting to refine the analysis of industrial districts, among other new or resurgent forms of industrial organisation. What are Amin's and Robins'? We know that they regard industrial districts and indeed any local economy possessed of minimal powers of self-determination to be marginal phenomena which cannot be extended through political intervention. What, other than some idiosyncratic curiosity, could cause anyone to be interested in such marginalia? If I am convinced something is negligible, I do not exhort others to study it.

Amin's and Robins' two substantive additions to the typology of industrial districts suggest further that they are less interested in discovering new possibilities in the mess of current reality than in confirming their view that the present is hostage to the past. The first is the "branch industrial complex". This is essentially a company town dominated by the new type of operating unit: fundamentally dependent on its footloose multinational parent, but autonomous enough to subjugate its suppliers and workforce. "This type of new production complex could be worse than the old branch plant since it could turn the entire locality into a branch plant" [p.206]. The second is the "product pioneering industrial agglomeration". These are areas at the early stage of Vernon's product cycle, when a standard design for a new product has not yet emerged. Given the rapid pace of development, production is carried on by networks of small and medium-sized firms rather than in the large, vertically integrated units that are suited to low-cost manufacture of standard goods [p. 207].

These distinctions seem to be straightforward efforts to reduce most apparently novel forms of industrial organisation to the familiar categories of mass production. I think this an error, but perhaps I err. If I did think such simplifying reduction was possible, I would simplify and not instruct those who disagreed that "reality is more equivocal, more ambiguous, more obscure" [p. 193] than they thought. If I were interested, as I am, in ambiguity and organisation equivocation, I would turn my attention not to the reductive cases, but to the many hybrids which show that there are indeed important distinctions to be drawn between the limiting cases of mass production and flexible specialisation.

Again and again Amin and Robins are drawn to defend the side of continuity in the false dichotomy of fixity and transformation which they themselves reject. They ridicule any analysis of the reorganisation of large firms which does not make reorganisation a matter of more of the same. They angrily ignore efforts to understand the connection which I believe exists between market volatility and corporate decentralisation [p. 201]. Yet, unless the markets have changed in some way, it is hard to understand why Amin and Robins believe they have observed such novelties as the "branch industrial complex". Instead of trying to explain these and other alleged changes, they present affadavits that the new is like the old.

Perhaps this is because Amin and Robins truly believe that those they criticise are "myth makers", [p. 185] whose spell can only be broken by another, more powerful myth. I urge a less Nietszchean, more platitudinous course. Suppose your opponents are as curious about the ambiguities of economic reality and concerned about its political implications as you. Then use criticism of their equivocations, false starts, and errors to help clarify the treacherous complexities that fascinate and trouble us all.

References

Castells, M.; Henderson, J. 1987. "Techno-economic restructuring, socio-political processes and spatial transformation: A global perspective", in Henderson, J.; Castells, M. (eds.): *Global restructuring and territorial development*, London, Sage.

Hirsch, J. 1985a. "Auf dem Wege des Kapitalismus? Die aktuelle Neuformierung des Kapitalismus und ihre politschen Folgen", in *Das Argument*, No. 151, pp. 325-342.

---. 1985b. "Fordismus und Postfordismus: Die gegenwartige gesellschaftliche Krise und ihre Folgen", in *Politische Vierteljahresschrift*, Vol. 26, No. 2, pp. 160-182.

II. Michael J. Piore replies

There are several portions of the Amin and Robins article with which I am in essential agreement. But their argument is played off a particular characterisation of *The second industrial divide* [Piore and Sabel, 1984]. It is a characterisation which has almost no resemblance to the argument Sabel and I intended to develop in that book and which, judging from other reviews, I thought we had developed. I have therefore asked for an opportunity to comment on their article in this forum in order to reassert the integrity of our own endeavour. I have tried to do this briefly in the following five points.

1. The argument of *The second industrial divide* was not meant to be deterministic. On the contrary, the "divide" of the title invokes the metaphor of the continental divide, where water can flow in either of two directions. The argument, as the metaphor suggests, was that further development in industrial countries might take place *either* through a revival of mass production *or* through flexible specialisation.

2. We never meant to argue that the existence of the dynamic regional economies of Central Italy established flexible specialisation as an alternative to mass production or even said very much in and of itself about that possibility. From the beginning, we took the position that, if it did, one would have to show how such economies would fit together into a coherent economic system; how that economic system, as a system, was different from Fordism (or mass production) and how one might get from one to the other. The argument of *The second industrial divide* is meant to have exactly this analytical structure, although we attempted to lay it out historically as well as analytically.

3. Amin and Robins assert that the argument of *The second industrial divide* has no sense of historical complexity or historical continuity. This seems to be the greatest distortion in their characterisation of our endeavour. We never argued that what we were seeing in Italy was completely new. On the contrary, Sabel's historical piece with Zeitlin [Sabel and Zeitlin, 1985], much of the material from which is incorporated in *The second industrial divide*, demonstrates the antecedents of Italian-like districts as historical systems. The point of calling the "divide" of the title the second one is to indicate that we have recovered the possibilities represented by these distant historical forms.

The argument we were constructing is meant to build upon history in at least two other ways as well. First, it attempts to show how an alternative system of development - flexible specialisation - can be built out of the same institutional forms used very differently in mass production and thus, how one might have continuity at one level of analysis and discontinuity at another. Secondly, it emphasises differences amongst countries in their historical development, and tries to show how these differences may be obscured by similarities in the systemic structures in one period and yet become central in governing the possibility of moving toward an alternative system at some point in the future.

The comparative material is also used to forestall normative judgements associated with what Amin and Robins term "utopianism". It demonstrates that systems with the same economic properties can be instrumental in institutional and social structures which have radically different implications for the felt experience of living within them. It is the nature of that experience, taken in all of its dimensions, to which one must turn to make normative judgements. Personally, I do not think that one can really make a normative choice among them at the level of analysis at which we are working. Flexible specialisation appears to yield a reintegration of conception and execution in the labour process, and it is the focus on that characteristic which gives a utopian flavour to some of our writings. On the other hand, mass production, because of its need for constantly expanding markets, creates an interest of each in the prosperity of all and, in that sense, it is more catholic or universal. Flexible specialisation admits a narrow parochialism which I personally find as disturbing as the alienation of work in mass production.

4. Ultimately, the major analytical problem with which Amin and Robins are concerned is one of how to generalise from economic and social phenomena. Or, to put the matter differently, how to introduce enough order in the chaos of experience to gain if not control over events, at least a space for purposive action and normative judgement. The many pejorative adjectives with which they characterise the "new orthodoxy" - utopianism, futurism, determinism - are so many ways of saying that the order which that orthodoxy creates is false. But the main thrust of their critique is the reassertion of diversity. The few concessions which they make to the viewpoints they criticise derive largely from a retreat from the chaos which their reassertion of diversity creates.

But *The second industrial divide*, as the preceding hopefully suggests, is not a retreat from this dilemma, but an attempt to resolve it. It attempts to capture *structure* through the notions of mass production and flexible specialisation and to capture the diversity in the unresolved choice between them and in the variety of historical experiences and national contexts out of which economically similar structures were built. It seems that Amin and Robins would have made more progress in the problem which concerns them by criticising this argument rather than distorting it.

5. Finally, it seems that part of Amin and Robins' discomfort can be traced to certain Marxian arguments, and that it will be helpful to address these as well. The literature of Marxist interpretation is so vast that it would be impossible to do justice to any particular reading in this context. My reading of Marx is that he had an integrated analytical view of capitalism in which technology, class, market processes, accumulation, and alienation all fit together in a logically coherent way. For a variety of reasons, the coherence of the original argument has been lost, and the analytical edifice as a single construct has fallen into a series of separate pieces. Marxist

analysts have tried to reconstruct an argument by working from one or another of these now separable elements. Most Marxists have built their analysis around social class and class conflict. For many, this is the defining characteristic of modern Marxism.

Sabel and I began instead with the technological trajectory: this seemed more in keeping with the processes we were observing. The choice was also consistent with the fact that the Marxian classes were no longer self-evident in the social structure as they had been even ten years before, and it admitted the possibility that class configurations which Marx had not anticipated were emerging. But the choice also posed a series of analytical questions which are not posed in orthodox theory.

Marx postulated a single technological trajectory; having done so, he was able to root that trajectory in nature. Postulating two trajectories, Sabel and I were forced to look for some basis for the commitment to one or the other. We found that basis in ideology. But this in turn raised the question of the source of the ideological commitment. The orthodox Marxist response would have been class conflict. But since, in Marx, the class structure derives from the technology, this would have made the argument circular. In *The second industrial divide*, we left this question open. That is admittedly the book's greatest analytical weakness. But the solutions which Amin and Robins seem to be proposing are not logically viable.

"Accumulation", another Marxist analytical category which Amin and Robins fault us for neglecting, poses similar analytical problems. Movement along the single technological trajectory which Marx postulated requires continuing investment and makes the system dependent upon capital accumulation. But capital accumulation may not be critical on other technological trajectories. At any rate, "regimes of accumulation" cannot just be introduced by fiat into the argument. If there are such things, they have to be derived from more fundamental postulates. This issue is discussed in the penultimate chapter of *The second industrial divide*, although not in precisely the same vocabulary as Amin and Robins employ.

References

Piore, M.J.; Sabel, C. 1984. *The second industrial divide*, New York, Basic Books.

Sabel, C.; Zeitlin, J. 1985. "Historical alternatives to mass production: Politics, markets and technology in nineteenth century industrialisation", in *Past and Present*, No. 108.

III. Michael Storper replies

Amin and Robins should be thanked for wanting to dismantle unduly "optimistic and celebratory visions" of contemporary industrial and regional change and for encouraging a debate about the significance of production flexibility in general and industrial districts in particular. They raise a number of very important questions in the course of their critique. In their anxiety to "disentangle realities from rapidly proliferating myths of a future golden age" of flexible specialisation and industrial districts, however, they frequently try to remould existing evidence and theory on industrial change to "prove" that flexible specialisation and industrial districts either do not exist or are essentially unimportant, instead of simply directly making their points about the social and political effects of this change and the fact that many unresolved questions about the organisation and geography of contemporary production remain. Once they do this, they are backed into the unsustainable analytical position of invoking discredited preconceptions about the "essential" nature of capitalist industrial development as a simple progress from small to big firms, from new products to mass production. Were we to accept this teleological view of industrial reality, we would not even be capable of constructing fruitful research agendas to respond to the valid concerns which motivate Amin and Robins.

For the sake of organising a coherent response, let me pose five questions which are implicitly raised by Amin and Robins:

1. What is an industrial district?
2. To what extent are flexible production agglomerations a widespread, and therefore, important phenomenon today?
3. Is this phase of industrial development significantly different from that of the Fordist/mass production period?
4. Are flexible production agglomerations changing so as to disappear as such?
5. What is the basic nature of contemporary industrial and geographical change?

1. According to Amin and Robins, there is only one genuine kind of industrial district, the Marshallian district, and this is defined by them in such a way that it refers not only to a localised production system characterised by a deep division of labour between producers, but as well by a social structure "characterised by a high level of small entrepreneurs, artisans, skilled workers, working wives and extended family or youth labour." Using this restrictive definition, Amin and Robins claim that only the Third Italy can be included and at that, only parts of the Third Italy. A certain irony should not escape us here, however: Marshall wrote about Amin's and Robins' own country of *England* in defining industrial districts, and now we

are told that *Marshallian* industrial districts can *only* be found in *Italy*. This reading of the Marshallian theory misses the point. Certainly Marshall worked from a set of concrete empirical cases. But Marshall's real significance, as Becattini has instructed us, is to have identified a district as consisting of a division of labour between firms on the one hand, and as a supportive tissue of social practices and institutions on the other. There is no reason, on the basis of a theoretical reading of Marshall, to think that such divisions of labour or social structures can take only the form found in today's Third Italy for us to be able to say that a Marshallian industrial district exists.

By engaging in this definitional sophistry, they back themselves into the corner of claiming that the Third Italy is *sui generis* without actually providing a convincing argument. They do, however, implicitly raise two potentially very interesting and important points: (a) that the specific social structures found in Emilia-Romagna and Tuscany are not reproducible elsewhere; and (b) that the specific form of the division of labour in Italy (i.e. *very* small average firm size and a tendency to not have large firm presence in the districts at all) make them very different from the other examples of industrial districts which have been treated in the literature. Nonetheless, these are claims that do not follow unproblematically from the empirical data; Amin and Robins would have to develop an argument to show why the Third Italy is *essentially* different from all other cases of production flexibility and industrial district formation, and this they do not do. In any case, it is not helpful to engage in a definitional game of mirrors simply in order to claim that industrial districts exist nowhere else.

2. Closely related to the definition of the industrial district is the question of whether such agglomerations are a widely generalised phenomenon. Amin and Robins claim that places such as Silicon Valley, Emilia-Romagna, Hollywood, and New York's garment district are too different to be grouped under the rubric of the industrial district. Amin and Robins fail to engage the case study literature, which shows that agglomerated flexible production zones exist which are not carbon copies of the Third Italy, but nonetheless have substantial affinities to the principles identified by Marshall and recognised anew by Italian scholars. Again, the question is *why* (one assumes in terms of essential developmental tendencies and/or social outcomes) these zones are different from one another.

In attempting to make the argument about difference, Amin and Robins make a double conflation. First, they reduce the question of production flexibility to that of flexible specialisation, which is only one of a number of varieties identified in the work of both Piore and Sabel and that of Scott and Storper; for example, one needs only think of the explicit recognition, in Scott's work on Silicon Valley, of the presence and importance of large firms, mass production units, and long-distance subcontracting and that these phenomena are explicitly theorised. Amin and Robins then reduce the question of *flexible production agglomerations* to that of the "pure" form of the "flexibly specialised industry in the Marshallian industrial district" (i.e. only small firms, few long-distance relationships,

Italian-style social arrangements). Many Italian scholars, by contrast [for example Garofoli, 1988], have already dealt constructively with this thorny problem of genus and species in developing notions such as the "area system" and the "localised production system", signifying forms of flexible production agglomeration which are different from the canonical form of the Marshallian district but are nonetheless analytically part of the same family tree. French [Courlet, 1987; Courault and Rerat, 1987; Ganne, 1983; Saglio, 1986; Leborgne and Lipietz, 1988; Veltz, 1988], American [Scott, 1988; Storper, 1989; Piore and Sabel, 1984; Lorenz, 1988], and German [Kern and Schumann, 1987] scholars have done so as well in the course of their detailed case studies.

Amin and Robins go on to make a number of specific claims about why many of the cases cited in the contemporary literature are not examples of flexible production. First, they go back into the past and suggest that places such as Detroit and Turin, the quintessential geographical symbols of mass production, are also agglomerations and that therefore there must be something wrong with our claims about the link between agglomerations and flexibility. Of course, we have never claimed that all agglomerations are examples of flexible production systems. More importantly, like many of its nineteenth and early twentieth century counterparts, Detroit once did have many of the characteristics of a flexible production agglomeration, i.e. high levels of vertical disintegration and rapid changes in products and processes. Later on, as mass production gathered force in the automobile industry, the organisational character of the Detroit agglomeration did indeed change, so that it became a mass production agglomeration. Eventually, Detroit's mass production agglomeration tended to break up as the car industry took on a more decentralised locational pattern. This is a point made well by Sabel and Zeitlin [1985] in their study of nineteenth-century flexible production systems, i.e. that they can evolve into something else. But - and here is the problem with Amin's and Robins' analysis - there is nothing deterministic about the course of development of such districts, and it has also been observed that mass production industries can become flexible and agglomerated after periods of vertical integration and geographical dispersion. The casual mention of Detroit and Turin does not help us understand whether some contemporary flexible production agglomerations are likely to survive while others are not.

Second, they allege that we indiscriminately include diverse types of growth regions under the rubric of flexible production spaces. Thus, high technology agglomerations such as Silicon Valley and Orange County are not flexible production agglomerations, but merely "product pioneering" industrial districts (and thus, one assumes, destined to follow Detroit). Here, their failure to deal with the theoretical problem of definition rears its head again. Marshall himself wrote precisely about a series of areas that were pioneering new products in nineteenth-century England. This fact alone has no bearing on whether an area is a district or not. Nor does it, in and of itself, shed any light on whether it will remain a district, for there are ample historical examples of both the survival and the dissolution of product pioneering agglomerations. Moreover, there are many examples of contemporary flexible production agglomerations which are manifestly not product pioneering in the sense of Silicon Valley: Prato, Emilia-Romagna, the City of London, Toyota City, the Rhône-Alpes, Baden-Württemburg, Bavaria, and so on. As we have repeatedly insisted, there are many specific developmental paths which lead to the formation of flexible production agglomerations, but nonetheless the central dynamics of the division of labour, flexibility, and formation of a supportive tissue of institutions characterises them all.

In any case, if one is going to criticise a theoretical abstraction by reference to empirical diversity, one has to get one's facts right. Amin and Robins are, for example, plain wrong in claiming [p. 200] that Orange County and Silicon Valley are dominated by large firms and have an international *rather* than a local division of labour and therefore cannot be considered to fall within the category of industrial district. These two areas have had declining average firm size for some time and have very dense local as well as long-distance divisions of labour. And the latter fact in no way impedes a locality from being an industrial district; indeed, insertion into wider divisions of labour has been key to the Third Italy's development, just as it was in Marshall's earlier English cases.

The result of all this effort to deny the generality of organisational and geographical tendencies in industry is the rather desperate claim of Amin and Robins that "London, Singapore, San Francisco, Boston, Toyota City, Orange County and even areas in the Third Italy, are exceptions and not the rule" [p. 213] for contemporary economic development. Yet to focus on the sectors and places where employment and output growth are rapid seems a straightforwardly logical way to understand important general tendencies in industrial and regional development.

3. Have we really entered a period in which mass production is no longer dominant? Here, Amin and Robins indulge in a "quantitative" critique which alleges that: mass production was never a majoritarian phenomenon; flexible production methods do not account for a majority of production activity now; and, the world of production is always made up of a complex mixture of methods. They say that we insist on a "simple and binary" replacement of mass production by flexible production. Here, the only simple and binary reasoning is that of Amin and Robins.

Our work on technological-institutional systems of production, like that of the French Regulationists on institutions and macroeconomic arrangements, is based on identifying *principles of dominance* at given moments in economic history, not on arguing that in each period absolutely no vestiges of past periods remain. We have argued that flexible production is becoming dominant in suggesting that three growing industrial ensembles, viz. high technology manufacturing and associated services; business and financial services; and craft-based or design-intensive manufacturing, account for increasing proportions of output and employment; in these three sectors, flexible production methods are favoured for many phases of production; and flexible production methods are increasingly favoured in many of the old consumer durables sectors as well.

We have explicitly written that, just as in the age of mass production there were many "flexible" production units, it is fully obvious that many activities (in the sense of individual establishments) remain Taylorised and essentially consist of forms of mass production. But these activities no longer account for the majority of output and employment growth, and the *principles* of mass production - standardisation, increasing internal economies of scale, non-adaptable capital goods, and long-term stability of inter-plant and inter-firm relationships - no longer dominate managerial decision-making in advanced capitalism. Let us briefly take up the "limit case", i.e. one which we would expect to be most favourable to Amin's and Robins' position, the automobile industry. One finds today a production system which consists of some units of production which produce via automated mass production (usually the producers of the most common inputs or components), combined with sourcing from many smaller firms who produce in medium-sized batches a set of more specialised, higher value-added components. These are then combined by the auto maker, which orchestrates the system, and manages the evolution of this complex system over time. The batch producers, along with the auto makers themselves, are the key new form of industrial enterprise: they dominate a kind of *savoir faire* which permits them to market a range of ever-changing specialised outputs to the auto makers, as their needs evolve, but to other clients as well, in order to smooth out their capacity fluctuations and minimise their dependence on auto makers. The *logic of the system as a whole* is different from that of mass production because: (a) the production system is much less vertically-integrated; (b) the time horizons of the large firm are shorter because markets are more contested and product development cycles shorter; (c) suppliers have developed greater internal flexibility and more complex and diversified inter-firm linkages to minimise their risks on large firms; (d) as a result of the latter, the supplier firms are increasingly developing a wider range of products, but within a given domain of specialised activity, and as a result they are tied to complex inter-branch input-output relations in which they engage in making other products with other firms. The flexibility of the production system thus resides in dynamics which are both internal to the automobile branch of production (shortened time horizons) and in how firms which are part of the automobile industry insert themselves into other technologically cognate branches of the economy. This is a story which has been empirically identified in so many recent case studies that I am at pains to imagine how Amin and Robins could miss its main point, which is *not* that every unit of every production system was once an assembly line and that every unit of every production system is now completely flexible.

Another "non-paradox" in this debate concerns the question of size and barriers to entry. It is most certainly the case that in large, capital-intensive industries, big firms continue to benefit from barriers to entry and that, at the level of the production unit, internal economies of scale exist. But these facts do not lead inescapably to the conclusion that we are in an age of mass production and oligopolistic competition, as Amin and Robins seem to think.

Amin and Robins also challenge our point that geographical agglomeration characterises this period of capitalist development and that this is different from the post-war period. The issue of metropolitan concentration seemed to disappear in the late 1960s and 1970s, when all attention turned to the decentralisation of production (whether to peripheral regions of developed countries or the Third World), deindustrialisation, and the hollowing out of the city. It is indisputable that, in the early 1980s in the advanced economies, the bulk of employment growth occurred in metropolitan areas or in highly concentrated industrial spaces which were often in different regions from those places which were dominant in employment and output terms in the period up to about 1970. This seems to signify reversal of a once-dominant tendency.

We have also noted repeatedly and explicitly that just as an era in which flexible production is dominant finds itself with many activities still accomplished by mass production methods, so an era in which spatial concentration is dominant finds itself with the development of an increasingly articulated international division of labour - the two are articulated. Even here, however, Amin and Robins fail to appreciate the fact that many of the most important dimensions of long-distance geographical integration are intimately dependent on production flexibility and agglomeration. Branch plants and the old forms of geographical spread on the part of multinational corporations are only a small part of the picture of inter-regional relations today. Strategic alliances between large firms which, in turn, are often closely tied into the dense tissues of industrial districts in their various places of operation, are now a principal form of internationalisation of capital. It would at best be premature to claim that the large firm is in this case necessarily the destroyer of the industrial district. The large multilocational firm might just as well be the agent of the combination of such districts into more organisationally and geographically complex production systems, as has been theorised by Phil Cooke [1988].

4. Throughout their chapter, Amin and Robins imply or assert that the real story of capitalist development is the continuing and ever-increasing dominance of large firms. Thus, even in the one place where they accept the existence of industrial districts *as they define them* (i.e. the Third Italy), it is implied that such districts are being rapidly eliminated by mergers and acquisitions and the formation of long-distance subcontracting relationships. The predictable conclusion is that the districts were a temporary aberration due to the crisis of Fordism, the weak spatial integration of the Italian economy, and the "vestigial, archaic" artisanal traditions there, and that things are now returning to the "normal" path of development.

There is widespread agreement that industrial districts are not static, self-contained, fully stable systems. The main reference on this point is precisely the work of Sabel and Zeitlin [1985] on the nineteenth century industrial districts, many of which fell apart due to internal or external forces, or both. But equally, as the empirical work of many on the contemporary scene in Italy, France, the United States of America and the Federal Republic of Germany has shown, today's thriving districts have been formed through complex histories full of twists and turns, and they are constantly subject to a variety of internal tensions and external forces. Some of these histories end with the destruction of production flexibility and of geographical concentration, but in other cases districts have manifested a remarkable capacity for adaptation, through elaboration of the division of labour as a whole as well as through the flexibility of individual firms. Many of the areas which we currently point to as the most highly developed districts, especially those of Emilia-Romagna and Tuscany, once looked like their more primitive counterparts of today, Veneto, Marches, and Abruzzi. Likewise, to claim the end of the flexible production agglomeration on the basis of a couple of references to long-distance subcontracting is at best premature; as we have already noted, successful industrial districts, even in the nineteenth century, were frequently inserted to a high degree into inter-regional, national, and international divisions of labour as well as serving geographically extensive markets.

In the much-debated "crisis of Prato", for example, it is by no means obvious that the disappearance of the district is at hand. This district has survived, even flourished, on the ashes of a number of crises in its history. The current crisis - competition by large firms in some markets served by the district - might simply push the district into doing what it has done several times in the past: move up the price-performance curve by specialising in higher quality items and leave the middle-range products to the large firms. Many *impannatore* are being encouraged to do just this at the present time. It is at best extremely premature to claim the death of the districts on the basis of exactly the kind of difficulties they have overcome many times before. This does not mean, *a priori*, that nothing is changing and, as I suggest shortly, the big questions today do concern change in the districts themselves and in the relations of the districts to the rest of the world. The problem, as we see next, is that Amin and Robins think they have already resolved these weighty questions.

5. Amin and Robins conclude that we have "an international capitalism which does not have much of a new face" [208]. They are of the view that "in terms of questions of power and control in the economy, the big multinational corporation continues to gain" ... "[It] remains the *most powerful* agent of the restructuring process" ([p. 209], italics added). This vision of the perfection of Fordism is carried forth into their view of the geography of contemporary capitalist development: "capital is increasingly mobile, hypermobile even, tending toward an increasingly nomadic existence", the "space of flows" [p. 210].

It is rather ironic that Amin and Robins, who persistently exhort us to respect the complexity of the world, end up with flat, categorical statements which essentially deny change and complexity. Indeed - and we come to the heart of the problem with the Amin and Robins analysis here - in their world, there appear to be just two possible paths of development, whose elements all come in indivisible packages:

(a) the world of monopoly capital, where small firms and flexibility are archaic forms of development which are used by large corporations, via the trick of labour market segmentation and geographical divisions of labour, to perpetuate nineteenth century forms of exploitation in the twenty-first; this is the "hard reality".

(b) the utopian vision of the "new orthodoxy", where small firms are equated with a democracy of artisans, the disappearance of the large firm, and the appearance of regionally autarchic economies.

Because of their haste to endorse the former view and to claim that it comes as a package, they fail to consider that the research on production flexibility and regional development really has called into question many of the received notions about the "essential" nature of industrialisation, and that it is precisely understanding the nature of a "third path" which presents us with our major theoretical and empirical challenge in the coming years. It is perfectly obvious - indeed, elementary - to observe that (a) corporate size continues to increase in absolute terms in many industries; (b) establishments using mass production methods continue to exist in many activities; the long production run is not gone, nor is flexible automation exclusively associated with short runs; (c) there are both "good" and "bad" aspects of production flexibility for the labour force, depending on the industry and the specific region at hand; and (d) agglomeration, spatial integration, and spatial dispersion are all occurring at the same time in many sectors. But making these claims in no way requires the definitional games that Amin and Robins go through, i.e. to trivialise the existence of production flexibility and the new industrial spaces, for this only hinders us from posing the questions of how these elements, once thought to be by definition incompatible in the process of economic development, might actually fit together.

It would be more constructive, both theoretically and politically, to use the opening which has been created by those who have studied production flexibility, the new industrial spaces, and cognate phenomena, to pose, collectively, a series of thorny theoretical and empirical questions, such as:

* What is the emerging nature of relationships between big and small firms in general?

* What is the relationship between geographically-concentrated forms of industrial production and the apparent diffusion and integration of production systems over wider (i.e. national or global) spaces? What about the regions "left behind" by flexible production?

* What is the relationship between the apparent concentration of financial and investment power in the hands of very large corporations on the one hand and declining average firm and establishment size in many industries on the other?

* What is the relationship between the drive to maximise the size of markets through geographical diversification on the part of many companies and the drive to minimise risk through flexibility?

* Under what circumstances do firms strive to minimise costs through traditional scale economies and when do they attempt to maximise super-profits (rents) by flexibilising so as to move up the increasingly steep dynamic price-performance curves which exist for more and more groups of products (precisely as a consequence of the existence of flexible production methods)?

* Do flexible production systems based around elaborated external economies represent competitive alternatives to the large firm? In all industries or only in some industries? Does the development of the flexible and externalised production system "crowd out" other organisational options (such as vertical integration) in an industry or, at the very least, in parts of its production process, and does this explain the current penchant for vertical disintegration on the part of large firms?

* Are flexible production agglomerations based on collections of medium-sized firms (i.e. 50-500 workers) qualitatively different from those based on small firms (less than 50 employees), such that the nature of entrepreneurial activity and their developmental trajectories can really not be said to partake of the same general phenomenon?

* What are the social effects of different flexible production systems, especially on the workforce, and can these be affected by policy?

These questions represent some of the elements of an agenda for serious progress on the momentous issues before us and, to the extent that Amin and Robins have (albeit in a rather inchoate way) raised them, they can be thanked. But Amin and Robins are wrong to imply that the answers to these questions can be deduced from old presuppositions about capitalist industrial development. Answering them accurately will require taking seriously the evidence on production flexibility and industrial districts amassed thus far and manifestly not falling back on outdated "conventional wisdoms" about development that have so often proved not only wrong but also politically irrelevant.

References

Cooke, P. 1988. "Flexible integration, scope economies, and strategic alliances: Social and spatial mediations", in *Environment and Planning D: Society and Space*, Vol. 6, No. 3, pp. 281-300.

Courault, B.; Rerat, M.F. 1987. "Un modèle de production régionale en transition: Le cas de la chaussure dans le Choletais", in *Cahiers du Centre d'Etudes de l'Emploi*, No. 30, pp. 91-112.

Courlet, C. 1987. "Coopération industrielle, PME, et développement local: L'exemple Savoyard", in Adefi-Greco: *Industries et régions*, Paris, Economica, pp. 191-204.

Ganne, B. 1983. *Gens du cuir, gens du papier: Transformations d'Annonay depuis les années 20*, Lyon, Editions du Conseil National de Recherche Scientifique.

Garofoli, G. 1988. "Modelli locali di sviluppo: Tipologia di aree e politiche di intervento", Pavia, University of Pavia, Department of Economics, Working paper.

Kern, H.; Schumann, M. 1987. "Limits of the division of labour: New production and employment concepts in West German industry", in *Economic and Industrial Democracy*, No. 8, pp. 151-170.

Leborgne, D.; Lipietz, A. 1988. "New technologies, new modes of regulation: Some spatial implications", in *Environment and Planning D: Society and Space*, Vol. 6, No. 3, pp. 263-280.

Lorenz, E.H. 1988. "The search for flexibility: Subcontracting networks in French and British engineering", in: Hirst, P.; Zeitlin, J. (eds.): *Reversing industrial decline?*, Oxford, Berg, pp. 122-132.

Piore, M.; Sabel, C. 1984. *The second industrial divide*, New York, Basic Books.

Sabel, C.; Zeitlin, J. 1985. "Historical alternatives to mass production: Politics, markets, and technology in nineteenth century industrialisation", in *Past and Present*, No. 108, August, pp. 133-176.

Saglio, J. 1986. "Petites et moyennes entreprises industrielles et environnement urbain", in: France, Commissariat Général du Plan, Plan Urbain: *Mutations économiques et urbanisation*, Paris, La Documentation Française, pp. 201-250.

Scott, A.J. 1988. *New industrial spaces: Flexible production and regional development in North America and Western Europe*, London, Pion.

Storper, M. 1989. "The transition to flexible specialisation in the film industry: Thc division of labour, external economies, and the crossing of industrial divides", in *Cambridge Journal of Economics*, No. 13, pp. 273-305.

Veltz, P. et al. 1988. "Nouvelle économie, nouvelle térritoires", Paris: Caisse des dépôts et consignations, Actes du Colloque Economie et Térritoire, "Vers une nouvelle dynamique du développement local".